THE
DRY-FLY MAN'S HANDBOOK

FRONTISPIECE

Landing a Trout

The
Dry-Fly Man's Handbook

A Complete Manual

Including

The Fisherman's Entomology

and The Making and Management of a Fishery

by

FREDERICK M. HALFORD

THE DERRYDALE PRESS
LANHAM AND NEW YORK

THE DERRYDALE PRESS

Published in the United States of America
by The Derrydale Press
4720 Boston Way, Lanham, Maryland 20706

Distributed by NATIONAL BOOK NETWORK, INC.

Original printing 1913
First paperback printing with french folds 2000

Library of Congress Cataloging-in-Publication Data

Halford, Frederic M. (Frederic Michael), 1844-1914.
    The dry-fly man's handbook : a complete manual, including the
fisherman's entomology and the making and management of a
fishery / Frederic M. Halford
    p.   cm.
    Originally published: 1913.
    ISBN 1-56833-154-1 (paper : alk. paper)
    1. Fly casting. 2. Aquatic insects. 3. Fish-culture
SH456.H3 2000
799.1'24—dc21   99-059351

CONTENTS

PART I

DRY-FLY FISHING

PART II

THE FISHERMAN'S ENTOMOLOGY

CONTENTS

PART III

THE MAKING AND MANAGEMENT OF A FISHERY

LIST OF PLATES

PART III

PREFACE

THE reader may well think that some kind of apology is due to him for the appearance of this work, because of the prediction hazarded in the last chapter of "Modern Development of the Dry-Fly," that "at my age it is scarcely probable that I shall write another book." Yet within two years I am again guilty of indulging in the *cacoethes scribendi* to the extent of producing the largest book I have yet written.

Pray bear with me while I explain. The fourth edition of "Dry-Fly Fishing in Theory and Practice," published in 1902, was out of print. Improvements in rods and tackle, and the better knowledge acquired by further experience of the habits of the chalk-stream trout and their many peculiarities and idiosyncrasies when subjected to the wiles of the modern dry-fly man, pointed to the necessity for something more than a mere revision. The question had to be squarely faced, and although I was loth to undertake a work so encyclopædic in character as the compilation of an entirely new book on the subject, this appeared to be the only solution of the problem.

Having determined to embark on the project, one's mind is naturally led to consider what should be the limits of the work. On the entomological side of the question it is evident that the practical dry-fly man would like to find in the same volume sufficient in-

formation to enable him to identify to some extent the
flies which are present on the water and on which the
fish are presumably feeding.   Hence the inclusion of
the second part of this book.

The addition of the third part, treating of the
making and management of a fishery, was desirable
because this branch of the fisherman's craft is every
day awakening more attention, and the dire results of
carrying out management without knowledge have
produced a state of degeneration among the south-
country chalk-stream trout which is a source of deep
anxiety to all who give their thoughts to the future of
such streams as the Test and Itchen.

It may be permissible to remark that I should not
have devoted so much space to this subject but for the
fact that since the publication of " Making a Fishery " I
have received so many enquiries—through correspondence and otherwise—that a little amplification seemed
to be essential in view of the widespread interest
taken in the whole matter.

These being in brief my reasons for including so
much in this book, I hope to be able to offer the
reader some degree of consolation.   If I have succeeded in my task, I have given him in the last two
books I have written, this and " Modern Development
of the Dry-Fly," a full and complete treatise on the
dry-fly.   The fishing, the entomology, the management, the patterns, and the modern methods of selecting and preparing the materials for them, as well as
the latest manipulation of fly-dressing—these are all
treated in detail in these two volumes, which should
thus cover the entire subject.

My friend Mr. E. Valentine Corrie has given me invaluable assistance in respect to the third part, and in many paragraphs his facile pen would probably be recognized by the many admirers of his style without any specific indication. His unique knowledge of everything pertaining to the making and management of a fishery has been freely placed at the disposal of my readers.

I am not sure that I could have undertaken the work without the active co-operation of my friend Mr. Martin E. Mosely, who has read, criticized, and, where necessary, revised every line of the book. It was at his suggestion that I went beyond the original scheme in the second part, because he assured me that many anglers would welcome a little information on the identification and scientific nomenclature of insects present on chalk-streams or other rivers in the United Kingdom.

The chapter " Dry-Fly on Lochs and Lakes " is, as far as I know, a novelty. For many years I have realized the possibilities and the manifest charms of the cult of the dry-fly under these conditions, but my personal experience was insufficient to warrant my launching out on this branch of the craft. Three good friends, however, nobly undertook to write the matter, and nobly have they carried out their promises. Mr. Hugh T. Sheringham, the Angling Editor of " The Field," has given his experiences of Blagdon Lake, Mr. A. C. Poole of Harris sea-trout lochs, and Mr. John Henderson of Lough Arrow in the west of Ireland. My gratitude to all of them is beyond the powers of language to express.

To the proprietors and editor of " The Field " my
grateful thanks are also due for allowing me once
more to reproduce all or any part of my many articles
in that great paper. They have also acceded to my
request and that of the author, Mr. M. E. Mosely, to
quote copiously from articles of his in " The Field."

My warmest thanks, too, are due to my dear old
friend Mr. William Senior, who has read in proof and
revised this like every other of the books I have
written. The practical advice of so able and experienced an author and dry-fly fisherman has contributed in a great degree to improving the style and
correcting many crudities in my composition. My
friend Mr. Hugh T. Sheringham has also placed me
under further obligations by reading the proofs, suggesting many valuable additions, and in many ways
improving the style of " Modern Development of the
Dry-Fly " and of this my latest bantling.

FREDERIC M. HALFORD.

6, PEMBRIDGE PLACE, W.

PART I

DRY-FLY FISHING

THE
DRY-FLY MAN'S HANDBOOK

CHAPTER I

ROD AND TACKLE

THE manufacture of fishing-rods and tackle has become highly specialized of late years, and realizing that no amateur can by any possibility be an expert on the subject, I have not hesitated to consult members of the trade in whose judgment and *bona-fides* I have full confidence. Mr. J. J. Hardy (managing director of Hardy Brothers, Ltd., of Alnwick, and 61 Pall Mall), and Mr. W. A. Hunter (manager of C. Farlow and Co., Ltd., of 10 Charles Street, St. James's Square), have given me freely the benefit of their knowledge and unrivalled experience, and I feel myself under great obligations to both of them for the incalculable assistance they have rendered to make this chapter descriptive of the latest modern improvements in rods and tackle designed for the use of the dry-fly fisherman.

B

The description of the modern dry-fly rod is a far
easier matter than it was in
Rods.   1888, when I first ventured to
offer advice to the angling
public on the important question of selecting a suitable rod.   Since those days the double-handed rod
has disappeared, and the single-handed one, with a
length of 9 ft. as a minimum and 10 ft. 6 in. as a
maximum, is nowadays recommended by all modern
authorities.   A vast majority of the twentieth-century
dry-fly men are strong advocates of the built-up or
split bamboo rods.   There are, however, still some
who prefer green-heart to split bamboo, as the material
for rods, and among these is Mr. John Henderson,
whose opinions are given in Chapter VIII of this
book.   I would ask the reader to give his very best
attention to Mr. Henderson's arguments, because he is
pre-eminently a practical dry-fly fisherman.   Personally,
I cannot agree with him, because in my own experience
no green-heart rod ever made has been comparable to
the split bamboo rods I have used for the last thirty years.

Mr. Hardy's opinion in reference to the class of
bamboo to be used for the
Material for split   modern rod is here set forth :—
bamboo rods.   " No   great   alteration   or
improvement   has   been   made
during the last few years in the method of construction.   In materials, split bamboo has become in-
creasingly popular, while in wood rods green-heart
still holds the pride of place."

"The so-called Calcutta bamboo (*Dendrocalamus strictus*), which was at one time almost exclusively used, has been largely displaced by a harder and tougher bamboo, called *Palakona* (a registered word). This bamboo is preferred on account of its greater stiffness, which permits rods of lighter weight being produced having greater resistance, which, of course, means greater line-lifting power and recovery."

"This material also lends itself well to the process of hardening and toughening, which has of late been introduced. So far as the method of construction is concerned, there is no advance on the ordinary hexagonal single and double-built bamboo rods. Octagonal and nonagonal rods are occasionally built, but their quantity is negligible."

Preparation of the sections and fastening them together. The preparation of the six sections of which each joint of a split bamboo rod is composed, consists in splitting out a suitable width of the bamboo, planing or in some other way shaping it with the greatest precision on two sides to an angle of 60°, leaving the bark, which is at once the hardest, most elastic, and most waterproof portion of the material, intact. These six sections are then cemented together. When the cement is absolutely dry and fixed, the surface is cleaned off and the joint cut to the requisite length. This is a matter calling for the highest technical knowledge, because the action of the rod and its stiffness are entirely governed by the judgment of the operative.   In an ordinary wood rod this is a comparatively easy matter, because if the joint is made of a diameter slightly greater than that required to give the necessary flexibility to the rod it is only necessary to plane it down a little to correct any excess of stiffness.

The maker of a split bamboo rod has no such means of correcting an error of judgment, because he must under no circumstances remove the outer skin or bark. If his joint is a trifle too whippy he can possibly correct this by shortening it ; but if the result of this shortening is to make one joint appreciably shorter than the others, the rod is not, from the view of the angling public, a very saleable one.   When the joints of the rod are prepared, the next point is to make the arrangements for fastening them together.

There are two methods of fastening the joints of a rod together ; splicing, or fitting with ferrules.   Most of the modern dry-fly men have

Spliced and jointed rods.

condemned the splice.   It is inconvenient when it is necessary to take down a rod at frequent intervals, and generally the spliced rod does not accommodate itself to the variety of casts effected when fishing the floating fly.

The rod-maker is thus confronted with the necessity of fitting his joints together by the means of metal ferrules—

Ferrules for joints.

male and female.   The old-fashioned plan was to

make the ferrules slightly conical or tapered to allow for wear and tear, and wire loops were fixed to each ferrule. A short length of waxed silk or thread was worked round these wire loops to fasten the joint securely together and obviate the possibility of their being worked loose or thrown apart when casting.

The first improvement made in this plan was the lock-fast joint with hook and spiral thread designed by Messrs. Hardy, and this lock-fast joint is probably the most usual one in use at the present time. The "Lloyd" treble-grip ferrule was brought out as an improvement on this, and, although in every way effective, it is, I think, unnecessarily heavy and cumbersome. Messrs. Hardy Brothers brought out later a joint with a spring lever arm on the female ferrule carrying a round peg. This peg drops into a hole through the female ferrule, and a certain distance into the male ferrule, and is held in position by a sliding sleeve.

The suction ferrule is advocated by some rod-makers, and the American rods are generally fitted with these. Of all these ferrules, I think that the old "Hardy" lock-fast joint is the best; but in my hands it invariably tends to work loose in use, and I generally discover this by noticing that the line will not run smoothly owing to the rings not being accurately aligned. It is suggested by the makers that if the spiral screw is made left-handed instead of right-handed, the tendency will be to tighten the fitting instead of its working loose. My objection to this plan is that every keeper or friend attempting to put up or take down the rod will, in all probability, ruin the screw by trying to work it right-handed.

I discussed the question with Mr. J. J. Hardy, and the following paragraphs in his own words will describe the result :—

"Joints can hardly work loose unless they can twist. It would appear, therefore, that some kind of a stop

Hardy's new ferrule.

connecting the two parts (i.e. male and female) is essential. The lever carrying the peg passing through both joints does this, and so does the 'Lloyd' joint, but I am of opinion that the arrangement of the hole in the former is not good, as it is liable to weaken the ferrule. Suction joints are good so long as they are perfect-fitting, but the frequent putting together and taking apart naturally wears the surfaces, and they become liable to throw out. Whatever form of joint is used it must be quite simple, strong, and capable of being turned when taking apart."

"The latest form which I have tested, and of which I think very highly, is one which Messrs. Hardy have provisionally patented and consists in the groundwork of the arrangement being an ordinary suction joint, supplemented by a locking arrangement which holds the two parts firmly together, so that they cannot possibly be pulled or thrown apart without first drawing back the locking ring."

"Fig. 1 shows the (A) male and (B) female portions. It will be noticed that on A there is a raised ring, F. On B the sleeve E is drawn back to show slot G and curved lip D. When A is pushed home the spring portion of the outer (female) lip D jumps over the ring F, when E should be pushed up to secure it."

Fig. 1

Fig. 2

"Fig. 2 is the joint closed, and shows the two portions locked together for work."

I have tried this arrangement for some days, and consider it is the best lock-fast fitting I have ever used. I cannot see any weak point in it, and think it should prove a decided boon to the dry-fly man.

The ideal rod should be made in one piece, and thus obviate the necessity of any splices, joints, or ferrules, but to the majority of fishermen to carry a 9 or 10 ft. rod in one piece is most inconvenient, and hence it is almost a necessity to make it in two or more pieces. The two-jointed rod is in practice quite handy, and with the thin metal modern ferrules the presence of metal at the centre of its length does not present any

Number of joints in a rod.

great disadvantage.   It is, however, overlong for the rack of a railway carriage unless the passenger has one side of the compartment to himself, so that, as a general rule, rods in three pieces are preferred nowadays.

Rod protectors. A solid wood protector, into which each joint is packed in a groove cut for the purpose, is often supplied, and when put away in a simple rod bag is a great boon.   A rod packed in the ordinary partition bag is liable to be injured or broken when travelling.   I believe that the idea of this solid wood protector was originated in the United States.

Spear. Personally, I always use a spear for the purpose of standing a rod up and saving it from the risk of being trampled on by fellow-anglers, cattle, etc.   Some anglers object to the spear, and of course its presence must to some degree increase the weight of the rod.   The arrangement patented many years since by Messrs. Hardy, by which the spear when not in use is packed in the thick end of the handle, is a most convenient one.

Rod rings. The following remarks by Mr. J. J. Hardy, in reference to rod rings, are the outcome of a discussion I had with him on the subject, and I think that the new agate rings referred to therein constitute a marked improvement on anything attempted before.

" Rod rings are a very important item in all kinds
of angling, but to none more so than in dry-fly
fishing. In some respects a perfect ring may be
compared to the barrels of a shot gun, which are not
of much value unless they *shoot* well. So with the
rod rings, which must be of such a character that the
line can pass easily so that it may *shoot* well. The
ring should present as little surface as possible in
order to reduce friction. Its inner edge must be
smooth, or the passage of the line is retarded, and,
worse still, the line itself is liable to get frayed, and
good shooting largely prevented."

" To refer to materials ; soft metal rings, such as
German silver, nickel, and untempered steel, soon
wear into grooves, which are most destructive to the
dressing of lines. Hardened steel is good, but unfortunately, when in contact with water or damp, it
rusts. It would appear, therefore, that we have little
choice, and that the best material, so far at any rate
as the surface which comes into contact with the line
is concerned, appears to be agate. Hitherto agates
have been largely used on fly rods as butt and end
rings, while on spinning rods which are comparatively
stout, they are often used throughout."

" The employment of these rings on fly rods has
hitherto been handicapped by the difficulty in mount-
ing the agates, which must be well protected. The
trouble has been to do this effectually without adding undue weight. This, however, has been successfully accomplished, and a perfect dry-fly rod fitted

throughout with agate rings is in Mr. Halford's possession. In using a rod so fitted, there is nothing to interfere with the shooting of the line, which is an advantage hardly to be overestimated."

FIG. 3   "Agates in their natural colour are a soft grey. After being manufactured into rings, they are frequently coloured red or blue. This colouring is done by heat, and as it renders them brittle, coloured rings should be avoided, and those only chosen which are the natural colour of the stone, as being tougher and less liable to damage."

"Fig. 3 shows the agate rings referred to as mounted on a 9 ft. 6 in. 'Halford' rod (1912 model), and gives the actual sizes."

"The ring nearest the hand is fairly large, while the others are reduced in size as they near the top, in order to reduce the weight forward as much as possible."

"*Top ring.* This should be of an area at least equal to three times the thickness of the line which is to pass through it. The illustra-

FIG. 4   tion (Fig. 4) shows a new design which is light and very strong. It may be noticed that the socket covers the full size of the end of the rod, and that the legs are hard soldered on the outside of it. This gives the arrangement very great strength, while the position of the legs prevents any possibility of the line getting fast round the top."

The latest form of winch fitting is described in the
following note by Mr. Hardy,
Winch fittings. and appears to me at once
simple and effective.

"The universal winch fitting invented by Dr.
Weeger, and originally manufactured by Messrs. Hardy
in 1883, has always proved a good, safe, simple arrangement, and has been adopted by the majority of
rod-makers."

"This firm have, however, lately introduced what is
called their patent *screw winch fitting*, for which they
claim that there is no liability of the ring which holds
the reel coming loose."

"In connection with this improvement they have in
some rods fixed the socket into which the reel end is
received (and which has hitherto been on the lower
end of the rod handle) the reverse way, and covered
it with the cork forming the handle. This arrangement prevents any irritation to the hand, as it cannot
come into contact with the metal parts, while using the
rod. The travelling screw grip is fixed on the butt
cap. In order to fix the reel in position it is only
required to push one end of the back plate into the
metal socket underneath the cork and then to screw
the travelling part over the other. The usual reversible
spear is fitted to the butt cap. This is undoubtedly one
of the most valuable of recent improvements in rod
fittings. It has occasionally happened to most anglers
that the reel has dropped off at a critical moment. With
this fitting such an accident cannot occur. The illustra-

tion (Fig. 5) shows how the locking ring B travels on the externally screwed ferrule A securing the reel."

Handle of the rod. It is most important that the diameter of the rod-handle should exactly suit the man using the rod, and having once decided on this dimension, it is well to calliper it accurately and have all rod-handles made to this diameter. Messrs. Farlow made

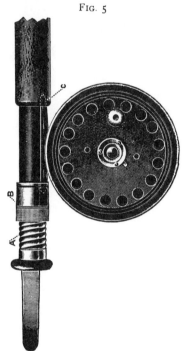

FIG. 5

a rod for me lately in which they introduced what is to me a novelty in the form of the handle. They describe it thus: " There is no cork or other covering to the cane, but the sections are continued right down and are double-built in the handle, the extra width being made up of strips of ebony let in on the corners, thus pre-serving the hexagonal shape while giving perfectly smooth edges. The result is a hex-agonal grip, shown in Fig. 6, which is cooler than the per-fectly round handle (which does sometimes cling to one's hand), and at the same time gives a feeling of firmness and control over the rod which is all gain."

This handle is certainly a most comfortable one, and

will be preferred by some fishermen—others will no doubt continue to use the old style of wooden handle or the cork handle, or the so-called inlaid handle, in which the six sections of the cane of the joint are inlaid into a solid cedar handle. A few anglers like the cane worked round the handle as is practised by some of the American rod-makers, and others have their handles whipped with water cord, dressed silk line, etc.

FIG. 6

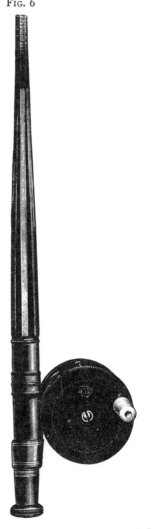

When the rod is completed the critical **Action of a rod.** question of its action is one to be carefully considered. The late Mr. T. P. Hawksley worked for years with me at a practical method of testing or comparing the action of rods, and devised the following tests which are given in pages 30, 31, and 32 of the fourth edition of "Dry-Fly Fishing in Theory and Practice."

"The points on which rods of the same material

and construction can be compared are length, weight, balance, stiffness, or pliability and speed. Length and weight require no definition and can be easily ascertained. Balance is best shown by finding the position of the centre of gravity or point at which the rod will balance, and for convenience the distance of this point from the butt should be measured. For the purpose of arriving at the stiffness and speed of the rod it must be firmly held in a horizontal position, with its butt in a vice, and the length of the portion projecting beyond the vice should be measured—this being styled the *length used.*"

" To measure stiffness the rod in the vice must be supported at the tip and at intermediate positions in a horizontal position and the height of the rod-point from the ground exactly marked on a staff. The supports being then removed throughout the length used, the butt being still in the jaws of the vice, the measurement of the height of the rod-point from the ground will show the deflection of the rod *free*, i.e. without any weight suspended from the top ring. A weight of 1 oz. is then hung on the point and the deflection again measured, and as a final test of deflection the measurement is once more taken with a weight of 2 oz."

" When an experienced fly-fisherman tries a rod

Slow and quick action of rods.

he usually advances the opinion that it is too slow or too quick for his own use. Generally the complaint is that it is too slow because the tendency of everyone using a fly rod is to cast and return more rapidly than the natural pace of the rod. This is a point on which considerable difference of opinion may well occur between the manufacturer and the proposing purchaser, and both should welcome the simple and practical test of speed as devised by Mr. Hawksley."

"The rod is still held horizontally, and the operator stands with watch in hand close to the place at which the butt is fixed in the vice. Placing his forefinger on the rod a short distance from the vice he presses down on it so as to set the projecting portion vibrating. After a short time, it will be found that the pressure of the hand can be relaxed until it is only sufficient to feel the vibrations, which will then continue at a fairly uniform rate. The number of vibrations in one minute are then counted and registered. It is perhaps as well, certainly for a beginner, to take an average of, say, three separate experiments. After the number of vibrations *free* have been ascertained those with weights of 1 oz. and 2 oz. respectively are also taken."

The method of rod-testing devised by the late Mr.

Rod-testing.

T. P. Hawksley, as described in the foregoing paragraphs, is the practical one used at the present time, except that the vibrations per minute are as a rule only noted free or without weight attached to the rod-point. Messrs. Hardy have further adopted the practical and admirable plan of recording the curve made by the rods free and with weights of 1 oz. and 2 oz.

Under the title of *the light rod craze* in an article published in the "Field" of **The light rod craze.** May 20th, 1905, I discussed at some length the origin of what is often called the *light rod* which has been adopted by our American cousins and to some extent in this country. The absurdity of grading rods by their gross weight in ounces is demonstrated in this article, and I have done my best to show that mere weight is in fact no criterion. A rod of 4 oz. may be, and often is, far more tiring to the hand, wrist, and forearm of the angler than a correctly balanced one of 10 or even 12 oz.

Mr. J. J. Hardy's opinion on the subject as a practical maker and a past-master **Mr. J. J. Hardy's** in using the fly rod must com- **opinion on the light** mand the attention of the **rod.** angler. He says in a carefully thought-out report on the subject :—

" During the last few years a considerable advance has been made in reducing the weight of rods due to the hardness of the material and reduction in the weight of the metal parts. In reference to this it is worth while to consider whether we have gained much and whether the reduction has been of any practical value, or whether in some rods it has not been overdone."

" In this direction the effort has been to decrease as far as possible the exertion required to perform a certain work and so render the day's fishing less fatiguing to the angler, but we must not forget that nothing must be sacrificed in point of efficiency. Actual weight is not of so much account in a rod as the disposal of it. Experiment has satisfied the writer that given two rods of unequal weight the heavier has frequently proved to be the more pleasant and lighter in use, and less tiring to the muscles of the forearm than the lighter one. Balance, i.e. counterpoise, is the important point."

" It is not desirable that the centre of gravity should be at the centre of the handle. As a matter of fact it will be found that (when the rod is mounted with the reel and line ready for use) the centre of gravity or balancing point is about $6\frac{1}{2}$ in. in front of the forefinger when grasping the rod in a fishing position."

" To attempt to use a rod by holding it at its centre of gravity makes it a very useless tool, and one greatly lacking in power. There must always be a certain preponderance of weight in the forward part to give force and effect to the cast. The exact amount of this is difficult to determine, and will vary with different rods and with different anglers according to their style."

" If we take as an illustration the 9 ft. 6 in. ' Halford' 1912 model, the centre of gravity when mounted for use is $15\frac{1}{4}$ in. from the end of the butt-cap. If the rod be balanced at the centre of the grip and a weight placed at the end of the butt to counterbalance the excess weight and leverage of that part of the rod which is in front of the hand, it amounts

c

to 14 oz. The weight of the rod alone is 8 oz.
14 drams, and with a suitable reel and line is 16¾ oz."

"For the purpose of comparison we will take a
9 ft. 6 in. rod 6 oz. 6 drams in weight of practically
the same balance. Now this rod with the same reel
and line mounted for use weighs 14¼ oz. If we
balance this rod at the centre of the grip we have to
add 16 oz. to counterbalance the leverage in front.
From this it will be seen that the heavier rod has
2 oz. less leverage in front of the hand than the
lighter one. This shows clearly that the 'Halford'
rod, although much the more powerful of the two,
is the easier rod to fish, and less tiring than the
lighter one."

Mr. Hardy sums up the proposition as follows :—

"Where the weight of a rod can be reduced without impairing its efficiency something has been
achieved. Some little reduction in weight, due to
improvement in material and the use of lighter
metal fittings, is quite practicable. With some men,
however, the notion of light rods seems to be quite
a mild sort of mania, and to such an extent is this
carried that short rods of 2½ oz. are actually in use.
These rods can undoubtedly place a fly within reasonable distance of a fish, and it may rise to the fly and
even be hooked, but here the trouble begins. This
little bit of bamboo has really become the thick end
of the line, and on a river you must follow Mr. Trout
wherever he cares to lead, and woe betide you if
there are snags or dangerous roots at the sides. The

rod being very thin, lacking in power and very short, you have nothing with which to stop or hold the fish out of the weeds, and therefore dis-aster is almost certain. Fishing from a boat in open water while drifting is the best place to use these rods, for there one has room, and may eventually draw the fish to the net."

FIG. 7

I can confirm every word of Mr. Hardy's dicta as to the comparison of the two rods, as I tried both exhaustively on the Test on May 7th, 1912, and found that the com-paratively heavy powerful rod was far more pleasant in action, and less tiring to the forearm than a rod of perfect balance which weighed $2\frac{1}{4}$ oz. less.

For the purpose of affording me an ample oppor-**The "Halford"** tunity of giving **1912 rod.** it a fair trial, Messrs. Hardy made for me the 9 ft. 6 in. rod, weighing with spear 8 oz. 14 drams on the model of the "Halford" 1905 rod, as shown in Fig. 7. This latter weighed $11\frac{1}{2}$ oz., so the reduction of weight is considerable. The 1912 rod was fitted with all the improvements referred to before, viz. the new form of ferrules, the small agate rings, and the screw winch fitting. I used it for three consecutive days, killed a considerable number of trout on it, and expressed to Mr. Hardy the opinion that, without exception, it is to my mind the best dry-fly rod I ever handled.

To compare it with the 1905 rod which was made on the model of one of the best rods built for me by Eaton and Deller in 1882, I append in tabulated form the particulars of weight, centre of gravity, vibrations and deflections free, and with weights 1 oz. and 2 oz. respectively hung from the top ring.

	Halford, 1905.	Halford, 1912.
Length	9 ft. $6\frac{1}{4}$ in.	9ft. $6\frac{1}{4}$ in.
Weight with spear . . .	$11\frac{1}{2}$ oz.	8 oz. 14 drams.
Length of handle . . .	15 in.	$14\frac{3}{4}$ in.
Distance of centre of gravity from butt cap . . .	$22\frac{3}{8}$ in.	26 in.
Number of vibrations per minute	106	104
Deflections free . . .	$5\frac{7}{8}$ in.	$5\frac{1}{2}$ in.
with 1 oz. weight . .	$16\frac{1}{4}$ in.	16 in.
with 2 oz. weight . .	$25\frac{1}{4}$ in.	$25\frac{3}{8}$ in.

In reference to the difference in weight I am assured by Mr. Hardy that the bamboo in the two rods is practically the same, but the new rod has less weight in its metal fittings and a somewhat smaller and lighter spear. The handles of the two rods are differently constructed. The 1905 pattern has a sheath of wood $\frac{3}{16}$ of an inch in thickness surrounding the rod proper to which the cork is attached in a sheet. In the 1912 rod the sheath of wood is only $\frac{3}{32}$ of an inch thick, and the thickness of cork is greater so as to make the outside diameters of the handles the same.

The object of this was to give a little more action in the hand, and this probably accounts for the slight increase of deflection with the 2 oz. weight. This rod thus bends slightly more in the handle and is a trifle more supple than the older one. The deflection of the new rod *free*, or with 1 oz. weight, is a trifle less than that of the old one under the same conditions, so that up to a certain point the 1912 rod is the stiffer of the two. This is probably due to the slightly harder nature of the bamboo, but when casting a longish line (represented in the experiment by the 2 oz. weight) it has a shade more play than the old rod.

The difference between the two rods in action is infinitesimal, and it is almost impossible to turn out two rods which will give under all conditions precisely the same deflections when compared by the delicate Hawksley tests. For all practical purposes, except the difference in gross weight, I consider these two rods absolutely identical.

It is useful for an angler to be able to effect small repairs to his own rod. Whippings may be worn or cut, a ring may come off or a new top ring required, or at times a broken joint can be spliced. The splice may be effected by using the rubber adhesive plaster as described by Mr. Henderson at page 181, or by whipping in the ordinary way with waxed silk. If waxed

Whip finish for whip-pings on rods.

silk is used for a splice or any other repair (after binding carefully with it) the necessity for an efficient finishing knot is very urgent. The whip finish is the only safe one either for flies, rods, or tackle, and I do

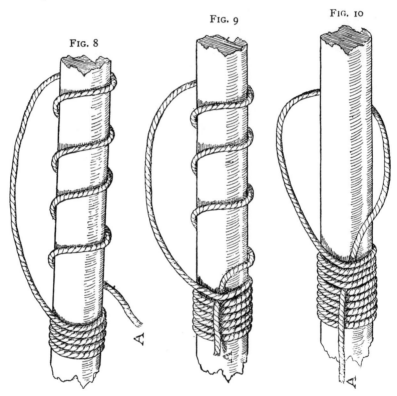

FIG. 8   FIG. 9   FIG. 10

not remember to have seen the method of making the whip finish in the middle of a joint described before in an angling book.

When the whipping is finished the end of the waxed silk (marked A in Fig. 8) is carried some distance down the joint in a loop and the turns

laid on inside the loop back towards the whipping.
The end A is then laid along the joint and one
turn of the silk taken over it as shown in Fig. 9.
Successive turns are then taken and laid evenly
side by side until all the turns in the loop have
been taken up. The finish then appears as shown in
Fig. 10. The end A is then pulled up with the
thumb and the finger over the turns of the finish until
the waxed silk is quite taut and the projecting end of
A cut off close. A little working with the thumb and
finger over the finish to smooth it and a coat of
varnish completes the work.

Brass or gun-metal reels are seldom seen nowadays,
and the ebonite reel is practi-
Reels.   cally a thing of the past.
Aluminium or aluminium alloys
of different kinds are almost invariably used by the
modern tackle maker for his reels. There is an inclination on the part of the manufacturers to fit reels with
an *adjustable check* in the form of a screw on the
outer surface of the reel, by means of which each
angler can arrange the check so that it is as light
or as heavy as he desires. In theory it sounds quite
good, but in practice I would urge that it is a mistake.
The angler carefully adjusts the check to his liking,
and the first friend, or keeper, who holds the rod for a
few moments, is irresistibly impelled to fiddle about with
this screw. The result is that either it is set too strong
for the fisherman, or it is eased to such an extent that
the line overruns and gets into a hopeless tangle.

Both Messrs. Farlow and Messrs. Hardy have

The latest improved reels.

introduced new reels, and both are admirable examples of good, sound, mechanical principles, and first-rate workmanship.

Messrs. Farlow's new reel is described by them in the following terms :—

Messrs. Farlow's new reel.

"The outward appearance of Messrs. Farlow's new reel does not differ greatly from some recent fly-reels of good repute, but the '*internal economy*' has undergone some further development and is surely the last word in mechanical ingenuity. Illustrations are given in Figs. 11 and 12 of the various parts as well as the reel assembled, and from the former it will be seen that it is fitted with ball-bearings throughout. Two sets of beautifully fitted journal-bearings take up all the running strain, and a third set of thrust-bearings takes up the friction between the plates, the result being a very free, easy-running reel, smooth and even—free from all jerkiness and shaking. It is made as far as possible of aluminium alloy, and weighs about 10 oz. The size is $3\frac{1}{2}$ in., which is not too much when you want to have a reserve of line, and the quicker winding afforded by the larger diameter is a distinct advantage. It is fitted with an adjustable check, controlled by a milled screw on the side of the handle plate, but this is an addition which, if so desired, can easily be dispensed with."

FIG. 11

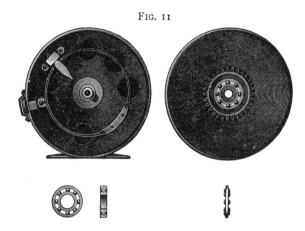

FIG. 12

The following notes on the improvement in reels and the description of Messrs.

Messrs. Hardy's new reel. Hardy's latest reel, are given in Mr. J. J. Hardy's own words.

"It is satisfactory to be able to report considerable progress in the development of fly-reels. In no part of the angler's equipment has so much valuable progress been made. The old form with its side plates held together by screwed intermediate bars, which were a big job, and required quite a number of tools to take asunder, has gone, and a good riddance. Imagine a reel getting wet or half full of sand and no means of clearing it out until one got home and found the tool-box. Those who have once used Hardy's 'Perfect' reels with ball-bearings, regulating check and line-guards, which can be dismounted in a minute without the use of any tools, would hardly be satisfied to go back to the older form, or indeed to any reel which requires a tool chest and some knowledge of mechanics before it can be dismounted."

"This excellent reel, which is so well known, was happily only the parent of others, of the same kind, which differentiate a little as has been found necessary to meet the special requirements for each kind of fishing. The original form is still retained in the salmon sizes, but in the trout series we have the contracted form for quick winding. The same reel is made with circular agate line-guide, and again another with agate bar and facings. The 'Halford' improved pattern of the 'St. George' is another of the class specially designed as a light, large drum reel for dry-fly fishing. Then, the 'Special Perfect,' for loch fishing where a very long line needs to be carried, and lastly, the 'Bouglé' as an extra light reel for small rods."

"A most notable recent improvement is the patenting of an arrangement by which all liability of locking in the check work (a thing which most anglers have experienced at one time or another) is avoided. Figs. 13 and 14 show the arrangement."

FIG. 13

FRAME WITH DRUM REMOVED

"The diagram shows the tongue, or *pawl*, held under a strong steel bridge, on the under side of which is a steel peg, on which the pawl works. The pawl is slotted, and this, while working in either direction, allows it to move at any angle, while at the same time it can rise or fall under pressure of the spring, and so take up wear and tear; or the pawl may rise away from the wheel in case of irregularity, and thus prevent any possibility of locking. The spring keeps the pawl to its work, but allows it to rise should any excessive pressure be applied. The form of spring gives a pleasant light and fine check when winding in. When the drum is turned in the direction in which a fish takes line, the check can be regulated to almost any stiffness by turning the screw of the regulator, which forces the arm to compress the spring,

FIG. 14

and gives the desired pressure." *

"Another improvement consists in the form of the section of that part of the reel frame which comes into contact with the line. The old form of frame is shown in Section 1, and the improved form in Section 2, carrying the raised circular part which forms the line-guard and prevents any scratching of the line on the sharp angles of the frame, as may be seen in Section 1 at B."

"For a special dry-fly reel, the 'Halford' improved St. George with the newly designed catch by which the reel drum, on pressing the lever A with the finger-nail, can be instantly removed (see Fig. 16), seems to be quite the best of all for the purpose. The very large diameter of this reel, $3\frac{7}{8}$ in., gives a large drum, which is so quick in recovering line as to

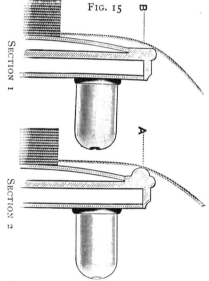

FIG. 15

SECTION 1

SECTION 2

* "The regulator here referred to is not shown in Fig. 13, as Mr. Halford prefers his reels without it.—J. J. H."

be almost equal to a multiplier. This is a valuable feature, especially in dry-fly work on weedy rivers, where a hooked fish is likely to bolt towards you, as by reeling in quickly you can often defeat him."

FIG. 16

" In selecting a reel for dry-fly work, any of those mentioned may be procured either plain or with agate line-guards and regulating checks."

Messrs. Hardy advocate the use of agate guards on their new reel, and they are

Revolving bar on reels. quite efficient. Some anglers, however, prefer a revolving sleeve of steel or other hard metal on the ordinary bar of a reel. It is entirely a matter of personal preference which of these guards should be adopted. I am to some extent of opinion that the revolving bar is quite as handy as the agate guards suggested by the makers of the new reel.

I hope that I shall be absolved from undue conceit in suggesting that all the

Reel lines. modern lines dressed in boiled linseed oil under an air-pump are the outcome of the experiments conducted many years since, at my suggestion, by the late Mr. Deller and the late Mr. T. P. Hawksley. The Hawksley lines are as good as any of the modern ones made to-day and are far smoother softer, and wear better than most of them. The dressing of lines by at least ten successive coats of the boiled oil rubbed down, as advocated by Mr. Hawksley, is in effect the same principle as and similar in manipulation to the methods employed by the modern manufacturer. I am under great obligations to the editor and proprietors of the "Field" for permission to give *in extenso* an article on the subject by my good friend Mr. Martin E. Mosely, published in the "Field" of May 4th, 1912.

DRESSING A TROUT-LINE

"When the first of October arrives and rods and flies have been packed away in winter quarters, the angling enthusiast who loves to keep his fishing by him, year in year out, might well do worse than turn his hand to dressing his own trout-lines instead of buying them ready made from the tackle-shop. He who would dress his own lines, however, must possess an unlimited supply of patience, as the work entailed extends over many months. In fact, the longer the time given to each successive dressing the more durable and lasting will be the resulting article, and in practice it will be found that a line cannot be turned out in much less than a year's time from the date when the first immersion in water-proofing fluid was made."

"The secret of successful line-dressing is contained in the three words—'time' and 'elbow-grease.' Ex-

periments with six different oils tend to show that it is
of great importance that the oil should dry, or, to use
a more correct expression, should oxidise very slowly
and gradually, and that the admixture of minute
quantities of litharge, gold-size, or other dryer is
harmful more in hastening this oxidizing process than
in effecting an injurious chemical or corrosive action
on the silk. I have, however, been informed by an
experienced chemist that the green linseed oil imported from the Baltic has better and more permanent
water-proofing powers than the ordinary yellow or
brown oils which come from Calcutta."

" Most amateurs are deterred from dressing their
own material by the idea that it is essential that the
lines should be stretched out at full length and in the
open air for the purpose of drying. This is quite
a mistake. It is better, if possible, to stretch the line,
as the tension of the silk tends to squeeze out the
surplus oil from the centre, which then has a better
chance of drying. But lines can be stretched on
frames when space is a consideration, and if, after
each coat, the places of contact of the line with the
bars of the frame be arranged so as not to coincide
and the line is not left on too long, the pressure of
the bars will have no permanent ill-effect upon the
surface of the line. It is advisable to remove the
lines from the frames as soon as the outside of
the dressing is dry, coil them up in loose hanks
and hang them up in a warm room to complete the
drying."

" The frames as shown in Fig. 17 may be made of two slips of wood connected at each end with a thin iron bar. I have found it an advantage to have these bars nickel plated, as the iron sometimes rusts and discolours and rots the silk. The larger these frames are made, compatibly with easy handling, the better, as there will be fewer points of contact of the silk with the bars. As eleven or twelve coats of oil are often required to dress a line, it is a convenience to fix a like number of very small brass hooks at equal distances along one side of the frame, and the end of the line can be fixed to these in succession after each coat of oil has been applied, thus

FIG. 17

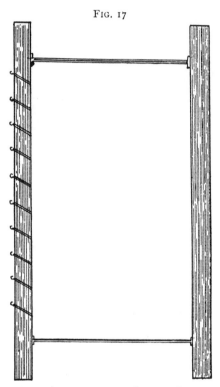

ensuring a new place of contact with the bars each time the line is placed on the frames. To protect the lines while the oil is wet, I have found it useful to have covers to fit the frames of fine gauze, which allow the air to penetrate, but prevent dust and hairs sticking to the line."

" The oil which I have found most suitable for line-dressing was prepared for me by Messrs. Naylor Brothers, of Southall. They took a great deal of trouble in the matter, making up several samples, with all of which experiments were made. Finally, they sent me Baltic oil, which was double-boiled, and which they guaranteed to be pure and free from any dryer whatever, and this has turned out quite satisfactory."

" The opinion is still held by some that the use of the air-pump is unnecessary in line-dressing. I can only say that the quantity of air that escapes from the silk when the pump is working is amazing, and that even with a powerful double-barrelled pump I have found it quite impossible to remove all the air, though the lines have been kept in a partial vacuum for the space of nearly a fortnight.* If such a pump will not completely extract the air, one would hardly expect to be more successful with the alternative method, namely, that of placing the line in a jar of oil, which is set on a stove and allowed to simmer very gently for several days, great care being taken the while lest the oil should become too hot."

" The line should be coiled in a loose hank and placed in the oil in a convenient receptacle under the receiver of the air-pump, supposing that this method is adopted. Care must be taken to raise the vessel containing the oil slightly above the outlet for the air in the footplate, otherwise, if the pump is a powerful

* Since this article was written, a more powerful pump was procured, which removed the air from the line in two or three hours.

D

one and the oil has been placed in a glass dish, it is by no means unlikely that a piece of the bottom of the vessel will be pumped out with dire consequences. Pumping should continue until the bubbles of air cease to rise out of the line in any appreciable quantity. The line is then taken from under the receiver, removed from the oil, and squeezed through the fingers, and subsequently through a piece of linen, in order to remove as much of the surplus oil as possible, for the less oil there is left in the line the more chance is there of the drying process becoming thoroughly effected."

"Next it should be wound on the frame with the end looped round the first hook. When the surface is no longer wet, take the line off the frame and make it up into a large loose hank, and hang it up in a warm place to get thoroughly dry. This may take any time up to two months, but after the second coat, as the inside of the line becomes filled up with the oil, the process of drying becomes much more rapid. When the line is thoroughly dry, so dry that when stretched between the hands no little beads of oil force their way out, the second coat may be applied and the line treated in the same way as before, and wound on the frame, beginning at the second hook. If the line appears to be at all stiff, it should be coiled up into quite a small coil, with a diameter of, say, four inches, and worked about in the hands until soft. A varnished line will not stand this treatment, but when pure oil is used, the dressing is so pliant that any

amount of such rough usage will be successfully with-
stood. The working also facilitates the extraction of
air under the pump, and will frequently betray the
presence of a small quantity of wet oil, which, when a
line has not been thoroughly dried, works its way to
the surface and gives timely notice that the line must
be hung up again before the next coat is applied."

" After the fourth or fifth coat the process of rubbing
down may be begun, and until quite the later stages
are reached a piece of loofah is as good a material to
use as one could desire. In rubbing down a line,
should it not be possible to stretch it at full length,
place it on an ordinary collapsible line dryer, taking a
turn of the line round the handle of the winder to
keep it taut, then hold the line between the thumb and
forefinger of the left hand, giving it a twisting motion
backwards and forwards, and at the same time rub it
up and down briskly with the loofah, held in the right
hand. If there be any very rough places which will
not yield to this treatment a piece of the very finest
glass-paper may be used ; but this is heroic treatment,
and the utmost care must be taken not to rub too long
or too roughly lest the fabric itself of the line be
frayed. After the eighth or ninth coat has been
applied something finer must be used for rubbing down,
and in order to get a really good surface to the line
pumice powder should be mixed up into a paste with
water and rubbed on with a piece of flannel, the
pumice being well washed out of the line afterwards.
When all the interstices of the silk have been filled up

with the hardened oil and the surface is quite round and smooth, the dull appearance left by the pumice powder can be got rid of and the line polished by rubbing it with the thumb and forefinger just smeared in oil. This will dry very quickly, and a final coat applied in the same way will cover over all marks left on the previous coat by the bars of the frame. Care must be taken that only the very smallest quantity possible of oil is applied in these last two coats, as if too much is used the surface will be spoilt, and the line will require to be rubbed down again with pumice. If all goes well, the line should be put away in a warm, dry place, hanging in a loose hank, and not used for at least a twelve-month; in fact, the longer the line is kept after having been dressed the longer will it last, the better will it wear, and the more satisfaction will it yield."

" It must be admitted, however, that a line dressed with nothing but pure oil, though extremely supple and delightful to use, will not stand the application of all the varieties of preparations sold for greasing lines. It has been found that pure deer's fat, for some as yet unknown reason, appears to act chemically on this dressing and cause a sort of eruption from within, which, though not making the line in any way tacky, yet breaks through to the surface of the dressing and allows the water to enter and rot the line. I have not yet ascertained what this action is and how it is caused, but it has been suggested that there is a certain quantity of size applied to the silk whilst being plaited up into the line, and it is the action of the fat on this size which causes the trouble. I am informed that the late T. P. Hawksley was under the impression that the use of animal grease with a pure oil dressing was inadvisable. But the amateur line-dresser need be in no way discouraged, as experiments have proved that the preparation sold as ' Mucilin ' has no ill-effect on lines dressed as above described, and possesses floating powers in no way inferior to those of deer's fat."

" MARTIN E. MOSELY."

I cannot agree with Mr. Mosely in reference to the use of deer fat for greasing the reel-line. For more than thirty years I have used deer fat or mutton fat for the purpose, and with the exception of the two lines he kindly dressed for me I have never found that it affected the silk or the dressing unfavourably.

In order to give the professional in juxtaposition to the amateur view of this question I append here Mr. J. J. Hardy's remarks on the subject.

"THE MAKING OF WATERPROOF REEL-LINES FOR DRY-FLY FISHING"

" You ask me to say a word about the manner of dressing high-class lines, such as the ' Corona,' etc. Really, there is not very much to tell about them. The silk used is of course the very best China silk that can be purchased. This is *boiled off*, that is to say, the gum is extracted from the silk. Naturally, this makes it softer and more pliable, but in the process of *boiling off* fully 25 per cent in weight is lost, which of course increases the cost of the line in the same proportion. From this degummed silk, the lines are plaited according to the size wanted, and in doing this it is usual to employ weights. These are attached to the strands designed to form the line, and vary according to the closeness of the plait desired. In this process it is very necessary to get the exact tension, so that the finished product shall be quite flexible and yet have a perfectly gut-like surface."

"After plaiting, the lines are carefully examined and all roughnesses attended to. The process of dressing is then commenced, the first part of which consists either in placing the lines with oil under the air-pump, or in tanks with oil until they are thoroughly saturated. They are then taken out and all the surface oil wiped off, when they are hung up to dry. The drying of course requires a certain amount of time, and varies according to the condition of the atmosphere and the particular nature of the oil which has been used. When sufficiently dry, they are rubbed lightly down and carefully examined, so that any little unevenness may be attended to. The line is then given another coat of oil, and again allowed to dry. This process is repeated eight or nine times, until a perfectly smooth surface is produced. When this stage has been reached, the lines are finally examined very carefully, and where necessary, extra rubbing down is done. The last process is to stretch the lines, and give them a coat of special varnish.

This is a delicate process, and can only be performed successfully in rooms which are heated to a certain and even temperature. The slightest draught causes what are called *devils* in the varnish, that is, roughnesses, so that all draught must be carefully excluded during the process of varnishing."

"It seems hardly necessary to say that none but the very best boiled oil must be used. The older it is the better, and before applying to the lines it must be very carefully filtered to ensure its being free from impurity."

Some differences of opinion exist as to the methods of attaching the fine end of **Attaching the reel-line** the reel-line to the loop at the **to the cast.** coarse end of the gut cast. Some fishermen use the plain *bend* with or without a knot at the end of the line, some prefer the figure of eight knot, and others again swear by the "Hi Regan" knot. My objection to all of these is that to remove the cast it is often necessary to break or cut off a small quantity of the reel-line. This continued from day to day shortens the taper at the end of the reel-line and thus curtails the life of the line. For many years I have adopted the plan of knotting on and whipping with waxed silk a strand of coarse gut with a loop tied at the end to which the loop of the cast is fixed. Such an attachment will last for months, and the only disadvantages as far as I know are that the loop and gut need to be tested at frequent intervals, and before commencing a day's fishing this strand of gut must be thoroughly soaked.

Mr. J. J. Hardy has kindly contributed the following note on the manufacture of gut, and it should be read with care by every fisherman who desires to make himself fully acquainted with the details of this most important part of his tackle.

Silkworm gut.

"THE MAKING OF SILKWORM GUT AND CASTS

" These form a very important part of an angler's outfit, and a few words on the subject may be of interest."

" The best gut produced is made in Murcia, Spain, where silkworms are produced regularly in large quantities. This is mostly done by the peasants, who cultivate the worms in their homes. The process of making the worms into gut is as follows : When the worms have attained the stage when they are ready to spin their cocoons, they are killed by putting them into a pickle, which somewhat hardens and solidifies the silk secretions. When this has been done, the worm is taken between the fingers of the worker, who deftly breaks it open and extracts from its interior two oblong sacs which contain the gluten, which had the worm lived would in the natural course of events have been converted into silk. These sacs are then gripped at either end and drawn out to their full extent, and fastened by the ends being coiled round a small peg. At this stage the material is of course soft, but by exposure to the sun it gradually hardens and becomes what we know as gut."

"The above is the first stage, and the product is called raw gut. This is sold to dealers who call themselves Bankers, because their business is to advance money in weekly payments to the peasants while the worms are growing, with, of course, a claim on the gut when it is produced. In this first stage of the gut the outer surface is covered with yellowish skin, which is removed by boiling in soap and water, after which it is further treated by polishing with special appliances. In this stage it is either handed over to the Bankers, or sold direct to the manu- facturers, by whom it is carefully sorted and graded in different thicknesses and qualities, after which it is packed in bundles containing a hundred each; these are again put up into bundles of a thousand, when it is ready for export. The thickest gut is called ' Hebra,' the second ' Imperial,' and the third ' Marana 1st.' Then there follow ' Marana 2nd,' ' Padron 1st and 2nd,' ' Regular,' ' Fina,' and ' Re- fina.' In all these various thicknesses there are at least three qualities, the best being called ' Selecto,' the second ' Superior,' and the third ' Estriada.' "

"When the gut is received in this country it again goes through a process of further sorting, each quality being put aside for the purpose for which it is best adapted. Much of it is used in the natural state, the very best being made into gut casts. The second, third, and fourth qualities are employed in making the commoner tackles and casts, down to the roughest of which much is used for sea fishing."

" In this short description it is not the intention of the writer to say anything about the great scarcity of very thick gut, which is used for salmon fishing, or the very fine long Refina which is used for trout fishing. Both classes are always very scarce indeed."

" The impossibility of procuring gut sufficiently fine for the end of gut casts has necessitated the introduction of the system of *drawing*. This is done by passing it through plates similar to those used by wire drawers. The majority of these plates are made of steel, but a limited number are made of stones of various sorts. The latter are somewhat expensive, but produce gut of a smoother quality than the steel, and, therefore, where the highest quality gut is required, stones are almost exclusively used."

" Before commencing to *draw*, the gut is made very soft by steeping it for some hours in cold water, when it is first pointed, i.e. tapered at the ends by rubbing them on a Bath brick with a soft pad. In drawing, the gut may be passed through as many as three holes."

" Drawn gut, like other articles, is made in various qualities, and where price is an object, it is naturally done by the shortest and cheapest method. Good gut, however, cannot be produced without a very careful selection of the material in the first instance, that is to say, if common or defective gut is used, the result in the end will be defective drawn gut ; on the other hand, if none but the choicest qualities are used, the product will be gut of the finest quality."

The knot shown in Fig. 18 is the one generally used **Knot for gut casts.** for making up a cast or other tackle from a number of strands of gut. It has been adversely criticised by some modern authorities, but I find no practical disadvantage from its use.

FIG. 18

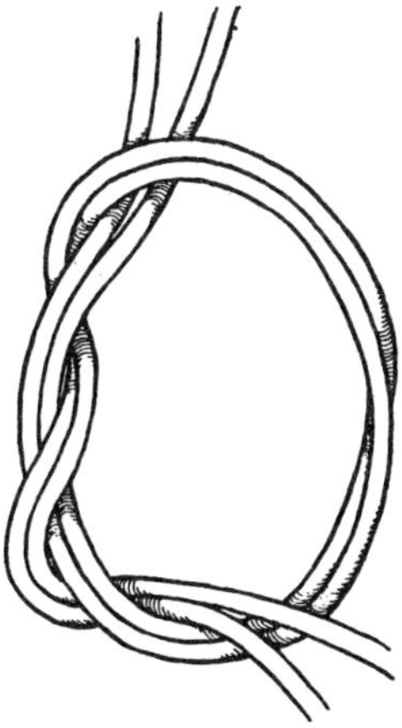

Gut must be thoroughly soaked before knot- **Cast damper.** ting, and a cast requires also to be softened in water before being fished. A number of boxes have been made for the purpose, but to my mind the very best gut damper is an ordinary indiarubber tobacco pouch with sufficient water in it to just damp the inner surface. This was suggested to me some years since by Mr. H. T. Sheringham, and, as in the celebrated soap advertisement, "since then I have used no other."

The upturned eyed hook is, to all intents and pur- **Hooks and their at- tachment to the cast.** poses, the only one used at the present time by dry-fly men. For attaching the fly to the fine end of the cast the " Turle " knot is the very best, and the successive stages of making it are shown in Figs. 19, 20, 21, 22, and 23.

The ideal fly-box has not even yet been invented.

Fly-boxes.

We know that fixing the points of the hooks into flannel, felt, cork, or any other substance is a mistake—resulting in rust which is fatal to the hook-point. Most of us carry our flies in boxes

FIG. 19   FIG. 20   FIG. 21

FIG. 22   FIG. 23

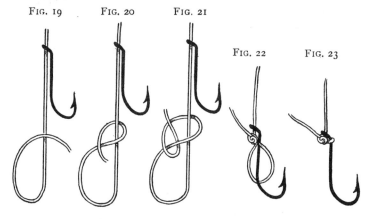

divided into a number of compartments. Messrs. Farlow have designed such a box to contain the new set of patterns in "Modern Development of the Dry-fly," and the following is their description of this box:

"THE MODERN DEVELOPMENT FLY-BOX"

"An adaptation of a well-tried form of fly-box to hold a complete set of the latest patterns is shown in Fig. 24."

"Size $7\frac{1}{2} \times 3\frac{7}{8} \times 1\frac{1}{4}$—a trifle large possibly for the ordinary pocket, but not for the bag or basket, and not too large for this set of flies, allowing say a dozen to each compartment."

"Compartments—27 of equal size with a lid opening over each row of 3. Six larger compartments for

FIG. 24.

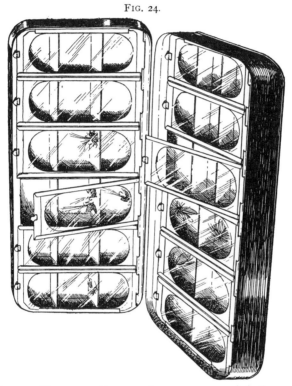

the 6 mayflies, or for one's own special favourites outside the 33."

" Nicely made and finished, and very compact, considering the number and variety of flies which it will hold."

Messrs. Hardy Brothers have brought out the " Halford Fly-boxes—Model 1912," for which they claim the advantage that the names and numbers of each pattern, as given in "Modern Development of the Dry-fly," being printed on the celluloid lids of the compartments, the use of these boxes tends to impress on the angler's mind both the names and numbers of the flies.

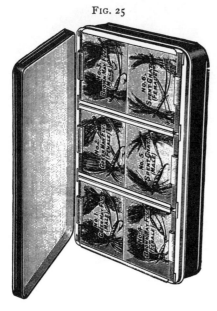

FIG. 25

The mayfly-box shown in Fig. 25 measures $5\frac{1}{2}$ in. $\times 3\frac{3}{4}$ in. and $\frac{7}{8}$ in. deep, and contains about one dozen each of patterns Nos. 1 to 6 inclusive, of the mayflies and spent gnats. The lids pull out from either side, so that only one compartment is open at a time.

The small fly-box shown in Fig. 26, measuring $5\frac{1}{2}$ in. $\times 3\frac{3}{4}$ in. and $1\frac{1}{16}$ in. deep, holds about one dozen each of the patterns Nos. 7 to 33 inclusive. The lids on one side are arranged on the same principle as those of the mayfly-box, while the other side has spring clip lids which lift up and expose three compartments at a time.

The flies can be seen without opening the compartments, because the celluloid lids are transparent and the boxes are made of tin enamelled in the usual way.

Where, as usual on chalk-streams, the fish run large, a landing-net is a neces-

Landing-net.

sity, and all the leading tackle makers make nets with a turn-over to hang in a sling. A strong, large, rigid hoop to the net, a net of moderately large mesh, and as long and as strong a handle as possi-ble are desirable. I should advise the fisherman when purchasing a landing-net, or in fact any other part of his rod and tackle, to go to a first-rate manu-facturer and select

FIG. 26

the very best, which as a rule is the highest priced one. It is true economy to do this, as inferior tackle (and most cheap tackle is inferior) is far more costly and less satisfactory in the end than the best.

A small bottle of paraffin to waterproof the flies, a means of applying the paraffin,

The "Curate."

a stiletto to clear the eye of the hook, a pair of forceps for picking them out of their compartment, or for extract-ing them from the fish's mouth, an implement to cut the gut when knotting up the cast or attaching the fly, and a short, heavy weapon to give the trout its *quietus* when landed, are almost all necessities. Messrs. Hardy have united all these in the little implement shown in Fig. 27, which is styled the "Curate (Registered No. 557672)." In this A is the cover of the paraffin reservoir, B the stiletto, used to apply the paraffin or clear the eye of the hook, C the paraffin reservoir, and E the gut-cutter.

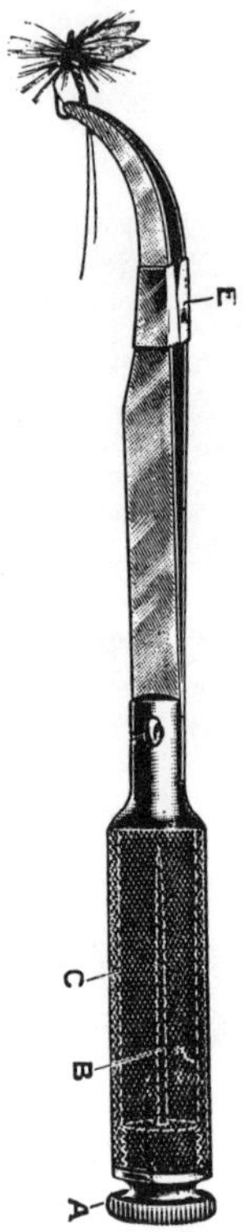

The forceps are specially useful for extracting the hook from a fish's mouth without injuring the dressing of the fly, and the use of it will save the life of many undersized fish which can be returned to the water.

FIG. 27

CHAPTER II

CASTING

FLY-FISHERMEN often assert that it is impossible to learn to cast from a book. This is to a certain extent true, but the beginner can, if he gives due attention to the subject, get from a book a number of hints which will greatly assist him. It is also said that the best plan is to get a past-master to give instructions and thus educate the embryo fly-fisher. This again is only to a certain extent true. A teacher must certainly understand thoroughly the subject he is teaching, but the greatest experts are often the very worst of teachers. The capacity for imparting knowledge to others is a natural gift just like an ear for music or talent for drawing. A moderate performer who possesses this capacity is a far better teacher than the highest exponent of the art who is without it. It is I believe a recognized principle of modern scholastics that the teacher who seeks to convey his knowledge to others requires very special training to do so successfully.

In " Dry - Fly Fishing in Theory and Practice " the following definition of cast-**Definition of casting.** ing is given : " Casting may be defined as placing the fly which is at the end of the collar, in a desired spot, in

E   49

a desired manner, and at a desired moment." I confess that I do not see how to improve on this definition.

The beginner when trying to teach himself to cast should let out a few yards of line, say eight or ten. The rod held firmly in one hand is raised nearly vertically to lift the fly, collar and line into the air behind the angler, and at the same time a slight backward movement is communicated by the wrist. At a certain point this upward and backward motion is checked, and the action of casting or throwing the fly is commenced by moving the rod forward and letting the point of the rod gradually assume a position more nearly horizontal so as to deliver the fly on the water. Before making a second cast the rod is raised and carried backwards into a nearly vertical position, and this is styled returning the fly.

The grip or method of holding the rod is most important. The majority of **Grip of the rod.** first-rate performers grip the rod (in the right or left hand), holding it tightly between the ball of the thumb and the second, third and fourth fingers, using the forefinger for regulating the line and pressing the thumb firmly, pointing upwards, along the handle of the rod as shown in Plate I. Marryat gripped his rod with both thumb and forefinger pressed against the handle and pointed upwards. He had an abnormally long forefinger ; possibly this was to some extent the effect of his peculiar grip. He always considered that this

Grip of the Rod.

PLATE I

Swan Electric Engraving Co Ltd

grip gave him a greater power of directing the line and fly with extreme accuracy. It is comparatively unimportant which grip is adopted by the tyro, but it is all-important that he should from the first learn to hold the rod as tightly as possible if he wishes to be a good hand at casting.

The first point to be impressed upon the student is that, if he will study and assimilate the hints given here, the direction of the wind, unless it is very strong indeed, is a matter of comparative indifference to him. There is no more difficulty in casting against a light wind than there is in casting with it. If the teacher can once persuade his pupil to look at the subject from this point of view, the progress of the study will be most rapid. I should like to see the experiment thoroughly tried of making the angler from his earliest efforts cast indiscriminately against or with the wind.

The most usual, the ordinary or overhanded, cast is effected by raising the hand holding the rod and carrying it slightly backwards with wrist action, until the position of the rod is nearly but not quite vertical. This action returns the line from the water, and is done without any great effort and at a slow pace. When the rod has arrived at the point where the backward action should cease, the fisherman makes an appreciable pause, and Plate II shows the position of the rod and line then. The casting-plates in this chapter are

The ordinary over-handed cast.

reproduced from instantaneous photographs taken for the purpose with exposures of 1/800 of a second by Mr. W. A. Rouch, who is considered to be the most successful operator of the day in this class of photography. These reproductions were made from the original negatives, and therefore represent with absolute truth the position of the rod and line. In Plate II the moment at which the plate was exposed was a fraction of a second too late, but the line is accurately shown, although the rod is just commencing to deflect backwards.

At the backward position the rod is bent neither forwards nor backwards, which must mathematically prove that, at what may be called the resting-point, the weight of line in front of the rod is exactly counterbalanced by the weight of line behind it. Of course, the line and fly at the end of it are moving backwards, and at once the excess of weight behind will begin to bend the rod backwards, i.e. with the concave side of the curve behind the angler.

The forward motion or act of casting is then begun, and the rod is brought forward at a very slightly increased pace. There is great danger of the beginner overdoing this increase of pace and making what is sometimes called a *flick*, or more or less of a jerk. Such action absolutely ruins the angler's chance of making a good cast; in fact, the acceleration of the rod as it comes forward is barely perceptible, and the movement throughout should be deliberate and

PLATE II

Overhanded Cast — Backward Position

Photograph by H. J. Smith

PLATE III

Overhanded Cast – Coming Forward.

Photograph by W. H. Busch

PLATE IV

Overhanded Cast – Forward Position

Photograph by W.A. Busch

uniform. Plate III shows the position of the rod and line as the rod is coming forwards to make the cast.

When casting down-wind this forward action is continued until the rod and line are in the position shown in Plate IV, and the rod is then perceptibly checked by tightening the grip slightly. This, again, is an action capable of extreme exaggeration, and anything like a sudden spasmodic tightening of the grip will ruin the best cast and bring the line on the water all of a heap and often with a perceptible splash. After the rod is in the forward position the line should gradually coil over forwards and deliver the fly in the desired direction, and it should land like the proverbial *thistledown* lightly on the very spot where it was intended to place it. This is the method of casting with a following wind.

There are diversities of style in casting. Some, and these, I venture to sug-
Style of casting. gest, the best of performers, do practically all the work with the wrist. Exceptionally when making an extra long cast they raise the whole of the arm well above the shoulder, but still use only the wrist in moving the rod. Raising the line high up behind in this way is called the *steeple* cast, and is useful not only for casting very long distances, but also for lifting the fly in the return above low bushes or other impediments behind the angler.

Some few fishermen cast with an almost stiff wrist

and use the forearm as the motive power. It is not a pretty style, but there are undoubtedly many first-rate fishermen who invariably adopt this method with overhanded or steeple casts. Again, Mr. E. Valentine Corrie, who is one of the most stylish and at the same time one of the most effective dry-fly men, has a peculiar method of his own. He brings his rod back to the resting-point (as I have called it before) when returning his fly, makes a distinct pause, and then drops his hand further backwards. He then comes forward in the usual way, stops at about the usual angle, and then deflects his rod further forward by dropping his hand forwards. It is difficult to explain, and as far as I can remember I have never seen another first-rate fisherman do this. His movements throughout the action of returning and casting are quite slow and without effort, and he places a fly with the greatest accuracy and delicacy combined.

In my former book this cast was described as the *downward cut*, but I have dis-
The downward finish. carded the expression *cut* and substituted for it the word *finish*, because to my mind the word *cut* suggests something in the shape of a hit or jerk, which is the one thing to be avoided at the finish of this cast. The downward finish is used by the best fishermen only in cases where the wind is nearly in their teeth. With a cross wind the horizontal or underhanded cast is used, and this will be described later in this chapter. The downward finish is made in the same manner

PLATE V

Overhanded Cast — Downward Finish.

Photograph by W.S. Reach

as the ordinary overhanded one up to the forward
position, when the rod and line are as shown in
Plate IV. Instead of the action at this moment being
checked, the forward motion is steadily continued
until the point of the rod is actually on the surface
of the water, and when this is properly carried out
the line coils out forwards and extends itself in the
teeth of the wind, the rod and line then being in the
position shown in Plate V.

In reference to these plates, it must be noted that,
whereas an ordinary dark-coloured line is plainly
visible against the sky, it is almost invisible against a
background of bushes, sedge, or water in shade, and
under these conditions the line has been whitened by
the application of chalk.

The position of the hand should be noted, and it is
above all essential that the action of the return and
cast should throughout be slow and without great
force. When the tyro fails to place his fly into the
wind it may be laid down that he is making one or
more of three mistakes : (1) he may be moving his
rod too rapidly ; (2) he may be using undue force ;
and (3) he may not be carrying the action through
until the rod-point is down on the water. Many
men make the cast in effect very like the ordinary
overhanded ; when they come to the forward position
check the motion of the rod for a moment, and then
let the point fall forwards on to the water. This
action will in every case fail, and the beginner must
learn to carry his rod right through from the back-

ward position to the finish when the rod-point is on the water.

The advice may be summed up in terms very similar to those given to the young golfer learning to drive—but the fly-fisher must not continue the acceleration of the action coming forward like the golfer. The golf professional says, "Slow back, do not press, carry your club through to the finish." The fly-fisherman's mentor says, "Slowly and deliberately back, a slight pause, a slight (very slight) acceleration of pace when coming forward, no great force at any part of the cast, and carry the forward motion slowly right through to the finish on the surface of the stream." There is one other very important difference between the golfer and the fly-fisherman—the golfer is taught to hold his club lightly with his fingers, while the fly-fisher can hardly grip his rod too tightly.

When you fail to bring off this cast you may, as before remarked, safely infer that your principal faults are casting too quickly, using too much force, and not carrying the rod through to the finish. The stronger the adverse wind the more rapidly the beginner casts and the more strength he puts into it. He should do exactly the reverse—the stronger the wind the slower should be the motion, and when once he has succeeded in getting the pace of the rod he will find the force required is very little more against a violent wind than against a light one.

PLATE VI

Horizontal Cast – Backward Position

PLATE VII

Horizontal Cast - Forward Position

Photograph by W. A. Beach

The length of the gut cast should vary according to the direction and force of the **Length of the gut cast.** wind. During a dead calm it should measure not less than $3\frac{1}{2}$ yards; with a strong following wind it should be increased say to 4 yards, or even a trifle more; with a moderate head-wind it may have to be shortened to 3 yards, and in a very strong one even to $2\frac{1}{2}$ yards. Under no conditions should the dry-fly man work with a shorter cast than $2\frac{1}{2}$ yards; as if he does his fly will inevitably land on the water with a splash, probably scaring the fish to which he is casting. It may be laid down that, the greater the length of the gut cast that a fisherman can manage, the lighter will his fly fall on the water, and the more likely will he be to succeed.

The horizontal cast is exactly similar in action to the overhanded one, but the **The horizontal cast.** rod is held and moved horizontally instead of vertically.

The position of the rod and line and appearance of the line at the backward position of a horizontal cast are shown in Plate VI, and at the forward position in Plate VII. All the instructions and hints given, in reference to the ordinary overhanded cast, apply equally to the horizontal cast. The beginner will find that his hand and forearm are cramped at first, this being due to a set of muscles being brought into play which are seldom used for any other exercise, but practice and perseverance will in time get over this.

Undoubtedly the horizontal cast is the most important of all for the dry-fly man, and it is especially useful when it is desired to deliver the fly in a direction across a moderate or even strong wind. One of the manifest advantages of this cast is, that the rod's position being horizontal throughout, its shadow is not projected over the water. The shadow of a moving object is specially likely to scare a shy fish when it is rising, and consequently close to the surface.

The beginner will find that there is a tendency on his part when learning this cast **Returning over and casting under rod with horizontal cast.** to return his line under and cast it over the rod. In fact, this would appear to be the natural method. I would strongly urge him from the very first to reverse this and return over and cast under his rod. He will find that his fly by this method will land more lightly, and that in the case of a fish rising under a bridge or plank not raised much above the surface he will be able to place his fly above the fish, whereas with the reverse action it would almost invariably strike the bridge and never cover the fish. Very little practice will enable the angler to acquire this particular mode in fishing the horizontal cast.

It is not quite easy at first to place a fly accurately with the horizontal cast, because the rod, and consequently the line with the fly on the end of it, move in a circle or parabolic curve, and not in a straight line as with the overhanded cast. The man who can make this cast has overcome the initial difficulty of dry-fly fishing, because with any breeze short of half a gale he can fish with ease across its direction. This cast will almost always land the fly *cocked* on the water, i.e. with its wings up, and in the natural position for may-flies, duns or sedges. This is caused by the wings of the fly as it falls on the water, acting like the feathers of a shuttlecock, while with the ordinary overhanded cast the fly is driven on to the surface of the stream.

Every fly-fisherman should, if possible, learn to use either right or left hand indiscriminately for casting. Most people can train themselves to be *ambidextrous*, especially if they commence in early life. A scientific friend of mine established a rule in his household that the table should be laid right and left-handed in alternate weeks. He himself not only used either hand to the knife, spoon, or fork, but even carved left-handed during the week devoted to that hand. His wife, children, and even guests were expected to conform to this rule. I commend it to my readers.

It is at times useful to the fisherman to be able to cast with either hand, especially **Horizontal cast, back-handed.** when he is on the right-hand side of the river looking up-stream, because when returning left-handed in this position his fly is over the water and cannot well catch up on the bank. There are places, however, where the left-handed horizontal cast will not deliver a fly properly to a rising fish. These places will be referred to in the chapter on "Drag." In such a place the angler (I am supposing him to be right-handed) must fish *back-handed.* No doubt, most readers will understand this term, especially the lawn-tennis players.

When one is fishing back-handed with the right hand, it is carried back in the return until it is against the upper part of the left arm, and the position of the hand is shown in Plate VIII. Throughout the return and cast the hand is kept with the side on which the little finger is placed, directed towards the point where the fly is to be cast. It is a most useful variety of the horizontal cast and well worth the trouble of learning thoroughly.

To make a very short cast is often difficult, and the reason is, as usual, that one **Fine and far off.** works too quickly and puts too much power into the action. The old school of fly-fishermen always preached the text "fine and far off." I venture to differ with them as far as dry-fly is concerned. The finest of drawn gut is unnecessary ; in fact, any drawn gut is to my mind a disadvantage. Every man can find out for himself the distance at which he fishes best, and wherever practicable, should place himself in such a position that this length of line should be used. It certainly will not in any case be what the modern school of dry-fly men would call *far off.*

PLATE VIII

Backhanded Horizontal Cast

From Gaskell Engraving Co. Ltd.

So far almost every word of this chapter would apply equally to wet and to dry-fly methods of casting. Drying the fly consists in returning and casting several times in succession without letting the fly fall on the water in front and, of course, keeping it up off the ground behind. The use of paraffin to render the fly waterproof or nearly waterproof has appreciably decreased the labour involved in drying the fly. Above all, the dry-fly man must keep his fly free from any moisture, so that it will float when it lands on the surface of the stream. There is no such thing known as a half-way house between dry and wet-fly fishing; either the fly is floating, in which case it is dry-fly fishing, or it is more or less submerged, and is wet-fly fishing.

Drying the fly.

Where there are impediments on the banks behind the angler the wet-fly man casts what is called a *switch;* this means that in returning the fly and while it is on the water in front of him it is cast with a sort of downward finish, and if all is accurately timed it will be propelled by the weight of the line from the water, and therefore at no part of the cast be behind the fisherman. Obviously this is impracticable with the dry-fly, but the fly may be dried up and downstream, and as the cast is made the hand turned over towards the point to which it is intended to direct the fly. Again the fly can be dried anywhere where there is space or even wiped with a

Dry switch.

handkerchief. It is then held in the left hand, the cast being made and the fly let go simultaneously ; if accurately timed a very fair cast may be made in this way.

It is often said that the presence of a stream or pond is not absolutely necessary for the beginner when practising the art of throwing a fly. This is true of every kind of cast except the downward finish, but in this case the finish on the water-level would in all human probability break the rod if tried on *terra firma*. I would suggest that the best possible practice of casting and the best method of improving one's style is to let out, say eight or ten yards of line, and while walking from one part of the stream to another at a considerable distance from the river to keep the fly moving backwards and forwards just as one does when drying the fly between two casts. This exercise is most beneficial in training the muscles and getting a correct notion of timing, and, above all, is most efficacious in thoroughly drying the fly.

Under all possible conditions it is·desirable that the dry-fly man should cast up-stream. The normal position of a fish is with its mouth pointing upstream, not only

Upstream and down-stream fishing.

because in that position it is best placed to intercept and annex any dainty morsel drifting down to it, but also because the respiratory organs of a fish work naturally with the water flowing towards its mouth. There are occasionally places where upstream fishing is barely possible, and at times, too, the force of the wind is so great that even with the downward finish and a cast of only $2\frac{1}{2}$ yards in length it is almost impossible to place the fly accurately into the teeth of the gale.

Then it is permissible to fish downstream or partly across and partly down even

Drifting. with the floating fly. The former direction, called *drifting*, requires that the angler should let out a length of line far greater than that required to cover the fish rising below him. As the line is descending at the forward position of the cast it is checked not only by tightening the grip, but also by bringing the rod-hand back towards the body. The result of this is that the fly is landed on the water above the rising fish with a quantity of slack line above it, and as the fly floats down the fisherman's hand is lowered and the fly allowed to proceed some distance below the feeding trout. It is recovered slowly either by drawing in line gradually with the left hand or by returning the fly laterally over the bank below the fish. In either case it is a manœuvre of desperation, and one can seldom get the chance of presenting a second fly to the same fish without setting it down.

Fishing partly across and partly downstream is called the *half drift*, and is

Half drift. achieved by dropping the rod-hand as the fly lands on the water and letting it float down, or even crawling or walking down after it as it proceeds down the stream and over the feeding fish. This cast is again seldom successful with trout, but at times grayling seem to prefer a fly cast in this way. The reader must study the chapter on "Drag" when devoting his attention to the questions of *drifting* and the *half drift*. He can safely sum up the question in a few words : whenever and wherever possible the dry-fly man should cast upstream, and whenever and wherever he deviates from this golden rule, his chances of success are indeed remote.

CHAPTER III

THE ETHICS OF THE DRY-FLY

THERE is, to my mind, no necessity to discuss here the relative merits of the dry-fly and wet-fly. The question has been debated *ad nauseam*, and there is room among true sportsmen for the votaries of either style of fly-fishing. The confirmed advocate of the dry-fly school will under all conditions float his fly. The wet-fly man will sink his fly or flies, and he who, like the late Francis Francis, believes that " the judicious and perfect application of dry, wet, and mid-water fly-fishing stamps the finished fly-fisher with the hall-mark of efficiency," will continue to use each method as and where he deems it to be the most likely to lead to success.

The dry-fly is, as its name suggests, an artificial fly used dry, i.e. with no water **Definition of a dry-fly.** held in suspension between the fibres of the hackles, wings or other feathers, etc., used in its construction. In this state it floats on the surface of the stream. Mayflies, duns or sedges should sail down *cocked*, i.e. the mayflies and duns with their wings erect and the sedges with their wings at an angle of about 30° to the horizontal. The spent gnat or spinner which represents the female imago after it has voided its eggs, or the male imago when its share of the work of procreation is complete, should float down in its natural position with wings laid flat and at right angles to the line of the body. A new fly which has never been wetted will float naturally at the first cast if it is placed lightly on the surface. After it has once been on the stream it will probably have collected some water, and in order to make it float it will require to be freed from adherent moisture, as pointed out in the chapter on "Casting," by waving it backwards and forwards in the air.

A sunk fly is constructed to absorb moisture from the water, and is de-

Definition of a sunk fly. signedly allowed to sink to a greater or lesser depth below the surface. The modern theory is that these patterns are taken by the fish for the nymphæ or pupæ—these being the scientific names of the immature insects at the stage immediately preceding the winged form.

I do not pretend to speak with any semblance of authority on wet-fly fishing. My first introduction to fly-fishing was on the Wandle where, for the last half century or more, the floating fly has been exclusively used, and later on the Test, Itchen and other south-country chalk-streams my allegiance to the floating fly has never wavered for a moment. Candidly, however, the presence of wings in sunk fly patterns has puzzled me, because in my ex-

perience I have never seen the winged insects submerged by the action of the stream. Sedges do at
times descend to oviposit and so do certain spinners,
but their appearance under this condition with an air
bubble between their wings resembles nothing so
much as a globule of mercury—an appearance which
bears no resemblance to the ordinary sunk fly
patterns.

When fishing dry, the angler must in the first
instance find a fish taking the
Method of fishing   winged insects on the surface,
dry-fly.   and it is essential that he
should locate its position with
the greatest precision. This is technically called
spotting the rise. If he should perchance catch sight
of a fish near the surface which is evidently on the
look out for duns or other flies but not actually rising,
he may cast to this fish. His chance of success is
in no case very good, and on club or subscription
waters, which are usually very much overfished, he
is far more likely to scare the fish than to induce it
to rise at his fly.

The artificial fly having been placed on the water
lightly and accurately so that it will float down over
the exact spot where the fish is feeding, the next
essential is that it should follow precisely the same
course and travel at precisely the same pace as the
natural insects under similar conditions. This branch
of the subject to be treated in a subsequent chapter
entitled " Drag."

The wet-fly fisherman does not as a general rule wait for a rising fish, but places **Method of fishing sunk fly.** his fly or flies (he frequently uses two, three, or even four) in a part of the river where, from his experience of the habits of the trout, he would expect a feeding fish to be located. Some fish upstream, some downstream, and some across the stream. In the hands of a past-master it is a most scientific and, under favourable conditions, a very deadly method of fishing.

The expression *chalk-stream* will occur frequently in this book, and it is well **Chalk-streams.** that the reader should clearly understand its meaning. The word chalk-stream refers to streams which have their sources in springs deep down in the earth, and from which the water rises to the surface through a considerable thickness of chalk, being thus filtered and freed from any visible particles of solid matter held in suspension. These chalk-streams abound in different parts of Great Britain. In my own limited experience I have seen several in Hampshire, Wiltshire, Dorsetshire, Kent, Derbyshire, Staffordshire, and Yorkshire, and very probably they exist in other counties as well.

The main characteristic of all chalk-streams is the pellucid clearness of the water, which is, as a general rule, unaffected by rain, except when unusually severe. Even then the discolouration is often caused by road washings, in which case these streams clear very rapidly, and in a few hours seem as bright as ever. The strength of the current in them is in most parts only moderately great, so that they flow smoothly and at no great pace. In exceptional places, below weirs or hatches, or where the fall of the river is very steep, there are short stretches of quite fast water, in some cases almost as rough and turbulent as a mountain stream.

In the late spring and summer they are usually covered with weeds, and, in fact, if the weeds are not periodically cut the rivers get choked up with dense tangles of vegetable growth. These weeds are well stocked with the immature forms of such waterbred insects as the duns, the caddis-flies, the stoneflies, some of the smuts or *curses*, etc. The weeds are also favourite haunts of crustaceans, such as the fresh-water shrimp and of mollusks, such as the various snails. Now all of these immature insects, as well as the winged ones into which they change, and the crustaceans and mollusks are the very best food imaginable for trout and grayling. As a natural consequence these fish are exceptionally well fed, grow to a large average weight, and are usually in the best of condition. These chalk-streams are pre-eminently the rivers in which the dry-fly is most used and most successful.

Those of us who will not under any circumstances cast except over rising fish are sometimes called *ultra-purists*,

Purists.

and those who will occasionally try to tempt a fish in position, but not actually rising, are styled *purists*. The expressions are often used by angling authorities as a species of reproach or commiseration, or even with the intention of being read as *chaff*. Now I would urge that the first rule to be observed by every man who wishes to be deemed a dry-fly fisher is to follow the example of these purists or ultra-purists.

Nothing is more gratifying to the true sportsman than to be able to give his **Sunk fly on dry-fly** enthusiastic friends an occa- **waters.** sional day on the water he fishes. Marryat used to say that a day at the river-side watching a first-rate performer was quite as enjoyable as one passed in solitude fishing oneself; and no doubt to an absolutely unselfish man like my late friend this self-denying ordinance presented many charms and had no disadvantages. Walking with his guest or varying the proceedings by trying some of the rising fish himself, the host can spend a delightful day in congenial society. At once the worst, and perhaps the best, feature of dry-fly fishing is its uncertainty and disappointments, and the fact that no amount of study of the subject, even when spread over many years, has to any appreciable extent enabled even the most observant to hazard a forecast of the probable basket, or pronounce any definite idea of the climatic conditions under which good or bad sport may be anticipated.

The mere fixing of a convenient date is often a

matter of some difficulty, entailing correspondence, and frequently requires to be arranged well ahead. When the day comes it may be all that could be desired, with a good hatch of fly, fish rising freely and fastening, and then everything is *couleur de rose*. Unfortunately such occasions are like the proverbial angel's visits, "few and far between," and when our long-expected guest arrives it is perhaps during a spell of unpropitious weather—often a dull sunless day with rough downstream wind. The past-master will in such case possess his soul in patience and wait for the appearance of the duns or other flies. He will then cast to the rising trout, fishing upstream, and, as shown in a previous chapter, there is no great difficulty in accomplishing this in anything short of a hurricane. If, however, the fly should be conspicuous by its absence he will shrug his shoulders and hope for better luck next time.

One who is not so well able to bear up under adversity, and is, perhaps, indisposed to waive the remote chance of killing fish, will proceed to the upper limit of the fishery and flog it steadily down with wet-fly. He will probably see some fish following his fly, occasionally even plucking at it and getting pricked ; a few, but a very small proportion, being landed, and of these the vast majority yearlings or two-year-olds. Perchance he may succeed in getting two or three killable trout, but these as a rule are only just up to, or possibly under, the legal limit of the fishery.

It is the very worst of taste for a guest to follow these tactics, because he should know that it is the unwritten law of the dry-fly man on a chalk-stream to eschew any but the legitimate method. An old hand has no possible excuse, because in addition to knowing the before-mentioned unwritten law, he is fully aware of the bad effect produced by hooking and rendering shy so large a proportion of the feeding fish. He ought to know, too, that his hospitable friend will abstain from making any remark on the subject, although his unspoken thoughts may be most eloquent.

One who is used to the sunk fly may be unaware of all this, and thus find an excuse. If by any chance he should kill an odd sizable fish he would probably be unduly elated. He might go away and talk of having wiped the eye of the dry-fly man, or even fly into print and proclaim *orbi et urbi* that he had made the astounding discovery that the dry-fly men are all fools, and that the sunk fly will at times kill on these south-country chalk-streams. Like many more, he will be deluding himself. Years and years ago it was well known to the *habitués* of the Test and Itchen that on *happening days* odd fish may be killed with wet-fly fished across or even downstream. Everything possible has been done by the dry-fly men to dissuade all and everyone from practising this lapse from their notion of sport on an essentially dry-fly stream, a notion which may perhaps be deemed ultra-orthodox by some of their *confrères*.

The larger chalk-stream trout is averse to taking any great exertion to satisfy its appetite, because Nature has provided an ample store of nutritious food in the form of duns or dun nymphs, caddis or caddis-flies, either in the winged, nymphal, larval or pupal stages, as well as the crustaceans and mollusks, which the feeding or hungry trout can secure by merely rising to the surface, or opening its mouth among the weeds. If it should prefer minnows or other small fish, a few strokes of its powerful caudal fin suffice to propel it at a pace sufficiently great to catch the very fastest of them. Thus the fish of the Test, Itchen, or other chalk-stream is not precipitate in its movements, it raises itself slowly and sedately so as to meet the natural insect floating down, and the larger the fish the more deliberate is its procedure when feeding.

In fact it may be laid down that one of the reasons why so few trout, and these few certainly not the monsters of the stream, are taken with sunk fly worked downstream, is that it is swept too rapidly across by the strength of the current to suit the measured pace of the chalk-stream trout.

It may also be admitted as an axiom that the comparatively large size and aldermanic proportions of the Hampshire trout are in a great measure due to their habit of moving slowly when feeding, which would be incompatible with their existence in a river where the food supply was not most bountiful and nutritious.

On some fisheries attempts have been made to frame regulations which preclude this form of wet-fly fishing, and such rules as : " No salmon or silver-bodied flies allowed," or simply " Dry-fly fishing only allowed," are printed on the members' and friends' tickets of some such clubs and subscription waters, and no doubt these are salutary laws in such cases.

On a length of water preserved by the lessee or owner for his own and his friends' sport, it is felt that the publication of these and similar regulations on the permit is almost an insult to the character of a guest invited to share as a sportsman in the pleasure of dry-fly fishing. Guests, too, should bear in mind that the very heavy rents paid for water, the great expense of stocking, weed-cutting, and other matters required to maintain the character of a first-rate chalk-stream fishery are based on the esteem in which anything like good dry-fly fishing is held at the present time. Mile for mile wet-fly fishing is not worth a quarter of the sum paid on the Hampshire streams, and nothing more surely tends to develop further the increasing shyness of the fish than the presence of a few persistent downstream fishers with the sunk fly.

The advocate of the winged fly, nymph, or pupa fished under water will possibly not be impressed by the last few paragraphs. He may skip them, or if he takes the trouble to read them may remark that as he almost

Wet-fly fished upstream on dry-fly waters.

invariably fishes upstream these scathing criticisms do not apply to him. I will at once freely admit that upstream wet-fly fishing is not so harmful on a chalk-stream as the same method pursued downstream. But in my view the continual flogging and the continual movement of the angler making his way along the bank, too often in full view of the trout, are, however, very nearly as destructive of the confidence of the fish as downstream fishing. Then, too, the distance covered by the persistent flogger is so great that the limits of any ordinary length of private water will be covered many times in an ordinary day's fishing. The excuse which is sometimes advanced to palliate the breach of etiquette committed in using sunk fly on a dry-fly stream is that the aim of a fly fisherman is to kill fish with a fly whether wet or dry—surely this should not be so on a water preserved entirely for dry-fly.

I am told, however, that there is a school of fly fishermen who only fish the sunk fly over a feeding fish or one in position if it will not take a floating fly. This, they urge, is a third method of wet-fly fishing, the other two being the more ordinary of *fishing the water* with sunk fly either upstream or downstream. Candidly I have never seen this method in practice, and I have grave doubts as to its efficacy.

The St. Andrews authorities, after compiling the rules of the game of golf and fixing penalties for any breach of them, supplemented these rules by issuing a separate document, entitled "The Etiquette of Golf." For the breach of the maxims laid down in this document they have imposed no penalties, but the true golfer is, if possible, more punctilious in respect to the etiquette than he is to the rules of the game. If a member of a golf club is unsportsman-like, or possibly only careless, and habitually commits the grave indiscretion of disregarding the etiquette of the game, he will find difficulty in persuading his fellow-members to make a friendly match with him. I would suggest that the ethics of the dry-fly on a fishery where dry-fly only is permitted should be regarded in much the same light.

After all, what does it amount to? A member of a club or subscription water has to practise a certain modicum of unselfishness so as not to interfere with the sport of his fellow-members. He must abstain from hammering a fish, whether rising or in position, so as not to add to the fish's already advanced education. He is expected to keep well back from the bank when walking upstream, so as not to scare the fish and injure the prospects of others who are following him. When making his way downstream he should take even greater precautions in this respect, because from the position of every feeding fish with its head directed upstream the angler is then visible at a far greater distance than when moving upstream.

If he has crawled into position over a rising fish with every precaution to keep out of sight, and has after a number of unsuccessful casts decided that it is better policy to abandon the pursuit of this and find another fish rising elsewhere, he should, when retiring from his position, double his precautions so as not to set the trout down. If he should start with the intention of fishing a particular stretch of the stream either because he has a preference for it, or because the wind or light is in his opinion propitious, and finds another member already in possession, he should either draw back and keep well below him, or, walking very wide of the bank, proceed a considerable distance above before even looking for a feeding fish.

If a fellow-member should hook a fish he should offer his assistance with the landing-net, and if this offer is accepted he should not volunteer advice as to the handling of a fish. He should at all times be ready to tell his fellow-member the pattern of fly which has proved successful, and if necessary give one to his friend in case he should be without the particular artificial. In a word, he should in every respect act as a true sportsman. If the *ethics* as before laid down are incumbent on a member of a club or subscription water in reference to his fellow-members, how much more stringently should they be observed by a guest whether fishing on a club or private water.

CHAPTER IV

CHOICE OF PATTERN

THE tyro is now equipped with rod, reel, line and other tackle. He has learnt to cast accurately either with, against, or across the wind. If my efforts have been successful, he is fully armed with the knowledge of the ethics of the sport. The next step is to help him in his choice of the pattern of artificial fly which is most likely to tempt a trout feeding and taking a fair proportion of the natural insects floating down to it on the surface of the stream. As a preparatory stage he should arm himself with the little net made for the purpose, and take from the surface a number of the duns or spinners which are sailing down the river.

He should examine them carefully with the aid of his magnifying-glass and determine their genus, and, if possible, also the species. To assist him in this work of identification he should refer to the second part of this book, which treats of " The Fisherman's Entomology," and it will not be unprofitable for him to devote some time to the study of the life history of the various insects described in detail.

If the angler has read the current literature on the

subject he will realize that there exists a great

Colour. diversity of opinion among the recognized authorities. Some deem colour to be the most important factor in the choice of the pattern. Some believe fish to be colour-blind, and there are a number of divergent theories between these two extremes.

Personally, I am charged with having apparently recanted to some extent the opinions enunciated in " Dry-Fly Fishing in Theory and Practice." The late Edgar Williamson, who was my fishing companion in 1902 and 1903, was a consistent and ardent advocate of the *exact shade of colour* theory, and persuaded me to devote all my spare time during those years to the congenial work of designing a new set of patterns imitating as nearly as I could in size, form and colour the natural insects of the Itchen which serve as food for the fish of that river. The result of my work on these lines is set forth fully in detail in " Modern Development of the Dry-Fly," published in 1911 by Messrs. George Routledge and Sons, Ltd.

I must ask my reader to arm himself with a copy of this book and read in it the history of the new patterns, their dressings, the modern manipulation of fly-dressing, and a number of chapters describing my practical experiences of their use. The numbers of patterns of artificial flies given throughout this book are those appended to these patterns respectively in " Modern Development of the Dry-Fly."

In page 2 of that book I said : " I am desirous of

placing on record here my own views of the colour question, views which I am told are shared by many others. I am not, and never have been, a believer in the theory advanced some years since by Sir Herbert Maxwell that fish are colour-blind. In justice to him it should be said that he himself has since to a great degree recanted some of the opinions he advanced on the subject.* While believing that the trout or grayling in the water can, to some extent, differentiate tones and colours, I do not think that the presence or absence, for example, of a tinge of brown in the body of a female iron-blue spinner, would suffice to account for a trout which is feeding on the natural insect (*Baëtis pumilus*) represented by this pattern fastening to the one with this brown shade, and coming short to one dressed with claret body like the old-fashioned pattern. At the same time there are occasions when, and places where, one is almost tempted to think that the colour perception of the Salmonidæ is developed to the highest degree. Every fisherman, however, who has

---

* Sir Herbert Maxwell takes exception to this, and writes in the "Pall Mall Gazette" of March 30th, 1911 : "First, I have never advanced the theory that fish are colour-blind ; secondly, I have never recanted any opinion previously expressed on the subject." He then suggests for observation and experiment three alternative hypotheses : "(1) That salmon and trout are insensible of colour. (2) That like human beings they cannot nicely distinguish colour in an object presented to them between their eyes and the light, which is the case with a fly, natural or artificial, on or near the surface of the water. (3) That if they have the power of distinguishing colour in flies so presented to them, they show indifference to it, provided that the shape and movement of the lure is life-like, and as regards trout provided the shade of hue (light or dark) approximates to that of the natural insect."

devoted himself to the entomological side of the question, and has also been interested in working out and dressing patterns of flies, must feel a great satisfaction in turning out one which is a truer and better imitation of nature than the generality of those he had seen before. No doubt he will fish this improved pattern with a fuller sense of confidence in its efficacy than he would with an inferior imitation, and, as has been so often written before, confidence in a particular fly is one of the most potent factors tending to render it successful in use."

I do not apologize for giving this extract *in extenso* because it sets forth succinctly my notions on the subject, and clears the ground before giving advice as to the flies to be used under various conditions and at different seasons of the year. I have every reason to thank critics for their favourable notices of my last book, but in one respect some of them have, no doubt unintentionally, misrepresented my views. They suggest that I have failed to adduce good and sufficient proof that the fish which were killed by these new patterns would not have succumbed to the charms of the old standard patterns comprised in the list given by me in " Dry-Fly Entomology." I do not think that I have ever advanced such a theory.

I have given numerous examples of their successful use, and summing up the results of the exclusive use of these said new patterns during seven consecutive seasons (to which since that time I can now add two more) I said : " Looking back and considering the

G

question in the most judicial frame of mind, I cannot find that I have on any occasion been placed at a disadvantage by limiting myself to their use." I certainly added that in some cases the natural appearance of the artificial flies had appreciably conduced to an amelioration of sport, but this is a far less sweeping assertion than that suggested by my critics. I think, perhaps, that one of the conditions which appealed to me most forcibly in reference to the new set of patterns was that by its adoption the full outfit of the modern dry-fly fisherman is reduced to thirty-three patterns, of which certainly six are unnecessary at any time, excepting during and immediately after the short rise of the mayfly.

In one respect my opinions have certainly become modified by further experience **Fancy patterns.** derived from continual observation of the fish and their habits, and from watching guests and friends fishing in Hampshire and other waters. At an earlier stage of my career I was, like many others, prone to think that at times fish, both trout and grayling, were inclined to take *fancy patterns*. By the word fancy patterns I mean artificial flies which are not imitations of any natural insects which the fish affect as food. Since discarding all the old standards and substituting for them the new set of patterns given in "Modern Development of the Dry-Fly," I have gradually arrived at the conclusion that seldom, if ever, is a trout tempted by one of these monstrosities. It is true that they kill at times, but when friends have scored with fancy flies I have almost always found that I could do as well with the new patterns for trout.

I am not so clear with regard to grayling, as at times they do seem to have an incomprehensible desire to rise at such patterns as wickhams, red and orange tags, furnace and other bumbles. I think that this is due to some such proclivity as curiosity. A rising trout is poised close to the surface, and, by merely separating its lips, can suck in the passing dun. The rising grayling is located at some depth below the water, comes up to each individual insect, and if it has succeeded in timing its movements accurately, arrives at the surface just in time to seize the fly. Immediately after securing the insect the grayling turns and goes down to the position it occupied previously. Often, however, it has apparently miscalculated the pace of the current and misses the fly. This may well account for grayling so often coming short to the artificial. It is, however, arguable that the feeding grayling cannot distinguish the object floating over it from a distance below with the same degree of precision as the trout close to the surface. The fancy fly is something moving and apparently alive, and when the grayling is near enough to see it clearly it is possible that it is tempted to try its flavour.

Comparison of rise of trout and grayling.

Some of my readers may have adopted my own plan of discarding the old patterns and confining themselves to the new set. Others may have full faith in one or more of the old standards, and will add them to the collection in their boxes or books. Others, again, will have nothing to do with the new-fangled notions, and swear by the old standards to the exclusion of any others. To all I would proffer a few words of advice. If you have a preference for a particular pattern by all means fish it. The fly you prefer is far more likely to kill than one in which you have no confidence. Do not, however, let yourself be blinded to the possibility of patterns being improved, and when you use one which strikes your fancy as an unusually good imitation of the natural insect give it a fair trial before condemning it.

Throughout this chapter it is my desire to cater for all sorts and conditions and to give the best advice I can to every shade of opinion. I therefore propose in each case to give my readers the alternative of selecting either from the set of patterns in " Modern Development of the Dry-Fly " or from the one hundred best patterns given in " Dry-Fly Entomology." For the sake of brevity I shall designate the former the *new patterns*, giving their numbers as before stated, and the patterns from the older book will be called *old standards*.

The trout-fishing season on the Test and Itchen opens on the 1st of April, a **Opening of the trout** date which, to my mind, is a **season.** month too early for the Itchen. Even on the Test it is quite early enough, and many of the large fish of, say, 2 lb. and upwards are not in first-rate condition. The

Test is certainly an earlier river than the Itchen, and no one, as far as I know, has advanced a good and valid reason for this. Test trout spawn earlier than those of the Itchen, they come into condition earlier, and perhaps to compensate for this the Itchen fish take well, and are in comparatively better condition than those of the Test towards the end of the season.

The policy of returning sizable trout taken at the commencement of the season if wanting in condition has been preached from time to time immemorial. In rivers in which the trout generally are the offspring of wild fish, and are bred and reared in a state of nature, it is, no doubt, a wise policy. Unfortunately few such rivers exist. As a rule the fish are raised from ova, taken from artificially bred parents; they are reared and fed in stews, and in many instances grossly overfed. The yearlings and two-year-olds which are turned into the rivers, as is the custom early in the spring, are frequently overgrown and degenerate specimens. This branch of the subject is dealt with in detail in Part III, "The Making and Management of a Fishery," and the policy advocated there of knocking on the head every dark, lanky, ill-conditioned brute whenever, wherever and however taken is the wisest one to pursue.

The hatch of fly in April, especially at the commencement of the month, is **Early spring patterns.** usually a short one, and it is as well for the angler not to waste too much time in the preliminary work of

identifying the insects on the water. The first of the
duns to hatch out is generally the dark olive, followed
by the olive duns, and the various patterns in the new
set, Nos. 7, 8, 9 and 10, are recommended during
the early and middle part of the month. Nos. 7 and
9 are the males, and 8 and 10 the females respectively
of the olive and dark olive duns.

The expression hatch must be clearly understood
to refer to the first appearance in the winged stage,
although, of course, the true meaning of the word is
the emergence of the larva or nympha from the egg.
The word has been used in this anomalous sense for
so many generations by anglers that I think it well
to continue to use it notwithstanding the knowledge
that it is not scientifically accurate.

The males of the majority of water-bred insects—and
especially in the case of the Ephemeridæ—assume the
winged condition first and largely outnumber the
females. The males are slightly smaller and distinctly
darker in colour than the females, and in the genus
Baëtis, which includes the olive and iron-blue duns, any
doubt as to sex can be quickly dispelled. A casual
examination with the naked eye will reveal the presence in the case of the males of a red-brown turban-
shaped cap on the top of the head which is absent
in the females. I have called this a cap from its
outward appearance, but as shown in Part II, "The
Fisherman's Entomology," it consists of two excrescences side by side on the top of the head, which
are covered with facets, and are in fact compound eyes.

The votary of the old standards should, when the olive or dark olives are up,

Old standard patterns for early spring. make his selection from the dark or medium olive quills, either winged or the hackle varieties of these patterns. The gold-ribbed hare's-ears, either winged or hackle, is perhaps all round the most successful old standard for the fisherman in April and, in fact, throughout the season. It has always been my theory that it is a fair representation of a dun in the act of disentangling itself from the nymphal shuck. It is a moot point whether it is good tactics to fish it over bulging trout, and in a later chapter some remarks will be found showing the deleterious effect of hammering away at these fish feeding almost entirely on the nymphs.

The rise in the early spring is, as before remarked, generally a short one. It may commence at ten, eleven, one, or even two o'clock, and last perhaps a few minutes one day, and on another with seemingly identical climatic conditions for as long as two or three hours. Temperature, direction or force of the wind, rain, sunshine, and even snow do not seem to affect the hour of its commencement or the length of its duration. There is only one golden rule to follow, viz. to start at a comparatively early hour in the morning and remain at the river-side until sunset, and in hot summer weather even later than that, and as long as the angler's fly floating on the water can be seen.

Even as early in the season as the middle of April on a warm calm afternoon the **Female olive spinners in April.** female olive spinners may be seen dipping and depositing their eggs in the water. As explained in the entomological portion of this book, the female spinners or imagines of the Ephemeridæ fall on the water soon after they have voided all their eggs, and fish rising at them take quietly and steadily, making little commotion on the surface of the stream. For trout rising under such conditions the female olive spinner No. 12 or the female olive (red) spinner No. 13 of the new patterns should be tried, or of the old standards one of the hackle red spinners, the red quills, or detached badger are the most likely patterns.

McLachlan, in his inimitable " Monograph of the Trichoptera of the European **The grannom.** Fauna," says of the grannom (*Brachycentrus subnubilus*) that it is a true spring fly, and that where found it is usually present in countless numbers. In my earliest recollections of the Test I can recall the swarms of this interesting insect from the middle of April to the commencement of May, and realize how true is the description given of it by the late eminent entomologist who made the family to which it belongs his chief study. Since those days it has gradually decreased in numbers and almost disappeared from its old haunts. I can say with truth that during the last nine years I have not seen a dozen examples of the fly on a part of the river where formerly it was most plentiful.

I have tried, with the kind co-operation of my good friend Mr. Martin E. Mosely, to reintroduce it, but unfortunately my efforts have been in vain. We imported from parts of the Kennet, where it is still plentiful, great numbers of the caddis—its immature form—as well as laying down thousands of the blue-green egg sacs from which the larvæ are hatched. I believe that it is still found in parts of the Salisbury Avon as well as the Kennet. Its disappearance from the Test is to be deplored, because it certainly was a capital fly to fatten the trout in the spring.

It was generally a source of deep disappointment to the fisherman. In the days of its biggest hatch, when the river from bank to bank was a seething mass of struggling pupæ, winged flies which had emerged from their pupal envelopes and empty pupal shucks, and the fish were boiling in all directions, his difficulty was to distinguish the large fish from the undersized ones. In such a commotion it is never easy to tell one from another, and in the hurry and excitement one generally selects the small fry. If one should hook a fish of any size the result is too often a smash. Seeing so many feeding fish and the continual disappointment of hooking little ones cause most of us to lose our coolness, and the natural result is too much power in the strike. Worse than all, after a few minutes the fish are gorged, and the rise at the grannom is over for the day.

Among the old standards there are two patterns, one each of the pupa and winged fly. I have killed fish with the pupa, but I am not keen on it, as, although I fished it and every other pattern quite dry and floating, yet I cannot conscientiously describe it as dry-fly fishing. This remark applies equally to all imitations of pupæ or nymphæ of the various angler's flies, and their use on streams reserved exclusively for the dry-fly should be strictly forbidden. Whenever, during the hatch of grannom, the feeding fish are not taking it, the before-mentioned patterns of olive duns or spinners are the most likely ones to try.

Grannom patterns.

In early seasons the first appearance of the iron-blue dun may well occur towards the end of April, but, to my mind, it is essentially a fly commencing to hatch in May, and continuing during the summer and early autumn. The iron-blue is present on the great majority of English rivers, including all the south-country chalk-streams. It is especially plentiful on the Test, where it is a great favourite with the trout, and the largest fish are particularly partial to it. Whenever it is up in fair numbers the patterns imitating it should be tried first, and if a carefully placed light and accurate cast with one of these artificials should fail to elicit a response the angler should fall back on one of the olive or dark olive duns. The male and female iron-blue

May patterns.

duns Nos. 18 and 19 in the set of new patterns are, I believe, the most lifelike imitations extant, and the votary of the old standards has, besides the iron-blues themselves, such patterns as the blue quill, adjutant blue, and blue dun, all of which, however, are lighter in colour than the natural fly.

The first appearance of the pale watery dun may be expected about the middle **Pale watery duns.** of May, and it continues to show up during the summer and early autumn. It is a smaller and much paler fly than the olive, and some angling authors probably refer to this insect when writing of what they style *pale olives*. If we could all agree to give the same English name to the same angling fly it would save an infinity of trouble and confusion, and as from time immemorial the name, pale watery dun, has been given to the subimagines of some three or more small pale species of duns, it would be well to adhere to it. On the Test the pale watery dun is not generally a very successful fly, but on the Itchen and many other rivers it is a great killer. Nos. 14 and 15 in the set of new patterns are the male and female respectively, and among the old standards the pale watery dun, pale olive quill, hare's-ear quill, little marryat, and occasionally the ginger quill all dressed on oo hooks, may be used with advantage when it is up.

On a fine calm and genial afternoon in May, spinners may be seen in the air, and when the

females are ovipositing a fish rising quietly may well
be feeding on them. Under
Spinners in May. such conditions, if one cannot
secure a few specimens so as
to identify them the choice of a fly calls for some
consideration. The species of duns which were most
plentiful earlier are those likely to have assumed the
imago dress, and their spinners are likely to be now
engaged in the act of oviposition. There are quite a
number to select from as olive, iron-blue, and pale
watery duns have probably all been *en évidence*. The
patterns representing the females of these in the
perfect stage should be tried first. Nos. 12 and 13
of the new patterns being female olive, No. 21 female
iron-blue, and No. 17 female pale watery spinners.
Of the old standards the olive badger, the various
patterns of red spinner, red quill, and detached badger
are the best, but not very good, imitations of these
spinners.

Very occasionally the male spinners are on the
water and are preferred by the fish. The males,
which as before noted largely outnumber the females,
are very prominent in the air, and when the angler is
nonplussed he may try their imitations. It must be
remembered, however, that every female soon after
oviposition falls on the water, while the males,
being polygamous, still continue their curious *danse
d'amour* in the air, and are available for their share of
the work of fertilizing the eggs of another brood.
Nos. 11, 20, and 16 are the male olive, iron-blue and

pale watery spinners respectively in the new patterns, but the only representative of these among the old standards is the jenny spinner.

Smuts or curses are sometimes to be seen in good numbers even in April, but **Smuts.** it is towards the middle of May that they may be confidently expected, and during fine or close weather are usually present throughout the summer. In olden times the angler generally lost his temper over smutting fish and, I believe, attached undue importance to the size of the artificials to be used. Some went so far as to get hooks made specially of extraordinarily fine wire and altogether very diminutive. The ooo hook was not small enough for their ideas, and some of the hooks made for them were marked oooo or even ooooo.

The description of smutting fish in a subsequent chapter will indicate that they are feeding and moving about under conditions likely to make them supernaturally shy and wary. If one of the large ones did fasten to a ooo or smaller hook it too often happened that the hold gave and the fish escaped. This occurred so frequently that I decided to abandon anything smaller than the oo hook. Of late years I have seldom failed to score off fish taking these irritating little Diptera with Nos. 26 and 27, the male and female black gnat in the new patterns—my preference being for the male. One of the best dry-fly men of the day, Mr. E. Valentine Corrie, has pronounced it to be the very best fly ever dressed for the purpose; he calls it "the chap with the red tie," from the ruddy colour of the horsehair at its head.

Of the old standards the curses and black gnat are the best imitations. Some of the old school of dry-fly men advocate the use of fancy patterns for smutting fish such as wickham, pink wickham, orange bumble, furnace, etc., also silver sedge dressed on oo hook, red quill, detached badger, or claret quill—but I am doubtful whether these latter should be classified as fancy patterns as they were probably originally intended to imitate some natural insects—the silver sedge, one of the small Trichoptera, red quill, detached badger, and probably claret quill, female olive and iron-blue spinners.

In olden days it was always said that quite at the end of May, or commencement of June, the first appearance of the mayfly might be expected. The hatch of mayfly has in recent years appreciably diminished in a large number of the chalk-streams, and in many this diminution has progressed by leaps and bounds, until at length some of the old hands have not thought it worth while even to include mayflies in their outfit, or to carry them during what used to be styled the carnival of the dry-fly fisherman. From my own personal experience, between 1903 and 1911, the new patterns of mayfly have remained almost untried in their boxes. In 1911

The mayfly season.

I saw an odd fish take a natural mayfly, and I did certainly succeed in killing two and a half brace of sizable trout with an imitation of the male green mayfly No. 1 in the Test. My experience in the years from 1903 to, and including, 1911 refers to a part of the river where in days gone by the show of green drake was quite remarkable. The spent gnat or imago of the mayfly has on a few occasions scored in my hands during the years referred to.

Some observant fishermen, although unable to adduce any logical argument in support of their contention, anticipate a further development of this gradual decline, until some day the mayfly on the Hampshire streams will become as extinct as the antediluvian animals. Others suggest that such vagaries have been noted in the past, and that after the lapse of some few years those of us who survive will witness, if I may so call it, a rejuvenescence of the green drake, and see hatches as great and sport among the big fish as surprising as ever—*Qui vivra verra.*

As I hope that this book may live after me and be of interest and use to generations of dry-fly fishermen yet unborn, I am inclined to hedge, and will therefore include here some advice as to fishing the mayfly and the patterns to use, and give a *résumé* of the life history and habits of this insect in the entomological part of the book.

The dry-fly man is now supposed to rent, own, or have permission to fish a stretch of one of the few

rivers where mayflies are still in abundance. He
will, no doubt, have impressed on his keeper the
importance of letting him have early information of
the first show of the fly. On some day, which may
be as early as the 15th May, and in any case at some
date between then and the end of the month, he will
probably receive a wire saying that the fly is up.
This will mean that the keeper has seen three or
four of the *jacks*—the slang name in the south for
the male subimagines—and very likely he will urge
his master to start at once.

My advice to him is to wait at least three or four
days, and then he will probably be too soon, and see
only occasional flies hatching out, and no fish taking
them. In another day or two the fish will appear to
have gone mad. They will be diving about in all
directions, splashing and taking something under
water with loud resounding *floops*. This is what
some locals call the fish running after the fly. It is
nothing of the kind. The trout are plunging about
after the active nymphs swimming up to the surface,
where they will assume the subimago or first winged
stage. To cast over fish under these conditions is to
prick and scare a number of them, and render all so
shy that it is quite possible that with the best hatch
imaginable the fish will not take either the natural or
artificial well.

A few days later, when the hatch of fly comes on
and the surface of the water is covered and the air
is full of the green drakes, the trout will settle

down and may take heavy toll of them. If they have been left alone during the flooping stage the skilled and cool fisherman will get quite a large number of the very biggest fish daily as long as the rise lasts. He must, however, play the waiting game, select his fish with care, keep well out of sight, use the underhand cast only, and throw once or twice accurately with a perfectly dry fly over the fish. If it is not taken, he must wait until the trout has taken two or three more naturals, and then cast once or twice more with the same care and with the same accuracy. Anything like hammering will very soon arouse suspicion in the trout and set it down for the day. When the fish rises he can hardly strike too slowly, and once hooked, all the strain possible must be put on and the fish prevented from plunging into the nearest weed-bed. If the trout goes to weed, the method of handling is worked out in detail in a later chapter.

Now for patterns. In the new set there are four, Nos. 1 and 2 being the male **Patterns of mayfly.** and female green, and Nos. 3 and 4 the male and female brown mayflies respectively. The green mayflies are imitations of *Ephemera danica*, the species usually found on the Test, and the brown mayflies are intended to represent *Ephemera vulgata* and *Ephemera lineata*. All three species are present on the Itchen and Kennet. Of the old standards " their name is legion " ; the best perhaps being the green and brown

H

champions, although all of those given in " Dry-Fly Entomology " are good.

As shown in the second part of this book the green drake or subimago sheds the **Spent gnat.** whole of its outer skin and emerges an imago or perfect insect.   The imago of the various species of Ephemera used to be, and is often still, most inappropriately styled a *spent gnat* by the angling community.   Some time after it has voided all its eggs, the female falls almost lifeless on the water, and at this stage is greedily taken by the feeding fish.   The great fall of spent gnat usually occurs on deep, slow reaches of the river on a calm and mild afternoon or evening, and the trout feeding on it are close to the surface, moving slowly and taking several flies in succession with a curious sounding *flop*.   They are very shy and easily scared, so that here again the waiting game and very occasional delicate casts with perfectly dry fly are necessary.   The rise does not as a rule last long, so that there must be no mistakes if the angler expects a big bag.

It is at times a good policy to try fish with the spent gnat during the morning, and fish will also rise to it for a week or so after the hatch of the fly is over. The male spent gnat is specially useful at this time because, as shown in reference to the smaller Ephemeridæ, the male imagines are polygamous and do not fall in great numbers on the water or land until the ova of all the females have been fertilized.

The old standard pattern of the spent gnat worked out by Marryat is dressed with **Patterns of spent gnat.** wings of four dark grizzled blue dun cock hackles set on horizontally; a grey partridge hackle at head, a badger cock hackle at shoulder, and another badger cock hackle ribbing the body which is of condor, dark at the point and white at the root, the white part at shoulder and two or three turns of the dark part of the quill at the tail end of the body ; a fine silver wire ribs the body and fastens securely each turn of the ribbing hackle ; the whisk is of gallina dyed a very dark brown, and the hook is No. 3 long.

In the set of new patterns Nos. 5 and 6 the male and female spent gnat respectively were worked out with the greatest care, and I firmly believe that, had he been spared to see them, my dear friend Marryat would have been the first to admit that they were more lifelike and nearer to nature than his own standard pattern. I think, too, that he would have warmly approved of my plan of representing both sexes instead of only the female, of which his pattern is an admirable imitation. The dressings of the two new patterns are given in detail on pages 34 and 35 of " Modern Development of the Dry-Fly."

I have given some space here to the consideration of mayfly fishing in deference **Welshman's button.** to the opinions of those who urge that it may in time to come be as plentiful as it was in olden days. An entire chapter of "Modern Development of the Dry-Fly" is devoted to the welshman's button, and I entreat my reader to study this chapter carefully. He may be one who regrets poignantly the decline of the mayfly. He may, like the late Mr. T. P. Hawksley, stigmatize mayfly fishing as a form of poaching almost as reprehensible for the dry-fly man as worming or spinning the minnow. Or he may hold an opinion somewhere between these two extremes. He will in any case agree with me that the presence and increase* from year to year of this interesting member of the family of the Sericosto-matidæ, known to all good anglers as the welshman's button, do to a great extent provide a fair substitute for the green drake itself.

Personally I do not regret the mayfly. It was, to my mind, the most disappointing form of dry-fly fishing. Hordes of men who never wetted a line during the rest of the season came down the moment they were warned of its first appearance. From *morn to dewy eve* they paraded the banks, hammered away at the fish whether bulging at the nymph, rising at the subimago, or imago, or even at times indulged in the time-honoured *chuck-and-chance-it* principle. They pricked and scared fish after fish, and often succeeded in rendering the big ones so shy as to be unapproachable for a considerable time. It was this that led to the erroneous belief that after the mayfly the trout were so gorged and lazy

* Unfortunately an exception to this occurred in 1911.

that they would not rise to any fly for at least six weeks.

Throughout this book it is my aim to abstain from unduly praising the new pat-

Patterns of welsh-man's button.

terns or depreciating the old standards. In this case I must pray of my readers, even those who are the most enthusiastic advocates of the old patterns, to take one of each sex of the natural welsh-man's button from the water and compare them with correctly dressed specimens of No. 29 the male and No. 30 the female. He should then compare them with flies dressed to the old standard pattern with wings from the peacock underwing feathers and the rough bronze peacock herl body. It will be surprising if he does not at once realize the great strides made towards imitating nature in the new patterns, and it is not unlikely that he will discard the old standard welshman's button from his list.

The male is, in my opinion, the more killing of the two, although I have known days and evenings when a rising trout would not look at the male and took the female. A notable example of this occurred in 1910, when, after a number of days during which the male had been almost exclusively successful, Martin E. Mosely, fishing with me on the evening of June 11th, could not get a rise out of a feeding fish with the male. He changed to the female and at once killed a handsome male trout of 3 lb. 11 oz. The next day, the 12th, was a Sunday, and consequently under the

terms of my lease a *dies non*.   On the evening of the
13th the female did not seem to tempt the rising
trout, but on putting up the male he killed in
rapid succession three perfect specimens of true
Test trout, weighing respectively 3 lb. 4 oz., 3 lb.
and 3 lb.

On rivers where there is no mayfly the welshman's
button is the most killing in
June.   the first part of June. Throughout this and the next months
the iron-blue or pale watery is the best of the
patterns of duns, the female olive, iron-blue and pale
watery spinners of the imagines, and the two sexes of
black gnat for smutting fish.   Of the old standards
flight's fancy, pale watery duns, pale olive quills, hackle
red spinners or detached badger are the most likely
patterns for fish taking the small Ephemeridæ, and
the various patterns of curses, black gnats, and fancy
patterns recommended for May are the best for
smutting fish.

The old school of dry-fly men were strongly in
favour of the alder during the
Alder.   early part of June, but the
majority of them are by now
convinced that my contention in reference to this
insect is correct.   The study of its life history shows
that at no time during its brief career in the winged
state is it voluntarily on the water, and prolonged
observation has proved that the flies struggling on
the water which were taken to be alders were, in the

great majority of instances, specimens of the welsh-man's button.

In hot weather generally there is not much fishing in the daytime for the fisher-man who is greedy and wants to make a big bag. The dry-fly man who is of a contemplative turn of mind and can find the necessary patience will often succeed in taking an odd good fish on the calmest and most sultry days. He must wait for a rise, spot the fish as a good one, and, casting at long intervals, take every precaution to keep well out of sight and place his fly lightly and accurately over the trout. The fish rising gently and slowly in the full blaze of the sun are generally feeding on smuts, spinners, or winged ants, so that the various patterns of black gnats and spinners, with the addition of No. 28 the brown ant, should be selected.

Fishing in hot weather.

Grayling in rivers where they are preserved should certainly not be killed before the middle of July, but they have a great tendency to increase very rapidly and in many cases crowd out the trout. Hence the policy of preserving them too highly is a doubtful one. Even the best chalk-streams can only provide food for a limited number of fish, and any undue preponderance of grayling is sure to react on the stock of trout. They take the patterns advised for trout, but many good judges prefer fancy patterns for them, such as the macaw tag, orange tag,

Grayling in the summer.

red tag, orange bumble, furnace, wickham, pink wickham, or green nondescript.

The chapter in " Modern Development of the Dry-Fly " on this subject should be

Evening fishing. studied in connection with the remarks I propose making. In fact it would be well for the reader to peruse this and the succeeding chapter on " Sedges," before considering the points now raised. The blue-winged olive (*Ephemerella ignita*) may be expected to show up about the middle of July, and continue during the remainder of the trout season. It is a fly which usually commences to hatch out in the evening and often continues until it is too dark to see. It is quite possible that the hatch goes on throughout the hours of darkness. The new patterns imitating it, No. 22 the male and No. 23 the female, are a great improvement on any of the old standards. If blue-winged olives are to be seen, and they are very prominent and visible on the water, these patterns should as a rule be tried first and persevered with over several rising fish before being discarded. When the trout are rising quietly and cannot be tempted by the blue-winged olive the imago stage of the same insect, i.e. the sherry spinner, is often successful. Nos. 24 and 25 are the male and female sherry spinners respectively. If the fish will have none of these the female olive (red) spinner No. 13, female iron-blue spinner No. 21, or female pale watery spinner No. 17 should be tried.

No. 31 small dark sedge, No. 32 medium sedge, and No. 33 cinnamon sedge are all the patterns of sedges in the new set. They are, to my mind, sufficient, although each of them is the representative of a number of caddis-flies of the various gradations of colour, and I cannot advise the dry-fly man to overburden himself with others which he will probably find superfluous. I must here remind the reader of the wonderful sport I had during some afternoons in July of 1907, with the small dark sedge No. 31, and the medium sedge No. 32, and the account of these red-letter days is set forth in detail in " Modern Development of the Dry-Fly," pages 196–9.

Sedge fly.

Sedge-fishing is usually carried on at or just after dusk, and its success or non-success depends almost entirely on the presence of the sedge flies. The later it is in the season the more prevalent are the natural insects ; I think, perhaps, there are more to be seen in October than in any other month in the year. Very fine gut is quite unnecessary ; in fact, fairly stout gut works better with large flies, and there is no practical advantage in handicapping oneself with flimsy gear when it is nearly dark. No place need be passed over on account of the natural difficulties of landing the fish when hooked ; even in parts overgrown with weed with mere patches of open water between trout may frequently be killed, as they seldom go to weed after dark. This is probably due to the fisherman being invisible until the fish is nearly tired out and practically in the net. Weeding is in many cases the result of a scare on the part of a trout from seeing the fisherman or feeling the strain of the rod.

The Test trout generally are in good fettle during the first half of September, and
September. on the Itchen, which, as before noted, is a later river than the Test, they are in good condition to the end of the month. I doubt whether the policy of killing Test trout after the middle of the month is a wise one. Some years back I suspected that the majority of the fish killed were then females getting heavy with roe, and since then continual examination has convinced me of the good grounds for this suspicion. The result of continuing the season after, say, September 15th must therefore be to unduly diminish the stock of female fish likely to spawn at the end of the year.

Mr. Sheringham suggests that it might be of use to anglers to give them a non-
Non-scientific deter- scientific means of differenti-
mination of sex of ating the sexes of the trout.
trout. With the view of obtaining the best possible opinion on the subject, I consulted Mr. G. A. Boulenger, of the British Museum (Natural History), Cromwell Road. He wrote me as follows : " I am afraid it would be impossible to draw up a definition of the two sexes in *Salmo fario* which could serve in all cases without reference to the

genital glands. Large specimens, of course, differ in the head, which is larger and hooked at the snout in the males."

My keeper is, as a rule, correct in his determination of the sex from outward appearance. He relies chiefly on the size and shape of the head, and also on the shape of the *gill-cover*, which he says is more pointed in the male and rounder in the female. If in doubt he examines the vent, in which there are two orifices or openings in the female (one the end of the tube down which the eggs pass, and the other the end of the excretory passage), while in the male there is only one opening.

On this point Mr. Boulenger is kind enough to say : " Big males of *Salmo fario* are, of course, easy to tell from females by the large head, but it is not so in smaller specimens, and I doubt whether the shape of the gill-cover would afford any help. As to the pore behind the vent (the peritoneal pore), it is, as you say, present in the female and absent in the male ; but it is not always easy to see, so that I would not recommend the character for the use of the non-scientific."

If trout are fished for during the second half of September on the Test, fishermen should make it a rule to return all female fish and kill only males. The males in all streams and especially in those which are much fished, largely outnumber the females, so that we can well afford to kill males during September. The patterns for day, evening and night are identical with those recommended for July and hot weather.

The trout season must close at latest at the end of September, and during the re-

October, November and December. mainder of the year only grayling should be killed. They are curious fish—some days seem quite simple and others *cute*. On their days one can literally *fill a sack*, and on their off days one often goes home utterly beaten and with an empty basket. They take iron-blue, olive and pale watery duns and even at times smuts, so that there is no difficulty in finding a variety of patterns, any one of which may be the particular medicine they want. Old standards such as adjutant blue, blue quill, little marryat, quill marryat and curses are at times successful. Fancy patterns such as wickhams, pink wickhams, red, orange or macaw tags, furnace, orange bumble and little chap are reliable patterns on all the Hampshire streams, and probably all these will kill elsewhere.

It has been my aim in this chapter to give the student the views of all schools of dry-fly men as to the most killing patterns, whether they be the advocates of my new set of patterns, votaries of the old standard imitations of natural insects, or those who pin their faith on fancy patterns. It would not be fair on my part to leave this branch of the subject without putting on record my own convictions.

Personally I want nothing more than the thirty-three patterns comprised in the series, and the rising fish that cannot be tempted by one of them is either preternaturally shy, or has reached so high a standard of education that I must retreat beaten, but I hope not disgraced. The fisherman who desires to take full advantage of these patterns must take the trouble to study and understand the entomological portion of this book. He must take from the surface of the stream specimens of the insects floating down, and with the assistance of his magnifying-glass identify them, so that he may select patterns which are imitations of the flies on which the rising trout has at least a chance of feeding at the moment. No casual glance at a passing insect whether on the water or in the air is a safe basis for identification. Perhaps readers will scarcely credit it, but with a number of iron-blue and pale watery duns rising off the water I have times out of number found it impossible to differentiate them in the air.

The reader may well ask what he should do if he cannot see any flies on the water when fish are rising. He should hold his collecting-net partly immersed in the stream in places similar to those in which he sees fish feeding. If on a periodical examination he finds no flies (spinners or smuts are the most likely ones) in the net his only chance is to think over the insects he has seen on previous days or in previous seasons at the same time of year, and fish the patterns of these. If he is still unsuccessful he must keep on changing his flies, and more important still, keep trying other feeding fish. The more often he hammers an individual trout, the less likely he is to get a rise out of it.

If, however, he should have the good fortune to land a trout, he can at times **Autopsy.** establish the identity of the insects on which it was feeding by taking some of the insects out of its mouth. If the mouth is empty and the fish undersized he is again beaten, but if it should be sizable he may be able to elucidate the question by means of an examination of the contents of its stomach.

In the accompanying Plate IX is shown the longitudinal section of a Test trout showing the air bladder, pyloric appendages, and giving a good idea of the digestive organs generally. A portion of the stomach is cut open to show the undigested food it contains, and below this a V-shaped valve called the sphincter muscle, beyond which the undigested food does not pass except as the result of some muscular exertion required to excrete indigestible substances, such as small stones or shells used by the caddis in making its case.

To perform an autopsy the best *modus operandi* is to take the trout after killing it, and holding it with its ventral side uppermost make a clean cut with a sharp knife or pair of scissors from the vent up the centre of the ventral surface to the pectoral fins. The whole of the digestive organs can be turned out of the slit, cut off close to the throat, and dropped into a

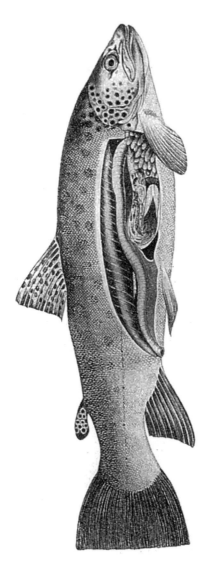

Autopsy of a Trout

Swan Electric Engraving Co.

PLATE IX

vessel of water. The stomach is then cut longitudinally down to the sphincter muscle, the contents
being turned out into a vessel of water, separated and
examined. If it is desired to keep and preserve
the contents of the trout's stomach, a small quantity
of washing soda should be added to the water so as
to neutralize the acid of the digestive fluid. If this
is neglected the process of digestion will continue
for a considerable time after death.

The conglomeration of food in the water if gently
stirred will separate by gravity into two portions.
The portion that sinks to the bottom is food taken
by the trout on the bed of the river, and the portion
which floats consists of winged insects and nymphs
or pupæ just on the point of emerging in the winged
state. The floating portion of the contents of the
trout's stomach is the only part which will interest
the fisherman when trying to decide on the pattern
of floating fly he should next try.

The angler must not be surprised at the small quantity of these floating insects, nor at the great variety
of genera and species represented. He may find quite
a number of ing le specimens of small beetles, *Aphis*
or green fly, *Corixæ*, a genus of water-bug, and many
others. He may also find some number of examples
of the duns, spinners, caddis-flies or smuts on which
the fish has been feeding, some winged and some, as
said before, just emerging from the nymphal or pupal
envelope.

An examination of the large mass of food, which is

of greater specific gravity than the water, will certainly be profitable. It will, in all probability, consist of different sorts of Ephemeridæ nymphs in their earlier stages, caddis of different sizes and enclosed in cases of diverse materials, fresh-water shrimps, water wood-lice, snails in great variety and very possibly minnows, stone-loach, miller's thumbs or even trout fry. It will give him ocular demonstration of the omnivorous nature and wonderful appetite of the fish, and show how bountiful a store nature has provided of highly nutritious food among the weeds growing in the bed of the river. It may also parenthetically serve to teach him why our wet-fly fishing brother can at times get such good sport, and it might possibly convey hints to the fly-dresser for new and perhaps killing wet-fly patterns.

CHAPTER V

DRAG

THE object of the dry-fly fisherman is to place his
fly in such a position and in
Definition of drag. such a manner that it will float
accurately over the rising fish
following a similar course and travelling at the same
pace as would the natural insect on the same run. Any
deviation from the natural course governed by the flow
of the stream, and any acceleration or diminution of
the pace of the living insect on the part of the artificial
fly, is designated *drag*. The use of the word *drag*, to
define any unnatural appearance of the artificial fly on
the water, due to its proceeding in a different direction
or drifting down at a slower or faster rate than the
natural, was, no doubt, in the first instance suggested
by the perceptible *wake* made by the artificial fly under
such conditions.

A natural dun floating on the surface will, under
normal conditions, follow the
The cause of drag. course of that part of the
stream on which it happened
to be when emerging in the winged state from the
nymphal envelope. It will not only follow the course
of the stream, but float down at the same pace as the

I   113

stream until its wings are dry. It will then fly ashore, and remain there until the time arrives for its next change to the imago or spinner. If a new and perfectly dry artificial fly on an eyed hook is dropped on the water alone it will float down the stream in precisely the same way as the natural insect. When, however, this artificial fly is attached to a gut collar and reel-line a new factor at once appears. The line is on the water, and the varying speed of the current acting on different parts of it will tend to retard or accelerate the pace of the artificial fly, or even pull it out of its normal course.

When fished directly upstream, if the fish is rising in the fastest part of the current in the length of the cast, the fly will travel at the natural pace, the line gradually slacken below it, and there will be no drag. If there should be below the rising place of the fish and in the length of the cast a portion of the stream faster than that in which the fish is feeding, this will cause the line to pull the fly down and make it travel faster than the pace of a natural insect in the same position, thus causing *drag*. The method adopted to retard this drag until the fly is below the rising fish is to check the cast at the forward position, so that the fly does not extend in a straight line, but falls on the water with some slack behind it. Until the fast part of the stream has straightened out this slack there will be no acceleration in the pace of the fly, and con-

Drag when casting directly upstream.

sequently no drag. This too is a strong confirmation of the advice so often given by dry-fly experts never to throw a straight taut line, but in every case to make the fly alight on the water with a curved or slack line behind it.

The same rules apply when the angler is casting across the stream or partly across and partly upstream. If the fish is rising in mid-stream or under the opposite bank the pressure of any part of the stream flowing faster than the run on which the fly is floating will tend to straighten the line, and thus cause the fly to travel faster than the natural pace. To obviate or at least retard this drag the fly should be cast so that the line is laid on the water in a curve with the convex side inclined upstream. The current acting on this convex surface will gradually straighten it, and if the position has been accurately gauged, the drag will be retarded until the fly is well below the spot at which the trout is rising.

Drag when casting across or partly across and partly upstream.

If by any chance the fish is rising in the swiftest part of the current the fly will not travel at an un-naturally fast pace provided the angler has cast a slack line. In all cases of casting across the stream another form of drag will occur, viz. that of the fly being pulled out of its natural course by the line as soon as it is straight or taut. These examples should convince the tyro that the beautifully straight line which is so often admired and praised by the onlooker, is a fatal mistake when applied to the cast of the dry-fly man. The slacker the line is within ordinary limits the better the cast and the longer the fly will float without drag.

A fly seldom drags owing to its travelling more slowly than the pace of the natural insect. Drag will occur when a fish is rising in such a position that to make the cast the lower part of the reel-line must be laid on a strong eddy. Here again a very slack line may retard the drag for a few seconds, but a place like this is one where none but the expert can hope to succeed, and such positions should be avoided by the beginner.

When casting a dry-fly downstream the pace of the fly will gradually slow down **Drag when casting** as the line begins to tighten, **downstream.** and when the line is straight the fly will stop altogether. If the direction of the cast is in any degree across the current it will also drag by being pulled towards the angler's bank, and thus travel across the natural course of the stream. A considerably greater length of line than that required to cover the fish must therefore be let out when fishing a drift or half drift, and the action of the rod must be perceptibly checked at the forward position of the cast, so as to land the fly on the water above the fish with sufficient slack line to allow it to float down well below the fish without any drag. As before pointed out, the drift or half drift is not usually a successful cast, and should only be adopted under conditions where it is impossible to get below and cast up to the rising trout.

Many fly-fishermen, and especially those who have gained their experience with **Advice to lower hand as fly lands on the water.** the sunk fly, get into the habit of raising the hand holding the rod as soon as the fly has landed on the water. The effect of this must be to straighten the line and cause the fly to drag. The moment the fly lands on the water the hand must be lowered so as to slacken the line, and this will effectually retard the drag for some time. This rule of lowering the hand as the fly falls may be laid down as a maxim with every style of cast and under all conditions, except when there is an exceptionally fast run immediately under the rod-point. In such a case the hand, or even the arm, must be raised so as to prevent the line from hanging in this fast run, which would at once cause drag.

The major portion of a chalk-stream consists of stretches in which the water **Fishing very fast runs.** flows at only a moderate pace, but there are lengths below weirs or hatch-holes, or where the fall of the river is very rapid, where the water flows almost at the pace of a mountain torrent. Such places are not easy to fish, and the angler to succeed must keep well out of sight by crouching, kneeling, or even lying down and fish a very short line. He must fish this short line most accurately with the horizontal cast so as not to scare the fish by the reflection of the rod waving over it. He must fish a perfectly dry, floating, and cocked fly, if he is using duns, smuts, or caddis-flies. The spinners must also be quite dry and floating, but with their wings flat on the surface and not partially submerged. He must fish a very slack line, and when he succeeds in hooking a large trout on one of these rough places, must expect a lively run and a well-conditioned fish. The miserable, lanky, dark, ill-conditioned stew-fed trout do not care to face the very fast water.

Great stress has been laid on the question of *drag*, because to my mind it is the most important factor in the dry-fly fisherman's art. Pattern of fly, judgment of the size of fish, combining accuracy and delicacy in the first cast over a rising fish, keeping out of sight not only the fisherman but his rod, these are all essentials to success. Every one of these essentials may have been carried out most effectually, but if the artificial fly, instead of following the natural course of a living insect, drags, the rising trout is set down by the abnormal procedure and the chance of rising or killing it is deferred for some considerable time.

As before laid down the most effectual means of retarding drag until the fly is **Methods for retarding** past the rising fish, when **drag.** casting across the stream, is by laying the line in a curve, of which the convex side is upstream. The action of

the current will straighten this curve, and until it is
nearly straight the fly will not drag. The beginner
may ask how he is to accomplish this. With a
downstream wind it is quite simple if the angler
will use the horizontal cast and exert only just
sufficient force to *cheat* the wind. The fly will then
land on the water a short distance below the rest
of the line. With an upstream wind it is not quite
so easy. The angler must take his position just
below or level with the fish, and to compensate
for the effect of the wind he must cast as if
he intended to place his fly below the fish. Here
again the force or downward finish must not be
sufficiently pronounced to put the fly directly into
the wind.

It is well not only to lower the hand the moment
the fly lands, but even to follow its direction down
with the rod-point, as this is a most useful adjunct
in retarding the drag. At times, and especially
when using the half drift, drag can be even further
retarded by walking or, better still, crawling down
the bank.

When fishing a difficult place the angler may find
that varying his method of casting will often be of
assistance in retarding drag. Thus, if with the overhanded cast he cannot manage to fish the place without
drag, he should try the horizontal, and if this is
unsuccessful, the back-handed horizontal cast. It is
perhaps as well not to try these experiments over a
feeding fish, but on adjoining water of similar speed,

and where the varying currents are arranged in the same way.

Many an apparently impossible spot can be fished by laying part of the reel-line on a weed patch, thus avoiding the action of the current on any part of the line between the said weed patch and the rod-point—and in this way retarding the drag until the fly is well below the feeding fish. Sometimes, too, in open water the line may in a similar manner be laid on a floating weed mass which is not located in the fastest part of the current.

Laying line on weed patches to retard drag.

A beginner is at times nonplussed at finding a fish rising a short distance above a fence or wire stretched across the stream. To stand or kneel at a point level with the wire or fence may place him too near the fish to be able to keep out of sight—or, possibly, so close to the trout that he is likely to scare and set it down. He should, without a moment's hesitation, take up his station below and cast boldly, with plenty of slack line over wire or fence, to the fish. Very often the stream will carry the fly down and it will trickle over the wire and fall in the water below. If it hangs on the wire a gentle pull will in many cases clear it. If, however, by any chance he should get foul a steady pull will, in the majority of instances, result in the loss of his fly only, or at most, of one or two strands of gut.

Casting over a wire or fence.

The importance of avoiding drag cannot by any possibility be exaggerated, and it may be fairly stated that nine-tenths of the ill-success of men who appear to cast well and understand their work is due to their want of appreciation of this most essential principle of dry-fly fishing.

CHAPTER VI

FAVOURABLE AND UNFAVOURABLE CONDITIONS

THERE are three separate and distinct classes of conditions to be considered in reference to this branch of the subject. (1) Those appertaining exclusively to the fish ; (2) The climatic conditions ; and (3) The nature of the locale.

Careful and prolonged study of the habits of the trout or grayling, whether feed-**Conditions appertaining** ing on the nymphs, larvæ, **exclusively to the fish.** pupæ, or the winged insects or taking crustaceans, mollusks, minnows or other small fish, should obviously be the first stage in determining whether the behaviour of the fish is such as to foreshadow at the moment a favourable or unfavourable opportunity for the dry-fly man. A man possessed of abnormally keen vision can, possibly, in a good light, discern with accuracy the nature of the animal food which a fish is taking, but even with the best of eyesight it is a fatiguing and wearisome business. When the light is fading it is practically impossible.

The use of instruments of precision for all scientific or semi-scientific purposes is to be recommended, and the manifest modern improvements effected in all

optical appliances are so great as to have brought
home to the angler the advan-
Use of the field-glass. tages of availing himself of
their assistance in carrying out
the class of observation required to enable him to
follow the habits and proclivities of the denizens of the
trout stream.   Hence for the twentieth-century student
of dry-fly work the field-glass has almost become a
necessity.   The prismatic binocular, as made by Zeiss,
of Jena, and many other continental manufacturers,
C. Baker, 244 High Holborn, and a few other British
opticians, is immeasurably superior to the old-fashioned
field-glass.   It is made in various powers, which are
designated by the degree of linear magnification
effected by the combinations of lenses in the oculars
and objectives.

When selecting a field-glass for any purpose the
purchaser should bear in mind that the greater the
magnification the smaller is the field, or in other
words, the greater the difficulty of finding the object
or objects to be observed.   Modern prismatic field-
glasses are made in magnifications of 3, 6, 8, 12, and
16 diameters.   The ×3 is essentially an opera-glass,
and the ×6 is the one I have personally used, but
many of my friends prefer the ×8 or ×12.

When once the student has focussed the field-
glass accurately and adjusted the interocular distance to his sight, he can distinguish the flies on
the surface of the stream, follow their motion, and
be quite sure at a glance whether the feeding fish are

taking nymphs or some other subaqueous creatures or rising at the winged insects. If he watches the artificial fly cast on the water by his companion, he will soon realize that the action of the line and gut will often cause the artificial fly, even when it does not perceptibly drag, to perform eccentric and un-expected antics on the water which are not indulged in by the living duns or spinners.

Let us now suppose that the student has spotted what he thinks is a rise, and **A rising fish.** that he has directed his field-glass on the place where it appeared to be. The next time the fish feeds he will see whether it has taken a dun, spinner, curse, or sedge fly on the surface. A trout or grayling feeding on any of these is designated a rising fish and is the fish to be selected by him for his cast. If he con-tinues to watch, he may well be able to make sure of the kind of fly the trout is taking, and an imitation of this is obviously the pattern to be selected.

When clouds of small Diptera are hovering over the water and occasionally **Smutting fish.** dipping on to the stream, fish are often madly on the feed. This usually takes place on a hot, calm, muggy day, when the trout will come to the surface and take in rapid succession quite a number of these tiny flies called *curses* or *smuts* by the modern angler. An accurately placed floating imitation of one of these insects will, at times, tempt even the largest and

shyest of trout. Smutting fish are generally, however, preternaturally on the alert, moving about in
a small area up or down, from one side to the other,
and are also as a rule very easily scared either by the
fall of the fly, the gleam of the gut, or the appearance
of the angler and his moving rod or line.

The fisherman may be unable to discern any insects
floating on the water where
Fish taking spinners in the rise is spotted. Under
broad daylight. these conditions he may find
his imitations of the smut un-
attractive to the fish. Very careful scrutiny may at
times reveal the gleam of the brilliant transparent
wings of spinners, but as a rule the imagines are
quite invisible as they float down with wings laid flat
on the surface and at right-angles to the line of the
body. As pointed out in a previous chapter on
" Choice of Pattern," he can then with advantage try
the patterns of spinners of the genus and species
prevalent at the time.

The casual observer's attention is too frequently
drawn to what he will, at the
Bulging fish. first glance, take for trout
rising rapidly. He will see
movements at or near the surface of a very pronounced
nature caused by fish ploughing their way through
the water upwards, moving from side to side, and
occasionally he may even distinguish the head of
a fish just showing above the top of the water. The
tyro thinks that he is now in for a good time and will

keep casting his fly over the fish. He will cast time after time in rapid succession, often get too excited to dry his fly and, as a general rule, will not get a rise or pluck of any kind. If by any chance he does get a rise he will most probably not feel the resistance of a fish when he strikes. If he should hook a fish, it is no exaggeration on my part to assert that nine out of ten hooked trout or grayling will get away.

The meaning of this is that the fish are busily engaged in chasing and securing the active nymphs of the duns coming up through the water to the surface, where they emerge from the nymphal envelope in the winged or subimago stage. Some of the nymphs will be taken at a considerable depth, some nearing the surface, some practically on the surface, and occasionally the dun itself will fall a victim just at the moment that it has emerged from the shuck.

With respect to the question of dressing imitations of nymphs, I have always **Imitations of nymphs.** urged that any fly-dresser who sets his mind to it can do this easily. Years and years ago Marryat and I dressed most effective patterns to represent the nymphs of duns and mayflies by tying in a few fibres of black feather at the head, constructing the fly generally with a quill body the colour of the abdomen of the natural nymph, hackle short and spare, and the whisks, which were also short, of gallina, were dyed to shade. When the body material had been tied in, the

fibres of black feather were bent down into a shallow
loop and fastened in at the shoulder to represent the
wing cases of the natural nymph, the hackle was then
turned, and the fly finished at the head.

We killed a few fish with them, but discontinued
their use for two reasons.   The first, that in our opinion
they were essentially wet-flies, and the use of them on
waters reserved for dry-fly only, constituted a breach
of the ethics of the dry-fly.   The second, which may
possibly be a more cogent reason in the minds of many
modern anglers, was that wherever and whenever we
used them we found that the number of fish hooked
and lost was out of all proportion to the total bag,
and that the fish rapidly became inordinately shy and
unapproachable.   This, I think, sums up the position
fairly from the dry-fly purist's point of view, and I
can only advise my readers to abstain from trying
bulging fish either on their own or their friends'
fisheries in all cases where the use of the floating fly
is considered *de rigueur*.

A disturbance having very much the appearance of
a rise is sometimes seen, and
Tailing fish.   when within a moderate distance one realizes that this
disturbance is caused by the tail or dorsal fin.   When
one can crawl up near enough to get a good view, the
fish itself can frequently be seen either in very shallow
water or at a place where the weeds are only submerged to a small extent.   When the tail is on the
surface the fish appears to be literally standing on its

head, energetically wriggling its body and busily engaged in exploring the weed patch. This tailing fish is feeding on shrimps, snails and similar creatures, or at times on larvæ or nymphs, taking them off the weeds, and if some of them rise up in the water, following them and taking them near the surface.

Obviously, to cast a floating fly over a fish which is intent on feeding among the subaqueous vegetation, and is only breaking the surface with the tip of its tail, is a futile effort. It has very occasionally happened that in very shallow water a fly on the surface has attracted the attention of such a fish just as it lowered its tail and raised its head, and in this way *tailing* fish have been killed with the dry-fly.

Minnowing fish. Trout in chalk-streams and other rivers are very fond of minnows, stone-loach, miller's thumbs, fry of trout and other small fish. When taking minnows they plunge about in pursuit of them, and the minnows themselves are often seen jumping from the water in their endeavours to elude the jaws of the hungry trout. Minnows spawn on the shallows about the middle or end of May, and trout are prone to take toll of them in considerable numbers at this part of the season. Very possibly this is the reason why there is often about this time of the year a space of many days when the fish do not seem to rise at all. Minnowing fish are not likely to succumb to the wiles of the dry-fly man.

At all times during the season trout are seen leaping into the air, and on some days **Trout jumping.** the number of fish indulging in this form of athletics is quite remarkable. What their object may be is more or less a matter of conjecture. Certainly they are not feeding, and the opinion frequently expressed that they are trying to kill or shake off the parasites adhering to their skin by jumping and falling on the water is open to question. As a rule the days on which the trout are behaving in this fashion are not favourable ones for the dry-fly fisherman. Small fish will at times jump at sedges and other flies just above the surface.

When trout are feeding they will sometimes rise fairly well and take a fly, then **Trout rising and** move upstream a few yards, **travelling.** take another fly, continue their journey, repeating the operation many times. It will be apparent to one who watches them carefully that generally they seem to occupy a beat of specific length. When they have arrived at the top of their beat they will drop back, usually tail first, down to the point at which they started. They may be seen to repeat this performance many times. If the angler follows such a fish up and keeps casting he will infallibly scare it when it is dropping downstream to the lower end of its beat. This is not a favourable condition, and the fisherman is advised to abstain from throwing over fish behaving

K

in this way until they have settled down to rise continuously at one and the same place.

When a trout has poised itself near the surface and is steadily taking duns or other **Fish in position.** flies without any great movement laterally or up or down the stream, it is said to be *in position.* When a fish in position is lying close to the bank and is rising freely, the angler on the same bank has found one under ideal conditions for the dry-fly fisherman, and may confidently expect a rise to his fly, if he is using the right pattern and succeeds in presenting it at the right moment and in such a way that the fish does not realize that it is being fished for, and its suspicions are, therefore, not aroused.

The rise of the fish is generally contemporaneous with a good hatch of duns, **Rise usually dependent** smuts, and other flies, with the **on hatch of fly.** fall of the spinners after oviposition, or of the sedges either at the time of oviposition or after this the most important part of their life's work has been completed. It is, however, by no means safe to predict that the angler's bag will be in proportion to the number of rises he sees. On some days every trout or grayling in the river seems to be feeding madly on the fly, and besides the difficulty of judging the size of fish from the nature of the rise it would seem that on such a day the fish appear to be endowed with an unusual degree of perception. They will take the natural flies one after another in rapid succession, but will allow the best imitations to float over them untouched, even when placed with the greatest delicacy and accuracy. Again, on a day when the natural insects are comparatively scarce the trout may be quite silly and rise at the artificial, fasten and get killed in great numbers.

We now come to the second class of conditions, those which are best described **Weather as affecting** by the word *climatic*. In this **the rise.** country the weather is of so changeable a nature, and we are all so much affected in various ways by heat or cold, rain or brilliant sunshine, snow or sleet, that throughout our short lives we are prone to attach undue importance to climatic conditions. The same rule applies with even increased strength to the angler. When he is successful he usually imputes his success in part to the weather, and when he is utterly beaten and returns at night with an empty creel he generally attributes his failure to a similar cause.

It is quite impossible to lay down any general laws which would enable the fisherman to predict even for a few hours ahead what his sport was likely to be from readings of barometer or thermometer, direction or strength of the wind, rainfall or any other climatic condition which can be measured by instruments of precision. With a rising, falling or steady weather-glass, in tropical heat, Arctic cold or temperature of the normal, the fish may or may not rise; there may be a good hatch, a poor hatch, or no hatch at all ; they may rise and fasten, or they may rise and come short, or not rise at all ; and we are not wise enough to be able to formulate the cause with any degree of accuracy.

In bygone days someone wrote a few short verses descriptive of the behaviour of **Direction of wind.** the fish under varying direc- tions of wind. I cannot re- member the exact words, but it was to the effect that when the wind was in the east it was good for neither man nor beast; when it was in the north the prudent fisher did not sally forth ; when the wind was in the south it blew the fly into the fish's mouth ; and when the wind was in the west all things then were at their best. Very ingenious and, like many more of these old sayings, in every way inaccurate and unsound.

More than thirty years of continual observation have convinced me that the south and west winds are no friends to the Hampshire chalk-stream fishers. The east wind is not as a rule a favourable one, and many of the greatest hatches of duns in the spring have to my certain knowledge been present with a northerly or north-westerly wind. South, west, or south-west winds mean heavy gales in the south-country, and the fly does not as a rule hatch well in stormy weather, nor do the trout or grayling of the Test or Itchen rise well when the surface of the water is broken or rough.

The Test runs more or less from north to south,

so that the north wind is a downstream wind, or what the old school of writers would consider an unfavourable one. Given a good hatch of fly, a downstream is more favourable than an upstream wind, because while the latter tends to lift the fly as soon as the wings are dry and erect, the former will ever force the dun down on to the water and cause it to float much further before taking to wing and flying ashore. In a previous chapter I hope I have convinced my reader that casting against the wind, unless it is a perfect hurricane, will present no difficulty to the man who can cast.

The reader must not magnify my statements. I am no lover of casting against a gale of wind, nor have I ever suggested that this is a favourable condition. What I do suggest as a favourable condition is a light downstream wind and as a most unfavourable one a gale blowing in any direction and especially upstream.

There are exceptions to every rule, and no experienced dry-fly man can say with truth that he has invariably found a south or south-westerly wind productive of poor hatches and bad sport. Nor can he aver that under all conditions is a northerly wind a precursor of a great hatch and a big bag. As said before, the only safe rule is for the angler to start as soon after breakfast as he can, and remain at the river-side until nearly dark, watching the water and studying the fish so as to take full advantage of the chances that a beneficent providence throws in his way.

Our non-fishing friends on a pouring wet day generally tell us that according **Rain and thunder.** to tradition this is ideal fishing weather. This may or may not be so. One of the greatest difficulties on a rainy day, that of keeping the fly dry and floating, has been enormously alleviated by the universal use of paraffin for waterproofing the feathers and other materials used in the construction of the artificial fly. The opinion that before a heavy thunderstorm trout do not rise, but generally take well during its height or after its conclusion, is to some extent a sound one. The barometer generally registers a sudden fall immediately before the outbreak of the storm and after the electrical conditions have subsided it usually assumes its normal height. A sudden fall is generally unfavourable, and the recovery, if not too rapid, is generally favourable to our particular class of sport. A very rapid recovery after a sudden fall is an indication of further unsettled weather, which is as a rule unfavourable.

The idea attached to the expression *hatch of fly* by the older school of angling **Temperature.** writers was based on the hatching of land-bred insects, which is accelerated by heat and retarded by cold. They therefore opined that similar conditions would attach to the hatch of insects which serve as food for the trout. The application of the word *hatch* by anglers to the metamorphosis of a water-bred nymph or pupa to the winged subimago or imago is, of course, a misnomer, as the word hatch means the emergence of the young larva or nymph from the egg. The late T. P. Hawksley when hatching Ephemeridæ and Trichoptera from eggs in captivity found those in a strong light invariably hatch sooner than others of the same brood placed in warmer positions but in comparative darkness. It is also suggested that warmth encourages the growth of weed which thus provides more food for the nymphs and thereby advances the date of the appearance of the flies in winged form.

The temperature of the air has very little effect on the temperature of the water in a chalk-stream, the more so as the volume of water is continually being increased by springs filtering up at many places throughout the course of the stream. The difference between the summer and winter temperature of the water in a chalk-stream is far less than one would imagine, and it is, therefore, not surprising to find that to the hands the water of these streams always seems cold in the summer and warm in the winter. This, too, is one of the reasons why our Hampshire rivers are seldom frozen, excepting in eddies or very still and nearly stagnant parts.

The object of this dissertation on the temperature of the water in the chalk-streams is to impress upon the student's mind the fact that his readings of the thermometer in the air are unsafe criteria of the probable hatch of fly. It may, too, serve to illustrate the absurdity of what we read at times in the sporting

Press. We are often told that the writer knows that he need not be at the river-bank on a specific day before one o'clock, because there was a hard frost in the early morning. Such a statement is founded on a misconception. The hatch of fly may be early or late, abundant or sparse, after a hard frost, on a hot muggy morning or a brilliant sunny day.

Two anecdotes referring to the unaccountable conditions regulating the rise of fish occur to me. A friend living on the banks of a chalk-stream, a portion of which runs through his grounds, has a number of pet trout which are fed with cubes of bread and other dainty morsels. He tells me that an infallible forecast of the day's sport can be arrived at in the early morning by feeding these fish. On mornings when they take greedily the fish in the river are always well on the feed later in the day, and, conversely, when the tame trout are disinclined to feed the wild ones are also *dour*.

In another case I have heard of a fisherman who, living some distance from the river, kept on his roof a tank with a few trout in it. When he observed that they were near the surface he put up his rod and hied to the river, but when they sulked at the bottom he knew that it was no fishing-day.

Light. Light has undoubtedly a great effect on the disposition of the fish to feed and the possibility of approaching it. On some days there is a dull, heavy leaden light on the stream, and every object is visible at a great distance. Looking down on the bed of the river it will be noticed that every weed-patch, every stone and, in fact, all objects including the fish, can be seen and are painfully visible from afar. It would appear that just as the fish and other objects in the water are plainly seen from the bank, so the fisherman and his rod are equally plainly seen from the river by the fish. In this light fish seldom if ever rise well either at the natural insects, if they are present, or at their imitations.

Bright sunshine is not as a rule favourable to the dry-fly man, and on a day of fleeting clouds, which at times obscure the sun's rays and at others allow them to fall with full brilliancy on the river, the past-master will invariably wait for a cloudy interval to cast his fly over the rising trout. This subject is treated more in detail in the next chapter, "The Psychological Moment."

The third class of favourable and unfavourable conditions, those appertaining **Favourable and un-** to the nature of the place and **favourable places.** its surroundings, will require very careful and prolonged study. I invite the reader's best attention to two plans of stretches of the Test which have been prepared to illustrate and explain my views on the subject, Plate X representing a shallow, and Plate XI showing a deep hole and the flow of water into and out of it. These are not fancy sketches, but enlargements of the Ordnance maps, and, as usual, the top of the map indicates the north.

In order to show the direction and strength of the current, it will be noticed that there are a number of arrows drawn on the plan. All of these point in the direction of the current—in places where the stream is slow the arrows are drawn thus : >—→ ; those indicating a moderate or normal current thus : ≫—→ ; and in parts where the stream is very fast, thus : ≫—→. A slack or still place is marked thus : ⊂▭⊃

As laid down in a previous chapter, the most important point for the angler **Necessity of avoiding** to remember is that he must **drag.** place his fly so that it floats down accurately over the rising fish without a semblance of drag if his object is to persuade the trout to take the imitation under the delusion that it is a natural insect. At the first glance it would appear that the fisherman's policy should be to eschew places where his fly is likely to drag, and only try the fish rising in the comparatively easy places where the artificial will float down at the same pace and in the same direction as the living fly. Unfortunately he will find himself confronted at the outset by a great difficulty. He may see fish rising, but a very small proportion of these will be in easy places.

A trout feeding on flies will almost invariably take up its position at a spot to which a large proportion of the insects floating down are carried by the action of the current, and in which they remain for an appreciable length of time; these are generally slack places, above, below, and at both sides of which the stream is faster, and into which the flies are carried. The result of this is, as shown in the chapter on *drag*, that the line will be acted on by this variation of current, and thus affect the pace and direction taken by the artificial fly, and make it travel in some way differently from the natural insect. I have shown before how the drag can be avoided, and if it can be retarded until the artificial has passed out of the trout's vision there is a chance of rising the fish with the first cast, and even giving it a second or third chance of being deceived.

Besides the fact that so large a proportion of the rising trout are located in draggy, and consequently difficult places, there is another reason which should impress upon the fisherman in any case, and pre-eminently when on a water which is heavily fished, the policy of trying to overcome the difficulty. Every one of his brother anglers will be as keen on finding fish feeding in easy places as himself, so that these fish will day after day and hour after hour have ample opportunities of studying the eccentricities and peculiar behaviour of the artificial fly. Nothing so surely tends to educate the trout feeding in clear water as continual casting over it by fishermen of different degrees of capacity and incapacity.

Before particularizing, the reader should devote a few minutes to a careful study of the shallow shown

in Plate X. Immediately above the shallow the
river is narrow and very rapid; it then widens out
on both sides, gradually getting shallower until it
arrives at the shallowest portion where the ford is
situated. From this it becomes contracted in width,
and consequently flows at an increased pace under
the footbridge and below it, attains almost the pace
of a mountain brook or torrent.

Above the ford a series of posts are driven, and
on these are stretched wires, thus making an effectual
fence which prevents cattle and horses from trespass-
ing on the shallow above. It will be noticed that
there are a number of piles driven into the bed of
the river at various points above the fence across
the river. The policy of driving piles in different
places is treated fully in the third part of this book
—" Fishery Management."

Supposing a fish to be rising at the place marked
a. It is evident that the
Places where drag can angler on the bank making
be avoided or retarded. an ordinary straight cast will
be handicapped by the fast
current near his own bank dragging the fly across
and at a greater pace than the flow of the stream.
Here a curved line with the convex side of the
curve upstream will retard the drag.

A trout is rising at the point *b*. If the cast is made
by the fishermen from the place B, the fast current
between him and the fish will make his fly drag, and
even with plenty of slack he will find it difficult to

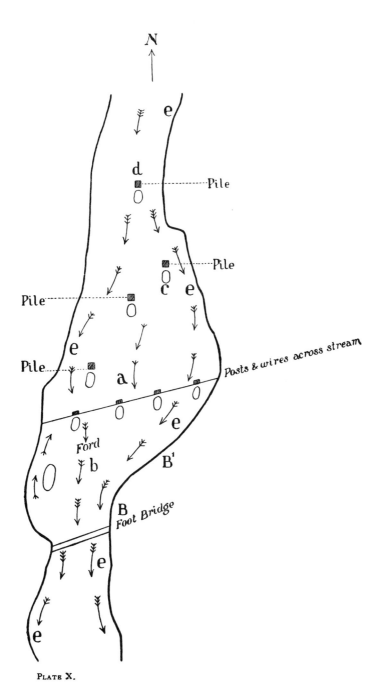

PLATE X.

PLAN OF A SHALLOW

make it float any distance before it drags. If he crawls up slowly, keeping himself well out of sight to the point on the bank marked B', his line will be above the rapid part of the current, and with plenty of slack he will be able to cover the fish without drag.

Below each pile or post, especially when some of the cut weeds have been lodged round it, there will be a slack place. The mark *c* shows a place such as big fish delight in when rising. Flies floating down rapidly on either side of the pile will sail quite slowly into this slack place and remain there for some few seconds. This is a difficult position. It must be fished from below, and the best chance is to put a very slack fly not far above the fish and hope for the best. The angler must not be chagrined if he finds that the first cast has set his fish down.

A favourite position for a large fish is marked *d*. Here a big trout will lie with its tail against the post and take the flies freely as they descend. There is no particular difficulty about such a place, and the only danger is that of hanging up the line on the floating weed which, lodging at or round the post, provides an admirable shelter for the fish, and should under no circumstances be disturbed.

In such a place the natural insect will float down at a great pace and the rising trout will often turn and follow it down. If in such a case the artificial has not been placed well above the fish there is a probability of the line on the weed stopping the fly before the fish has decided to take it—a proceeding which usually results in scaring the trout.

A number of places are marked *e* on the plan in Plate X. They are all favourable ones, if fished from the angler's bank, preferably with the horizontal cast and with the fisherman, of course, well down and out of sight.

Many of the difficult places on the plan could be quite easily fished by an angler **Wading.** wading and placing himself directly below the trout. The shallow depicted on this plate is a comparatively narrow one, as the stream on which it is situated is one of two, and the smaller of the two branches into which the Test is divided at this part of the river. Wading this shallow is strictly prohibited. Every part of it can be covered by anyone able to cast a moderately long line, and in most places drag can be retarded or avoided ; of course, in some places this is very difficult. Possibly the fisherman whose whole aim it is to make records might find fault with this regulation, but I venture to suggest that a true sportsman would glory in it and not be annoyed even by his incapacity to fish parts of it.

Wading on every shallow should as far as possible be avoided, and when wading the fisherman should make his way from the nearest point on the bank to the station from which he intends to cast. He should move slowly, and when once arrived at the station should as far as possible keep absolutely still, and,

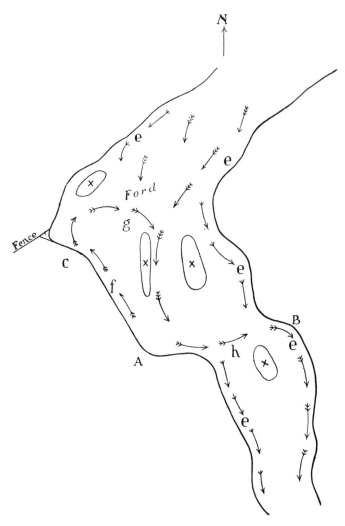

PLATE XI

PLAN OF A DEEP HOLE AND EDDY

above all, not sway his body backwards and forwards, which sends up, down, and across a wave which may well give warning to a shy fish of the fisherman's approach.

Wading on shallows in narrow streams is fatal. Two or three years ago a well-known dry-fly man had a day on this shallow, and not having made himself acquainted with this regulation, or possibly disregarding it, stepped boldly into the water and fished it wading. He killed two or three good fish and went away quite pleased with himself. For at least a fortnight after that trout were conspicuous by their absence from parts of this shallow, where the keeper and those fishing it had previously spotted them. The keeper declared that he had told this gentleman of the rule prohibiting wading, and the answer was that it was a rotten rule and wading did no harm. The said dry-fly man has not since been invited to try his luck on that stretch of the Test.

The reader's attention is now directed to the plan in Plate XI. This is on the main Test, and the normal width of the river above the ford is about twenty yards. At the lower side of the ford there is a sharp dip, and the water flows over this at a great pace, the bottom being very hard bright gravel. This fast water deepening suddenly flows down to the point marked *A* on the bank, where the current divides into two parts, the main run flowing in a curve across the river to the point marked *B*, and the smaller portion turning in what we must call an upstream direction, thus forming a large eddy, which curves out again and rejoins the main run. From B the current is uniform and moderately fast along the eastern bank, while the flow under the western bank is much slower. The slack places, four in number, are indicated as before and marked X.

As in the other plan, the marks e indicate places under the banks which are easy and favourable ones so long as the fisherman is casting from the same side of the river. None of these are, however, easy to fish from across, as the varying currents will tend to cause drag, but in many of them the use of the slack line or curved line with the convex side upstream will to some degree retard or obviate the trouble.

The large eddy opposite the letter C on the western bank is a great holt

Fishing eddies. for fish and some of the largest and best-conditioned ones have been killed there. Of the trout which live in this deep hole (twelve to fourteen feet) some go up to the ford to rise when there is a good hatch, while others rise on the main run, on the slack water on the eastern side of it and in the eddy itself.

Fish rising under the bank in the eddy at places like that marked f must be cast to from above, the fisherman placing himself as close to the bank as he conveniently can. It is a high overhanging bank, so that under all conditions he must keep himself well down and use every precaution possible to keep out of sight.

Trout rise freely in all parts of the eddy, and the careful and observant angler will reap his reward if he will exercise his patience and make sure with each feeding fish of the direction in which the stream is flowing and place his fly accordingly. For example, the trout is at g. He creeps to the river, and taking his station at C, may see the trout take a fly sailing out from the side directly across the natural direction of the river. This is not a favourable position because to fish it without moving he must drift, and this, as we know, is seldom successful. The direction and force of stream in an eddy are always changing, and when in position to rise a fish lies with its head up current, although this may not be the normal direction of the flow of the river. Hence, the next position of the same trout may be taken with the view of rising at flies moving in a direction totally different from the normal up, down, or across.

Wonderful sport has been obtained, and some very large trout have been killed in this eddy, but it is essentially a difficult place, requiring great patience and a fixed determination to cast seldom and then with great accuracy and avoidance of drag.

To cast directly up the main run the fisherman must locate himself somewhere near the letter A. If he takes up his station lower down than this the cross-current from A towards B will hasten the pace and drag his fly across towards the eastern bank. A favourite place for a big fish is at h. If the fly is placed much above the fish it is dragged across

L

towards *B*, if it is placed very close to a shy trout it is very likely to scare it, if it is placed well above in the fast water in the bay below *A*, it will generally sail over the fish without drag.

It is surprising how the experienced fisherman can, after a little study of the position, realize intuitively what is necessary in each case, either in reference to the station from which he should throw or the kind of cast he should deliver in order to avoid or delay drag. It is, perhaps, owing to the necessity for this continual study and the ever-varying nature of each position that we are able season after season to keep up our enthusiasm. We go on casting floating flies over those shy chalk-stream trout without the sport or absence of sport affecting us very much, and the cult of the dry-fly never seems to pall on those who take it seriously.

On a well-kept shallow there are clean gravel patches behind beds of weed **Gravel patches.** plentifully dotted about, and in the part of this book devoted to *fishery management* it is shown how effectively the modern plan of driving piles in different parts causes the water to wash away the weed so as to scour and leave exposed the bed of the river. It is safe to predict that when the trout are feeding on the surface or below the surface, or when they are taking up their positions ready to feed, there will, in a well-stocked river, be one at least lying over every gravel patch. No experienced dry-fly man ever fails to scan each of these clean bright places for the big fish which may enable him to save his blank on an unfavourable day.

The short bright green compact masses of water celery (*Apium inundatum*) are **Celery-beds.** the homes of great numbers of fresh-water shrimps, nymphs, caddis, etc., and fish will generally be seen lying over them and feeding. The beginner will imagine that these trout are rising and taking the duns and other insects on the surface. As a rule, he will be disappointed, and find himself unable to get a response even to the lightest of casts with the very best imitations in his collection. If he will once more exercise his powers of observation instead of casting and, in fact, fish with his head rather than his hands, he will soon realize that the class of food taken in such a position is in the form of shrimps, snails, nymphs, caddis, and other larvæ rather than winged insects.

The advisability of selecting fish rising close to the bank, and fishing them **Recovering fly when** from the same side of the **hung up.** river, has often been referred to in this book. With the usual fringe of rushes, etc., along the margin, the tyro is generally obsessed by the dread of getting his fly caught up. He imagines that such an occurrence is the precursor of the loss of tackle or of the necessity of showing himself to the trout when disentangling it. If he will try the experiment at a time when, and place where, there are no fish rising, he will find that, so long as he abstains from any jerk when returning, the hook will very seldom catch up. If it should be fixed in a rush or a bough, he should take the line in his hand and draw gently and steadily without jerk, and in the majority of instances the hook will come clear. If this action is unsuccessful, swaying laterally may at times clear it, and if again this does not effect his purpose he must draw steadily until he breaks, and as a rule this will only entail the loss of the fly or, at most, one or two strands of gut in addition to the fly. A fly hung up in a branch of a tree, whether the hook has actually fastened or not, can often be cleared by holding the rod in a horizontal position and drawing the line gently through the rings without jerk and keeping the rod motionless. If it is hopelessly fixed a good plan is to reel up the line until the point of the rod is as close as possible to the fly, and then steadily draw and break, thus only sacrificing the fly and a few inches of gut.

When casting to a fish under the bank in a place where there is a projection of the bank between the angler and the fish, he is sometimes haunted by the notion that in recovering he will infallibly get caught up in the herbage, and on this subject I will quote the advice given in "Dry-Fly Fishing in Theory and Practice." It runs thus: "Brother anglers, will you take the advice of one who has passed through all these stages himself, and after some careful study of the subject has found that there is no cause for despair? When returning raise the rod slowly, smoothly, and without the semblance of a jerk, and you will find that the fly will generally come free. If, however, it should hang in the grass, drop the rod and, taking the line between the thumb and forefinger, draw gently, and the fly will probably come clear. If not, a slight swaying motion will often disengage it. Drawing the line through the rings with the rod in a horizontal position will at times work wonders in recovering a fly when hung up. A difficult place with long grass can thus be safely fished, and if perchance you should get fast it becomes a question of breaking off the fly on the chance of retrieving it later, or crawling slowly up to the place, keeping quite low, disentangling it, and coming back with the same precautions to keep out of sight."

All our study of favourable and unfavourable conditions in reference either to **Coming short.** the fish and its method of feeding, the force and direction of the wind, the easy or difficult nature of the spot where the trout is feeding, has led up to the point when the fish rises at our artificial fly. If all has gone well, at the action of raising the rod and hand we experience the delightful sensation of resistance and realize that the fish is on. Unfortunately our experiences are not all quite so satisfactory. We may find no responsive tug of the hooked trout when we raise the rod, and if we do in a few seconds the fly may be seen in the air, and we are only too conscious of the fact that it is another case of disappointment.

In a subsequent chapter it is the intention to discuss striking, and for the moment let it be conceded that when a fish is badly hooked and gets away it is not usually due to any want of rapidity or other fault in the action of striking.

It may be laid down almost as an axiom that when a trout which has risen at the angler's fly is not hooked at all or is so lightly hooked that it soon shakes the hook out it has *come short*, i.e. for some reason either turned at the last moment away from the tempting morsel, or only taken it so gingerly into its mouth that the barb of the hook is not driven home by the act of striking.

Why do fish come short? Experience goes to show that the shyer and more highly **Reasons for coming** educated are the trout the **short.** greater is their tendency to thwart all the angler's hopes at the last moment. This sentence I fully believe if worked out *au fond* contains within itself the entire theory of the subject. On a heavily fished water, trout are certainly more wary and more prone to come short than on a stream where the fisherman's presence is a comparative rarity. In exceptionally bright sunshine the proportion of rising fish which come short is greater than in dull, cloudy weather. A fish rising well in windy weather when the surface of the stream is strongly rippled is less likely to come short than the same fish taking surface food in a dead calm. Some authorities go as far as to say that a badly dressed fly, one out of proportion to the living insect, or one in which the shades of colour in the different parts of it are not accurately matched to those of the natural fly, will often result in the trout coming short, while with the well-dressed, properly proportioned and perfectly coloured imitation it would fasten.

When a trout is lost at the first run it is not unusual to find a tiny scale affixed to the hook. As there are no scales inside its mouth, the fish has evidently been hooked outside, and it is another case of coming short.

Anything like the smallest trace of drag, or even an unnatural gyration of the artificial as it comes over the fish, may well tend to rouse its suspicions at the last moment and impel it to try to eject the bundle of feathers and hook instead of sucking it in, as would be the case if it had taken a dun or other natural fly.

CHAPTER VII

THE PSYCHOLOGICAL MOMENT

SOME of our humorous critics may well be heard exclaiming with horror at the above title. They will say that these ultra-scientific dry-fly purists who fancy that they know everything on the subject and, in fact, do not know anything, even of the rudiments, are now trying to introduce a new factor into the complicated problem of succeeding with the dry-fly. Not only must we use rods of particular length and action, lines dressed *in vacuo* with pure boiled oil, gut casts of a specific taper and thickness, and flies dressed according to the latest ideas of the expert. Not only must we throw the fly in a particular style, place ourselves crouching or prone in the recognized attitude; not only must we spot a trout rising in a favourable position and make sure that it is rising, and not, as may well be, bulging, tailing, or minnowing; not only must we identify the fly on the water and select a pattern which is a good imitation of this fly; not only must we deliver it at the first attempt delicately, cocked, and accurately placed, so that it will float over the fish at the same pace and following the same course as the natural insects on which the trout is feeding, but in addition to all this we must wait for the psychological moment to place the fly on the water.

Marryat used to say that the great secret of rising a trout with the dry-fly is to com-

Marryat on the first cast.

bine accuracy and delicacy at the first cast. When indulging in his best epigrammatic style he summed up the proposition in something like the following terms. He said that if the calculated odds are three to one against a fish rising to the fly at the first cast provided it comes accurately and without drag over the spot where the trout is rising, at the second cast it is ten to one, and at the third or any subsequent cast it is at least fifty to one.

How often does this successful combination of lightness and precision come off at

Policy of making the first cast short of the fish.

the first attempt ? It requires great judgment to be able to let out precisely the length of line required to cover the fish under all conditions of light and shade or wind and calm. If at the first attempt the fly is placed too far above the fish so that a considerable length of gut and possibly even part of the coarser and more visible reel line is shown to it, its suspicions may well be roused ; and if it is at all shy, it will certainly be set down or so effectually scared as to beat a hasty retreat. To obviate the possibility of overcasting it has become the custom among the majority of modern dry-fly men to let out designedly such a length of line for the first cast as will place the fly some distance short of the fish. This cast, unless the reflection of the rod or line moving through the air has been visible to the trout, should not disturb its equanimity. Careful observation of the precise spot where the fly fell at this trial cast will enable the fisherman to let out sufficient additional line to place the fly at the next attempt exactly where it should land to rise the fish. It may be well to note here, too, that in failing or poor light, and especially at or just after dusk, the invariable tendency of every angler is to place the fish further off than it actually is.

The case of the ideal fish rising under the angler's own bank taking practically every fly of the hatch coming over it with its nose close to the surface is, when found, the one in which the fisherman need not give any consideration to the moment he should select for presenting his fly to the trout. If it is taking, say, one out of six natural insects floating down, a comparatively small disturbance of the water, a slight inaccuracy and sometimes even the gleam of the gut on the water may be sufficient to set it down. Here it is important that the moment selected should not be immediately after the fish has taken a natural fly, but should, if possible, be timed so as to coincide with the fish's desire for another morsel of food.

If there should be a great variety of natural flies on the water another difficulty occurs. As a rule, one is too far from the rising fish to be able to distinguish with any degree of certainty the genus and species of the insect on which it is feeding. To keep changing flies, and cast each over the feeding trout, soon degenerates into hammering, which is an infallible means of educating a trout and making it shy. It may be that the fish is taking almost indiscriminately, but at long intervals, specimens of the different insects. In this case the pattern is not important, although, no doubt, those who are still wedded to a multiplicity of very similar patterns will wish to try every likely one in succession.

One of the modern golfing experts brought out a little handbook consisting almost entirely of advice as to the various mistakes made by the beginner or moderate amateur. It took the form of a great number of pithy maxims each commencing with the word "don't." To parody this here : Don't cast to a fish taking a number of smuts just at the moment when it has gone down to swallow the mouthful it has collected in the gullet. Don't cast to a trout feeding on any fly just as you see its head turned downwards and its dorsal fin or tail coming up towards the surface. Don't select on a dull day the moment to cast when the sun suddenly blazes out and lights up everything on the surface with a strong glare. Don't select the moment when the wind suddenly drops on a blustering day to place your fly on the water. Don't wait for the very strongest puff of adverse wind to cast to your fish. Above all, don't lose your head and keep on hammering and forgetting to dry the fly.

Of positive advice I would say : With a number of

insects coming down in single file try to place your fly just below the leader of the drove. Select, as a rule, the moment when the sun's direct rays are obscured by a cloud. The principle enunciated by Ronalds more than sixty years ago of " casting into the ring of the rising fish " on a calm bright day is often a successful plan to adopt. Having cast over a rising fish without effect, wait until it has taken one or more natural insects before making a second cast. If you can see a smutting fish, watch it carefully and place a perfectly dry and floating fly close to its nose just as it is coming to the surface to take a natural insect. It will often annex both the natural and artificial. Above all play the waiting game. The most patient angler who can be contented to bide his time until the fish he is trying is fully on the feed is the one who is most likely to succeed, while the man who is impatient and casts the moment he sees a rising fish without due consideration is more likely to scare than to rise or kill his trout.

On a day when there are few fish feeding and these only taking at long intervals the keen angler slowly making his way up the stream may well discern the disturbance of the surface caused by a rise. He will proceed at his best pace to the place whence he thinks he can cover the trout. After waiting some minutes there may be no repetition of the movement. His patience is getting exhausted, and he is confronted with a choice of two alternatives. One is to let out what he deems to be a sufficient length of line and at once cast over what he deems to be the spot where the fish rose. In nine out of ten cases he will fail to cover the fish, because it is almost impossible to spot a rise accurately from any great distance.

If his first cast lands his fly many yards above the feeding fish he will in all human probability set the trout down. If, as is far less likely to happen, his fly has fallen some distance below the fish, he will do neither harm nor good.

The second alternative open to the fisherman is to wait on in the hopes of seeing the trout come to the surface once more. If it comes off he will hug himself with satisfaction, and if perchance he should succeed in rising and killing a sizable specimen, he will be a convert for life to the principle enunciated on an historical occasion of "wait and see."

CHAPTER VIII

DRY-FLY ON LOCHS AND LAKES

IT has often occurred to me when travelling in Switzerland and elsewhere without rod or tackle to find myself on the bank of a lake containing a certain number of trout. The natural impulse of a dry-fly man under such conditions is to be on the look-out for rises, and to devote some time to studying the habits of the trout when seen and the class of insect on which they are feeding. In lakes where the flow of the water is very slight a rising or feeding fish does not move in the same way as in a stream. Instead of waiting for the floating insect to be carried down to them by the strength of the current, the trout cruise about to find and pick up the surface food.

During the hot weather smuts as well as duns, spinners, caddis-flies, and winged ants are generally present, and the trout are not, as a rule, loth to take goodly toll of them. In olden times I have frequently thought that instead of getting inferior sport with sunk flies an enthusiastic fisherman could probably do well with the floating fly. It has, however, not fallen to my lot to follow up the casual study of this branch of the subject by anything like a serious attempt to cope with the intricacies of it. Like many others,

when touring with lady members of my family, I
have steadily refrained from carrying fishing gear or
trying to fish, because unless the ladies are themselves
ardent votaries of the fly rod, the pursuit of angling
by their male escorts is likely to mar their pleasure in
the trip.

At the same time, I have ever felt that this pursuit of dry-fly on lakes and other comparatively
stagnant waters should be a charming variety and be
full of interest for the enthusiast.   When working out
the scheme of this book, Mr. Martin E. Mosely at once
suggested a chapter on this branch of the subject, but
the difficulty was that my own personal experience
was not sufficient to warrant my trying to hammer
my opinions down the throats of my readers. The
desirability of including this mode of dry-fly fishing
in a book pretending to be a *complete manual* was so
self-evident that I determined to try to enlist the
sympathies of dry-fly men who could write on the
question with some degree of authority.

After a little consideration I addressed myself to
three friends, each of whom possessed the necessary
experience of dry-fly on lakes or lochs.   The result
of the disinterested and sportsmanlike manner in
which my good friends met my suggestion is that
I am able to give any dry-fly men who wish to try
their hands at this form of fly fishing valuable hints
and a mass of well-digested maxims derived from
long experience.   Each of my three friends is a past-
master in the art of dry-fly work on lakes or lochs

in one of the three divisions of the United Kingdom, and I am thus able to carry out the ambitious
project of my title page of making this a *complete
manual.*

At the outset I must ask my readers to note that
I am giving the opinions of my friends in their own
words and without comment. It is, however, necessary that I should place on record the statement that
I do not necessarily agree with the *dicta* of these
gentlemen as to rods, tackle, flies, etc., but I think it
right that their opinions as undoubted experts should
be set forth in accordance with their own ideas. It is
manifestly impossible for me to express my gratitude
for the able manner in which they have all presented
their views and for the great kindness towards me
personally evinced by their undertaking the arduous
task of writing these articles for this book.

The three friends whom I desire to introduce to
any of my readers who are not yet acquainted either
with the men or their efficient work are :—

(1) Mr. Hugh T. Sheringham, the Angling Editor of
the first sporting periodical in the world—"The Field"
—who has devoted some part of his leisure time to
studying dry-fly on Blagdon Lake.

(2) Mr. A. C. Poole, who having for some years
spent a few weeks each autumn among the Harris
sea-trout lochs, was from the first struck by the possibility of getting great sport with the dry-fly. After a
number of trials he systematized the work, and has
succeeded in killing some of the largest sea-trout

besides a great number of smaller ones with the floating fly.

(3) Mr. John Henderson, who has for the last ten years or more fished lakes in the West of Ireland. As will be seen from his own narrative, he was not greatly attracted by the *dapping* with the natural mayfly, and prolonged study convinced him that when the dapping season was waning or even after it was over there was a chance of quite extraordinary sport with the floating spent gnat or mayfly imago. To call his sport extraordinary is no exaggeration, seeing that he does not kill any fish under 3 lb. and gets specimen fish even of 7 lb. or more. The greediest of dry-fly fishermen would not feel dissatisfied with his sport if he could secure trout of such dimensions, and these, too, in the pink of condition.

The three articles so kindly contributed by my good friends follow here in the order named :—·

(1) "Dry-Fly at Blagdon," by Mr. Hugh T. Sheringham.

(2) "Sea-Trout Loch Fishing with the Dry-Fly," by Mr. A. C. Poole.

(3) "Dry-Fly on Lough Arrow," by Mr. John Henderson.

M

"DRY-FLY AT BLAGDON"

" In setting out to offer some observations on dry-fly fishing on lakes with special reference to Blagdon, I feel that I embark on a presumptuous venture, because I am acutely conscious of the fact that I know very little about it, at any rate, from the point of view of scientific study, which is the important one. It is also an unfortunate fact that, though I have been to Blagdon with dry-fly intentions a good many times now, I have for the most part been hampered by the weather, which has usually been too rough and cold, and once, last September, too hot and fine. Ordinarily, I should say, it is impossible for it to be too hot and fine at Blagdon for dry-fly work, but on the occasion mentioned there had been a drought lasting some months, which doubtless upset things. At any rate, there was then very little fly about and but few fish of any consequence were to be seen rising."

" It will be clear therefore that my impressions of themselves cannot have much solid value, but putting them down may be of some use if they suggest to other anglers lines of further inquiry, and if a more intensive study of the conditions on a lake like Blagdon should be practicable for one or more of them. One cannot be dogmatic from observations taken at a few random visits paid when opportunity allowed, and it is desirable that somebody with better luck in the matter of weather or more frequent chance of fishing should take the inquiry in hand."

" The thing that has most impressed me with regard to dry-fly fishing at Blagdon (and I presume this would to some extent apply to other large lakes also) is that the angler is confronted with a need for learning a quite new fisherman's entomology. A certain number of duns there probably are on the lake, but I do not remember to have seen more than one or two. The mayfly has so far been practically non-existent, but I have been told that it is gradually increasing in numbers, and it may be that in future years it will be a serious factor in the fishing there. I think it would be a welcome addition to the menu of the trout, and it would certainly give scope for some very interesting and attractive sport."

"Of other flies usually valued by river fishermen I cannot say that I have seen much sign at Blagdon, but this is not to say that they may not be present in considerable numbers on favourable days or at the proper seasons. Doubtless there are plenty of sedges of the commoner kinds, there must be periodical falls of brown ants ; and black gnats, smuts and so on must be forthcoming on a sheet of water formed by damming up a river like the Yeo as well as other streams. Probably too, the daddy-longlegs which plays an important part on some Irish loughs is a thing to be reckoned with at Blagdon also. I have noticed a good many on the water at different times, and once or twice I have seen specimens taken by fish. It may well be that the trout look on the daddy-longlegs as an important item on their bill of fare."

" But my experience has caused me to think less of such possibilities by reason of the definite hatches of other flies which I have seen and on which I have depended for such sport as I have had. Three kinds of fly have most impressed themselves on my notice. The first is the brown silverhorns, which appears in vast quantities in both July and September—probably also in August, but I have never been to Blagdon in that month. The fish certainly take this fly on the surface to some extent, but not, I think, so eagerly as its abundance would seem to warrant. Nor have they taken very kindly to such imitations as I have been able to offer them, but that may be because none of my imitations have been worth much. The grannom of the ordinary pattern on a No. 2 or No. 3 hook has secured me one or two fish which were rising at silverhorns, and a hackle-fly, known in Wales as the early brown, has also killed a fish or two."

" But the two flies which really did make the trout rise were respectively a midge with a grass-green body * and a midge with an olive body. The first was about in myriads one September and a friend, who was fishing with me, imitated it with the simple material of some green wool, snipped from the anti-macassar of our long-suffering hostess, and a white hackle. The imitation was quite effective and, fished both dry and wet, gained a number of rises. The weather at the time of this visit was hot and steamy, and the midges could be seen like columns of smoke

* Mr. Mosely informs me that Mr. Sheringham's grass-green midge of Blagdon is called *Chironomus viridis* Macq.

in the air at various points of the lake shore. I must confess that I have never seen them since myself, but I am told that they still make their appearance in appropriate weather. They should be hailed with joy when seen, for they certainly cause more enthusiasm among the fish than do the silverhorns. We found that most of the fish we caught on that visit contained numbers of the insects in their gullets and stomachs."

" These midges are biggish flies, quite as big as the biggest gnat one encounters, to one's sorrow, in the Broads and other marshy districts, if not bigger ; and they have, I think, rather more substantial bodies, and I do not consider that a light-wired No. 3 hook is too big for the imitation. This is an advantage for a place which contains such large trout as Blagdon. Where the fish average 2½ lb. and may run to 5 lb. or more I personally feel much happier with a hook of reasonable size."

" The olive-bodied midge is bigger still, and it can certainly be tied on a No. 3 hook without risk of overdoing the hook. This fly was for a long time a great puzzle to me. I used to see extraordinary rises of big trout going on on calm evenings, and I never could make out what the fish were rising at. Flogging away with the salmon flies which one used to use as a matter of course would have not the least effect, and I got to despair of doing any good when the Blagdon fish began to move to fly of an evening. It *seemed* to me that they were taking some minute form of white fly which it would be absurd to try and imitate. This was a simple deduction from the fact that the fish were rising furiously all round, and that all one could see on the water were whitish specks which seemed to be cruising about on the surface."

" Later, I discovered that these whitish specks were not smuts at all—they were the inadequate wings belonging to the substantial body of our friend the olive midge. It was no wonder that the trout were rising, for they had something solid to rise at. Then the ranger, Mr. Donald Carr, sent some of these flies to me for examination and identification. Thanks to the good offices of my friend, Mr. Martin Mosely, the midge was identified at South Kensington as *Chironomus tentans*, an insect which in this or closely allied forms is common on many lakes and pools."

" It seems to me not a little curious that a fly which is common on such well-known lakes as Killarney, Arrow, and Leven, and which is evidently so welcome to the trout, should hitherto have escaped notice among anglers. Possibly it does not elsewhere appear in such numbers or have such an effect on the fish as at Blagdon. Possibly, too, the fact that it does not appear till dusk (that at any rate is my experience) has helped to keep it unknown. Certainly, I myself should have gone through life believing that the Blagdon trout rose in the evening at a whitish midge unless Mr. Carr had shown me what the beast really was. The big body is of course invisible on the water in the dusk and the wings are all that one can see. The habits of the fly and its effect on the trout remind me somewhat of the blue-winged olive, which also puzzled me for a long time. Appearing late in the evening, and only imperfectly visible then, the blue-winged olive has given me many bad quarters of an hour."

"Besides getting the midge identified, Mr. Mosely was also kind enough to tie me an excellent pattern to imitate it, and I take the liberty of giving the dressing as it appeared in an article on *Ch. tentans* by him in 'The Field' of September 9th, 1911. He there wrote :—

'An imitation of *Ch. tentans* may be dressed on a o long hook with dark olive condor quill unstripped for the body, a very green olive hackle for the legs, two short blue cock hackle points set along the body for wings, and, to represent the prominent thorax, a few fibres of heron or any bluish feather tied in at the shoulder and humped over to the neck of the hook, where they should be fastened in and the fly finished off. If the water contains big fish, such as are found at Blagdon or Lough Arrow, it would be better to dress the fly on a stouter hook, and as the natural fly has a body nearly half an inch in length, the use of a No. 3 or even No. 4 hook would in no way detract from the likeness of the artificial to the natural insect.'

"I have to confess that the trial of the pattern lacks a good deal in thoroughness so far. I had three days at Blagdon last September, but, as I have already said, the conditions were very unfavourable and the evening rise was much less than usual. I do not consider that the fly had a fair chance. But using it either dry or just below the surface on one evening when there was some little semblance of a rise I succeeded in hooking five fish with it. Three were landed, but they were small for Blagdon, the best not being more than 1½ lb. They were returned, and the others, which were bigger fish, got off. A friend got a good fish of over 2½ lb. the same evening with the pattern, and another friend got one a little smaller with a wickham fished dry. I cannot therefore do more than record the genesis of the olive midge pattern. I trust that ere long, however, it will prove its value fully."

" For Blagdon, of course, fishing is divided into two portions, big-fly and small-fly rather than wet-fly and dry-fly, that is to say, there is, to my thinking, no very hard and fast line to be drawn between small flies dry and small flies wet so far as efficiency goes. Probably either method will kill fish when the fish are in mood to take flies at all. The small wet-fly has some slight advantage over the dry-fly in the fact that much of the trout's food consists of beetles, and is, of course, subaqueous. Fishing with big or salmon flies pays when the trout are bent on sticklebacks, or perhaps not bent on anything in particular but ready to have their appetites tickled by bright and tempting lures."

" But in the whole course of my trout fishing I have known nothing more fascinating and exciting than the two or three *good* evening rises which I have experienced on that wonderful lake, and which have given me a fair chance of using a dry-fly. It is a thrilling experience to see really big trout cruising round and round all over a calm bay of the lake and taking in floating trifles with all the aplomb of a Test fish. The worst of them is that they sometimes, indeed generally, cover a great extent of water in their patrols, and it takes one some time to discover the route taken by each. Once you have made sure of that you can place your fly somewhere along it and wait till the fish returns—he usually travels on the same line or near it. If the fly is properly presented he ought to take it. This process of waiting for the fish's return and then covering him is often a long one, and the result is that one does not cover nearly so many fish in an evening as one would if they were not such cruisers. I should regard a brace of fish caught during an evening rise from the bank as satisfactory work and two brace as very good. But I can imagine that in ideal circumstances one might easily get more. Once for a few thrilling minutes I found several big fish cruising in such close proximity that one cast would probably suffice for two or three of them. I only caught one, but I missed another through my own fault. Similar opportunities might recur on any evening."

"So far wickhams, zulus, coch-y-bondhus, and sedges have been the floating patterns most successful within my knowledge, over and above the kinds mentioned earlier, but no doubt others would serve."

"One ought, I think, to have the water calm, or very

nearly calm, for dry-fly work at Blagdon, and I always make for the sheltered side or bays in the expectation that the fish will begin to rise there sooner, or at any rate that one will be able to see them doing it. I believe that a dry-fly cast at a venture and allowed to sit on top of the water will catch fish, just as it does with sea-trout in the Hebrides—in fact I know that it has done so. But there is not the same charm about fishing blind in this way. The essence of the sport is to find a huge fish visibly rising and to try and catch him by the orthodox dry-fly process."

"I need hardly say that a powerful rod, plenty of reel line, and strongish gut are advisable at Blagdon. Personally, I prefer a rod of about eleven feet, like to have at least seventy yards (with backing) on my reel, and for dry-fly use gut which might be described as medium mayfly gut. With this equipment one is prepared to meet anything in reason. The biggest Blagdon trout I have had with dry-fly weighed $4\frac{3}{4}$ lb., but it is quite on the cards that one might get into something a good deal heavier. I can conceive nothing more triumphant in a fishing career than the subjugation of a Blagdon 10-pounder with a dry-fly from the bank, and every year as I revisit the lake I am buoyed up with hopes of such a victory. Rivers do not give us such promise as this, or very rarely indeed, so here is another inducement to study the art of the dry-fly on big lakes where monster trout are to be found."

"H. T. Sheringham."

"SEA-TROUT LOCH FISHING WITH THE DRY-FLY"

"There can be little doubt that in the south of England—the home of the dry-fly—there are some anglers who have become so proficient in the art, and, in consequence, have given so much time and practice to this special branch of fly-fishing, that they use it more or less exclusively, even when choice or circumstances find them in other localities."

"It is also common knowledge that dry-fly fishing has been steadily creeping northward and westward in the British Islands for some time past, and there are many north-country anglers who have become so practised in the art that they have adopted it in conjunction with their usual method. Even in Scotland, where it was always supposed to be unsuitable for the type of water usually found, it is becoming evident that the idea of unsuitability is an erroneous one, for the very simple reason that nature has endowed flies, especially water-bred flies, with so much buoyancy that they can, and do, float in any type of water, and that their artificial counterfeits may be employed to advantage in all water that is possible for the usual orthodox method; but, curiously enough, although sea-trout have fallen victims to the dry-fly when employed on Scottish rivers under favourable conditions for several years past, it has only been within the last five or six years used with success on purely sea-trout lochs, but the success has been so surprising that doubtless there are many anglers (not necessarily dry-fly specialists) who quite naturally wish to obtain some little enlightenment upon the subject ; and really there is nothing in the way of unusual skill or acquired knowledge necessary to prevent the frequenter of sea-trout lochs from substantially increasing his bag by the dry-fly method."

" Dry-fly fishing is (although not usual) quite possible for the wielder of a double-handed rod, indeed such a rod might under certain conditions prove of greater utility than the short one, even to an expert. It has, however, become usual to employ the single-handed rod in loch fishing, but where a long cast has to be made, shooting the line is essential, and that method is not apparently very generally adopted, although it does away with the necessity of the long double-handed appliances."

" Some anglers of my acquaintance prefer to use two rods, a twelve or fourteen feet rod for the orthodox method, and ten feet for dry-fly. This is quite unnecessary, and only adds to one's impedimenta, the exchange of the wet cast, with its attached droppers, for one with a single (previously paraffined) floating fly attached, being all that is really necessary. The wet part of the reel line (it is inferred that the line in use is thoroughly sound as to its waterproof dressing) should be wiped dry, and greased. For this purpose there are several preparations on the market, which are best applied with a small piece of thin flexible leather, kept in a tin box for the purpose. It is important not to allow any of the reel line to sink beneath the surface of the water, for should it do so, when it is retrieved, the fly gets hopelessly wet."

" The condition best adapted to the tyro is one of dead calm, or very light airs, when the majority of sea-trout loch fishermen give up any further attempt to angle, and patiently await the hoped-for breeze.   A little perseverance on the part of the tyro under these conditions will probably be rewarded if the loch be at a fishable height, but he should endeavour to go to that part of the loch which the big fish are known to affect, and to do so as quietly as possible.   There is no need for the cast to be a lengthy one, excepting where the fish are very shy.   The fly should be allowed to remain on the surface without any motion being given to it for a matter of ten to fifteen seconds, or even longer, and then a fresh cast should be made to a point a few yards from the last."

" Do not stand up in the boat, and remain as quiet as possible, and should a rise reward your patience and skill, you must remember to let the fish hook itself, or disaster will certainly occur.   This applies especially to *big fish in deep water.*"

" The foregoing are simple instructions for anyone wishing to make a first trial, and do not necessarily apply to dry-fly men who are well acquainted with the general practice."

" With regard to allowing the fish to hook themselves, there must be no spasmodic action, nothing quick or hurried, just a deliberate tightening of the line being all that is required—it is impossible for the line to be too free, but it must be taut."

" Most of the casting is a matter of prospecting, and it is only upon rare occasions that the usual procedure of fishing the rise becomes possible."

" It is questionable if anything is to be gained, as far as the sport is concerned, by any entomological study of the lochs, but there can be little doubt that those who have the inclination and opportunity to indulge in it might obtain much useful information."

" Occasionally one sees single specimens of the olives, or a few sedges, round the shores or banks of the lochs.   There are, noticeably, two kinds of sedges —a small dark, and a medium-sized brown."

" Of land-bred flies the red ant appears in very large quantities.   Clouds of this insect are sometimes to be seen during hot, calm weather, but the heather-moth and heather-fly appear very sparsely during the period of my annual visit, which is from the middle of August to the second week in September."

" Success may generally be expected in dead calm, or light airs, when the orthodox method is at its worst ; but at the same time sport is good when the conditions are equally good for the sunken lure.   Success should be expected in likely places, such as well-known bays or promontories."

" Sea-trout apparently rise indiscriminately in general, i.e. they are not partaking of a regular meal, but are attracted by the lure much in the same way as salmon. There is no definite hatch of fly, and consequent rise of fish, as occurs on the majority of rivers, and the only occasions when dry-fly fishing on sea-trout lochs assimilates to that of our southern rivers is when there happens the afore-mentioned fall of red ants.   In a minor degree, the crane-fly, which is always more or less in evidence, may be regarded as productive of rises, and is one of the best insects to take as a model for a floating sea-trout lure.   It is not placed first on the list, but should certainly be given the second place.   There may be, of course, for the purpose, many artificial representations of this fly. The tying generally adopted is that of a modified large blue upright—wings, medium starling rather long and narrow, body well marked undyed peacock quill, long blue dun or grizzled cock hackle, hook Nos. 0, 1, 2, 3 long."

"The medium, or small sparsely tied spent gnats, of any pattern, may also be used as representing the crane-fly."

"The artificial of greatest importance is undoubtedly a black palmer tied with stiff cock hackle to float well—sizes 3, 2, 1, 0, and 00—in fact any fly tied palmer fashion is useful."

"Colour is of little importance, excepting as it affects transparency, or opacity."

"There is one general principle it has been found well to bear in mind—heavy, cloudy sky, darkest possible lures of the larger sizes, especially if the

wave is big ; bright clear sky, flies of greatest transparency. Tinsel may also be used sparingly on the
lighter flies ; it is of no use with a dark heavy sky
as it produces no scintillations under these conditions."

" The small blacks, 1, 0, and 00 sizes, with fine tinsel,
or lightly tinselled (the tinsel should be *fresh* and
bright) may also be used in fine weather, but they
should be more sparsely hackled than the larger sizes,
which are used with a cloudy sky."

" During a fall of red ants, 0 and 00 red quills or
lightly hackled wickhams, and the 00 lightly hackled
black palmer, will prove effective, possibly more so
than the usual so-called imitation of the red ant—as
ordinarily tied."

" To those who are acquainted with dry-fly fishing,
as practised in the south of England, a word of
warning with regard to the tackle may not be out of
place, although there is nothing to prevent the usual
tackle being employed."

" *Beware of a heavy rod.* Of necessity there is much
more casting to be done upon a loch than is usually
necessary in river fishing. A nine-feet rod is long
enough, and 5 to 6 oz. should cover its weight. The
reel also should be a light one, of not more than $4\frac{1}{2}$ oz.,
and the casting-line about thirteen drachms for 35 yd.
length, with 50 to 60 yd. of fine, strong, undressed
silk backing, so that all told 12 to 13 oz. covers
the total weight of equipment."

" Heavy fish must be played upon the butt of the rod

of this weight, otherwise top or middle will be unduly strained."

"The heaviest sea-trout it has been my good fortune to take during dry-fly trials is one of $8\frac{1}{4}$ lb., but this is hardly claimed as a dry-fly fish, for owing to the big wave running at the time of its capture I had not troubled to keep the fly perfectly dry, and it was taken just under the unbroken crest of a wave—a particularly beautiful type of rise never to be forgotten. It had commenced to blow from the south rather suddenly, and a southerly wind makes a high wave upon the Hebridean lochs, as most of them are positioned with their length north and south."

"Another very perfect fish of 5 lb. 15 oz. was captured with a o red quill."

"There was a slight swell at the time, but no wind. The fish rose with a long diagonal rush from a depth of seven or eight feet. These furious rises are more or less characteristic of sea-trout when taking the floating fly on lochs, and somewhat disconcerting to the angler; upon the other hand, with a dead calm and a fall of red ants, the rise is similar to that experienced when brown trout are taking fly in our southern rivers."

"The variety in the type of rise to the dry-fly that a sea-trout gives you lends charm to the sport. It is doubtless caused by the different depths from which the fish rise."

"As a break in one's usual routine these annual visits to the Harris sea-trout lochs have certainly proved a

N

very pleasant change, more especially since the adoption of the floating lure, and for the last three years no other than dry-fly equipment has troubled me when preparing for the expedition, the floating fly not only holding its own, but having been the means of capturing the largest sea-trout of the season (with the exception of one) since it was adopted six years ago."

"Considering the number of fishermen who for a period of about three months fish these Harris lochs in the orthodox manner, and that my use of the floating fly has never exceeded three weeks during that period, it appears well worth while to adopt its use much more generally, and not alone for sea-trout lochs, but experimentally on lochs and lakes in general throughout the British Islands."

"A. C. POOLE."

"DRY-FLY ON LOUGH ARROW"

" It is with great diffidence that I comply with
Mr. Halford's request that I should write this article
on dry-fly fishing on an Irish lough.   I do so mainly
in the hope that it will be a beginning, and that others
will follow on and relate their experiences on other
lakes."

" My first attempt at dry-fly fishing for *trout* in Ireland was not a success.   I could only catch peal as
they are called in Ireland, this being the synonym of
what are called *grilse* in Scotland and elsewhere, but
I never saw trout come into position and feed on fly
(sedges) better than those 4-lb. peal did."

"Subsequently I went over to *dap*, but could not
take sufficient interest in that primitive method of
angling to keep awake over it, and although I gave
it a fair trial, can only look upon it as a sort of
"duffer's godsend," success depending entirely on the
skill and knowledge of your boatman *and luck*.   But
the splendid trout were there, and there was no apparent reason why they should not give good sport
and be interesting to fish for, even though the bag
should not be a record one.   It is the *sport*, not the
number of *fish*, one should fish for."

"At first I encountered much ridicule and discour-
agement ; was told that it was useless ; that you could
do no good with the artificial fly ; that trout would
only take when there was a good breeze on, etc. etc.   I
was then living on the shores of the lake, and had an

excellent opportunity of watching the fish and their ways, and soon found that a breeze was the worst thing you could have, and that the largest trout fed as a rule only in the calm sheltered places where the fly became settled on the surface."

" The patterns of flies were at first a great trouble ; there were no satisfactory ones to be bought, so I have been forced to work out my own, and after many failures I am fairly contented with the patterns I have made and now use, but it has been ten years' work. I started well with the green drake, having an *answerable* hackle pattern, but it was two or three years before I found that the trout seldom took the green when the gray or spent drake was on. I tried all the patterns of gray and spent drake that were on the market, but none were satisfactory for lake work ; those tied with hackle points were best, but would not stand the work, and soon got limp, the wings broke or got tucked into the bend of the hook, and they came to pieces ; they were all tied with hackle points from the neck. A better and stronger feather can be obtained from the shoulder and back of an old cock."

" The rod and tackle I recommend are not intended for small fishing, but for waters where the trout will average 3 lb., and go up to 7 or 8 lb. (and over)."

" Spliced greenheart with plenty of wood left for strength at the splices, 10 ft.

Rod. 6 in. to 11 ft. long ; it should not be too stiff, with easy play down to the handle of the butt. The best material for splicing is ¼-in. rubber adhesive plaster on *linen or brown holland* made by Ferris and Co., Bristol. If the rod can be kept up it is advisable to give a coat or two of good varnish over the splices. The rings throughout should be small, of brown porcelain, lashed directly on to the rod with strong silk ; metal supports are too heavy and spoil the balance of the rod. Good hard metal bridge rings with agate linings to the ring at the tip and the lowest ring at the butt may be used. I like having a pair of rods in the boat ready for use—it often saves very valuable time. The rods should be varnished with matt or dull varnish."

"A good oil-dressed single tapered 30-yd. silk line with 50 yd. of backing is **Line.** required. It should taper from D to G, or fly end ·024 in. ; 2nd yd., ·027 ; 3rd yd., ·032 ; 4th yd., ·035. It must be a good, soft and easily handled line that will palm and shoot well. A *really* good line is a priceless treasure and worthy of care being taken of it. It should be taken off the reel after a day's fishing, dried, and before use rubbed over with Mucilin (maker, Aspinall, Carlton Street, Bolton)."

"When not in use lines should not be kept on reels for any length of time. The dressed part can be taken off the reel, made into loose coils, tied in places to keep the coils together, and the reel and line hung up out of the way; after a season's fishing the dressed portion should be cut from the backing, washed in soap and water and well rinsed in plain water, dried thoroughly and redressed with pure linseed oil under the air pump. A line thus treated improves each year."

Floatant. "I use Aspinall's Mucilin thick for both flies and lines, and find it excellent."

Cast. "The cast should be 6 ft. to 8 ft. in length, tapering from light salmon, or 'Marana,' to 'Regular'—not finer if the trout run large. When fishing on hot bright days, the gut should be kept damp by being constantly trailed overboard, either with the fly on or off, as it becomes very dry and brittle, and in this state is the cause of many good fish being lost. A well-made fly mucilined and properly *groomed* will not absorb moisture, and will lie on the surface if only the gut cast is placed on the water, and will float well when subsequently cast to a fish."

Landing net. "The landing net should be large and V-shaped for open waters where there is not much weed, not less than 18 in. across and about 22 in. in the arms; it must be deep and roomy. In weedy waters an oval or round wooden frame is better; a strong 5 to 6 ft. handle for boat work is required; if you are wading or fishing from the shore a net you can carry in a sling is necessary."

"The boat I have found most suitable for single-handed work was built from patterns supplied by the

PLATE XII

Boats on Lough Arrow

Photograph by John Hardcastle

Pioneer Boat Co., Detroit. It is about 15 ft long

Boat.

with 4-ft. beam, flat-bottomed, and with sharp stem and stern.

The boat is the centre one of the three in Plate XII, reproduced from a photograph. It is easy to row or paddle, draws little water, and, with fair handling, is an excellent sea-boat for an open lake; it is a steady boat to fish from. For anchors I use stones and a piece of strong tanned deep-sea fishing line with the kinks well worked out. One anchor, either at bow or stern, will generally do, but sometimes it is necessary to use two to prevent the boat swinging and placing the fisherman too far from the fish's rising beat, or, what is worse, swinging the boat on to it and setting the fish down. Small jamb cleats are very handy for fastening the anchor cord."

"A light handy *cot*, such as is used on the Shannon about Castle Connel, with a good boatman used to the handling of cots with paddle or pole, would be much better for approaching the fish and casting from than the ordinary boat. To attempt to fish dry-fly from a drifting dapping-boat is of little use, as the boat is moving too fast for you to fish properly any fish you may see rising in front of you.

"It is a mistake for two men to fish from the same boat, as it spoils sport for both."

"I have tried most of the hooks on the market, have had several patterns made specially, and have found the best a plain round bend hook with *no sneck or*

skew; in all cases where there is a sneck I have
had some of these hooks open
Hooks. out or break—you can never
trust them. Round bend
straight hooks with strong wire (gauge No. 5 ·021 in.,
No. 6 ·024, No. 7 ·026), Nos. 5, 6, 7, 8 Hutchinson's
Kendal sizes loop eye, are the most satisfactory as yet.
It is important that the eye should be a fair-sized one,
sufficiently large to take the gut twice through it, but
still neat. Warner's brazed eye is a nice shape and
size. I have found little difference between *turn up*
or *turn down* eyes; I tried small double hooks, but
found little or no advantage in their use."

" I have found hackle patterns best, but much care is
necessary in choosing suitable
Flies. Green drake 1. hackles, the shape and strength
of fibre of the large wing
hackles being most important ; they should be taken
from old winter-killed birds."

" 1. Tail.—Cock pheasant tail, three strands."

" Body.—Rofia grass, sometimes dyed green, ribbed
with fine gold tinsel or wire. Body hackle.—Cuckoo
(Plymouth Rock) cock's neck dyed green."

" Wing.—Barred feather from side of French partridge, slightly dyed green, tied hacklewise."

" Head hackle.—Gray feather from breast of English
partridge, or hen pheasant, dyed green in Crawshaw's
Green Drake."

" Canadian Wood-duck drake makes an excellent
hackle for wings, undyed, but Egyptian goose is not

satisfactory, being too soft, and it does not sit well. For bright days I have found gold tinsel bodies answer."

Gray drake 2.

" Tail.—Cock pheasant tail, three strands."

" Body.—*White* or bleached rofia grass, quill or celluloid over flat silver tinsel, as the quill especially darkens from the wax on the tying silk being dissolved by paraffin or Mucilin ; silver wire ribbing."

" Body hackle, if required, cock's neck hackle with black centre rib."

" Wing hackle.—Guinea fowl with small spots, or cuckoo (Plymouth Rock) cock's hackle from wing or back, a good stiff, strong and clear feather, dyed, first in Crawshaw's *slate* and then in *iron blue*, not too darkly."

" Head hackle.—Undyed English partridge gray feather from breast of an old winter-killed bird."

Spent drake.

" This is much the most important stage of the fly, the larger fish feeding almost entirely on it when lying flat on the water. I use the term *spent drake* instead of *spent gnat* because it is not a gnat, and there are several true gnats on which lake trout feed at times."

" My method of tying is as follows :—"

" Tie in a good, clear hackle from the *shoulder* or *back* of an *old* cock, stiff and clear in the fibre ; some may be got a good enough gray, but are rare. The best result with dyed feathers has been with cuckoo

black and white speckled hackle, dyeing first in Crawshaw's slate lightly and then finishing in their iron

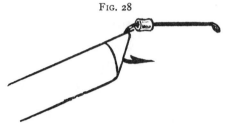

FIG. 28

blue. This feather
should be wound on
so that when finished
it leaves about $\frac{1}{8}$ to
$\frac{3}{16}$ in. bare shank to
the eye. Before ty-
ing the hackle a small
piece of india-rubber tubing about $\frac{1}{8}$ in. long (a
piece from the small tubing used for snapshot camera
shutters is about the
right size of bore) is
put on to the shank
of hook and left rest-
ing on the jaws of
the vice, as shown in
Fig. 28. The hackle
is now divided and
spread out in two
equal parts on each
side of and at right
angles to the hook
shank ; the silk is
then taken over and
under in a figure-of-
eight to keep the
wings in position, as

FIG. 29

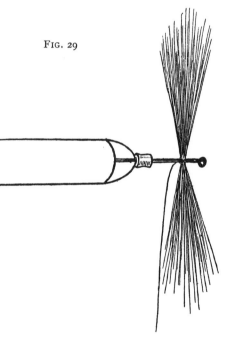

in Fig. 29 ; then make a half-hitch on the tail side
of the wings, pass the silk through the rubber tube

and the tube over the wings towards the eye, leaving it thus Fig. 30. Then tie in with the silk at the base of wings three strands of cock pheasant tail, a length of fine silver wire, and piece of white rofia grass about 6 in. long and $\frac{1}{16}$ to $\frac{1}{8}$ in. wide; fasten the silk and cut it off. Hold the tail and wire straight on top of hook and wind rofia evenly down to tail and back to base of wings; pull the tube off over head, and take rofia in double figure-of-eight over and across the separated fibres of hackle so that they stand out well and at right angles. If the rofia grass is good, a half-hitch in it will hold at head; if not, put the hackle pliers on the end and let them hang down while you put two turns of the wire under the tail to make it sit up, and wind the wire spirally up the body with tight figure-of-eight turns over the rofia between the wings. Finish off with tying silk, fastening in both the rofia grass and wire together. Now give the body several coats of celluloid cement or Zapon enamel, allowing each coat to dry before putting on the next; it dries quickly."

FIG. 30

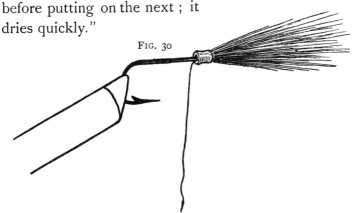

"When dry put a piece of rubber tube back over wings, shown in Fig. 31, and finish by tying on a head hackle of partridge gray breast feather ; a small portion of the shank next eye should be left bare.   When the

FIG. 31

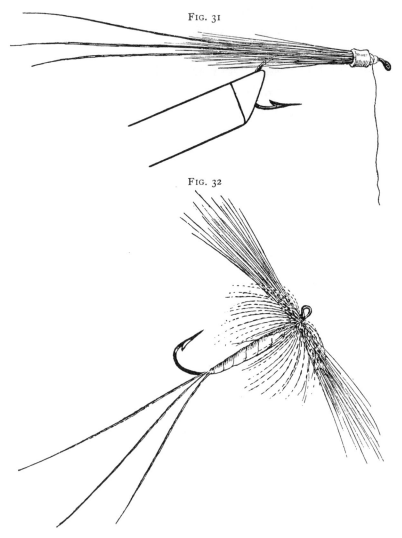

FIG. 32

fly is finished (Fig. 32) the tubing is passed over the tail and bend of hook."

" I give this mode of tying at great length, as it is useful in tying the winged green drake and the up-right winged gray drake ; tying in with rofia grass figure-of-eight sets the wings more upright. This method succeeds too with all the spinners of the duns, which should be tied in this way ; hackle point wings do not float as well, and soon break up ; they make good show-case flies, but are of little practical use for lake work. One trout generally finishes them. The hackle patterns and those tied as above will last well, and a worn and chewed fly sits and kills better than a new one."

" With the exception of the mayfly or drake I know too little as yet to say much. **Other flies.** It requires someone who lives on the shores of a lake, and is constantly and carefully observing what is going on during the whole of many fishing seasons to be qualified to do so."

" I give briefly the other flies which I have noticed trout feeding on and with which I have killed fish."

" A small black fly, not unlike the hawthorn fly, but without the long hanging legs ; the only local name I have heard for it is the *young duck-fly ;* it comes out about 15th to 20th April, when the young wild ducks are about, and they feed on it."

" The trout come really well on the feed on this fly ; even the larger trout that, as a rule, only come up to the spent drake, feed well on it. The trouble is that it occurs in such countless numbers as to be too thick on the water, and is so small that it is difficult to make a good floating pattern."

" March brown, few seen on lakes. A fly locally called the olive dun, which is a larger fly than the true olive, and somewhat similar in colouring. It has been identified as *Cloeon simile*."

" Blue-winged dun. Fish feed well on both these, and take them and their spinners even when the drake is on."

" Claret dun. This comes on just before the mayfly, and is often taken well. It is a fly that sits well on the water and seems very weather- and water-proof. The scientific name of this fly is *Leptophlebia vespertina*.

" A large gnat comes out in May, rising mostly from a peat or mud bottom. I have sometimes, when it is still on the surface, seen trout take it well; at other times they do not seem to care for it, although taking other flies. A difficult pattern to tie."

" A green gnat comes on later (August) slightly smaller, an evening riser (the gray is about all day), and is worth trying to copy and fish with."

" In Ireland called *wallflies*."

Caddis sedges. " The *murragh* in lakes rises only from a peaty bottom at sunset, comes to the surface in a shuck which splits open and allows the fly to emerge. So far as I have seen trout only take this fly when stationary, either when leaving its case or when drying its wings—not when it is scuttling about on surface of the water. It is probably *Phryganea grandis* or *P. striata*."

"There are very many of the Trichoptera to be found on lakes, and all are more or less taken by trout. A small clear-winged sedge that comes out early in the afternoons of July is taken well."

"Welshman's button (*Sericostoma personatum* McL.). I have killed with hackle pattern of it dressed with peacock herl body and land-rail hackle. It is well worth trying on a fish picking about amongst drakes, but not taking them."

"Alder (*Sialis lutaria*) comes on in May and June, but the drakes kill better."

"*Cænis halterata*, a small white dun, comes on very thickly on calm evenings towards the end of June, and the trout sometimes take it well, but the artificial requires such a small hook that you lose most of the fish hooked."

"The daddy-longlegs are sometimes blown off from the land in large numbers, but I have not seen trout rise to them, except to a bunch of them when dapped."

"I have seen wonderful rises to red or brown ant when a swarm of these insects gets on the water, but I am not sure that it was all at the ant; it looked more as if perch fry had followed the ant out when blown off shore, and as if the trout were feeding on the perch fry."

"The mayfly has for several years past had a very

bad time of it. Hard, cold winds have killed the
flies in their early stages, and the black-headed gulls
have increased greatly, and take a heavy toll of them.
The drake usually comes up about 25th May, but last
year, 1911, the fly came up ten days earlier. There
was a very heavy rise the first few days, and afterwards there were comparatively few females, and
although you saw plenty of the male gray drakes
kiting, there were no females to take them out over
the water, and they died in the trees and on land in
great numbers ; there were not enough on the water
to bring the trout up to them. I saw no schools of
trout that year."

"It is most interesting to watch trout and their
ways carefully in a lake. Most
Habits and manners of of them when surface feeding
trout in lake. have their regular feeding
places, which they come to,
often from a considerable distance, as you can sometimes see from a fish's rises as he cruises along until
he finally settles down to a regular beat close in
shore, but always where it is calm, with the wind off
shore and where the flies are likely to collect and
remain settled on the surface. These feeding spots
are often clearly marked by a rock standing out in the
water, the end of an old wall carried out into the lake,
or a clump of trees on shore, especially sycamore,
which give good shelter for the flies. Such a spot is
illustrated in Plate XIII. These are the fish that will
provide the best sport for the dry-fly fisherman. To

PLATE XIII

Calm on Shelter of Point

fish cruising fish means going out *abroad* and hunting them ; this requires *very careful* boat handling, and even with the greatest care, especially when oars are used, many fish are scared and set down for the very few brought to the net. There is no doubt that the dry-fly affords most fascinating sport *if* the boat is well handled and the fisherman is a good quick caster, and if both boat handler and fisherman thoroughly understand each other and the game ; but on public or open waters it certainly leads to spoiling sport for others by scaring and making the fish shy."

"Trout occasionally cruise and feed in pairs, and towards the end of the hatch of mayfly often in schools of twenty and more. They will travel on the surface like a school of porpoises, but when travelling I have never known them feed (although there may be plenty of fly on the water) if there is a breeze on and the surface ruffled, but when they come on some sheltered shore or bay where the spent drake are lying thick on the surface they feed greedily and soon clear off what flies there are ; they will then cruise off *abroad* for a time and return when flies have had time to collect again. When in a bay or on a perfectly calm evening they often feed in circles. On a shore where the wind strikes so as to leave a calm streak along it they will feed up and down it sometimes if there is much fly, coming close in amongst the stones. They are then best fished from the shore. After the mayfly is over, in some years they have been seen to

o

remain in small schools when feeding on the perch fry. Some trout again never seem to join the schools, and are always to be found about the same spot. Islands with trees on them to give shelter from the wind are the best fishing grounds, as shelter can generally be found somewhere round their shores if the wind changes, and also from their position out in the lake, islands collect fly with every wind and have a more certain supply. A rush-covered island sometimes collects a great quantity of fly which will lie close amongst the rushes during the day while there is a breeze, and if it becomes calmer in the evening rise go to the water in a cloud and drift away from the shores like a great raft of spent drakes. I am inclined to think that it is in following such a raft that trout get collected into schools."

"The edge of the breeze and calm is a favourite place for fish feeding, but it is generally better to anchor in shore or in the reeds and fish out to your fish when they feed in, as they will do if not disturbed, or if the wind does not change and blow on to the calm piece of water. It may be laid down as an axiom that calm evenings are favourable ones. The appearance of the lake on such an evening is depicted in Plate XIV. When anchoring in reeds I have seldom known a fish run into the reeds when hooked ; it usually makes out for the open. When fishing from very light boats or canoes not securely anchored, a 3 or 4-lb. fish is quite

Where to fish.

PLATE XIV

A Promising Evening

Photograph by John Henderson, Esq.

capable of towing the boat and starting it to run
on to the fish, and you hear of fish running at and
under the boat, but in reality it is the boat running
at the fish. On rocky open shores without reeds and
points much can be done wading, especially in the
early mornings and evenings. The contour of the
land where there are high trees near the water's edge
and hills behind often produces eddies in the wind off
shore, and at such places in certain winds fly, etc.;
collects and makes good feeding ground, but troublesome to fish on account of the uncertainty of the
wind. They are worth watching for and their positions noted. Leaves and other rubbish collect in
them, amongst which all sorts of fly and spinners
lodge, and you are rather apt to find a trout there
which is not taking mayfly, but feeding very quietly
on small fly and spinners. Such fish will often give
some interesting fishing."

"A *school* feeding in to you requires watching, and
the larger fish should be spotted. It is as well to
have a little patience and only go for the best ; it does
not always come off. I once watched, waited, and
selected two large trout, feeding side by side, and cast
carefully to them, but they were not quick enough ;
an active four-pounder got the fly and the school
sheered off ; they will generally return after a slight
scare if there is plenty of fly on the surface. I once
got four weighing 19½ lb. out of a school, and I did
not get a chance at the *schoolmaster*. I did next day
and he broke me up."

"It is simply pitiable to see the paltry hooks and
tackle that are generally thought
Inadequate tackle.   sufficient for these trout. There
seems to be a mistaken idea
that with the dry-fly you must have finest of gut and
tackle combined with a powerful split cane rod and
heavy line well suited for tournament casting, but very
rough on hooks and gut and the trout's mouth ; also
bad to handle a fish on."

"When you have cast to a fish without result, you
do not want to lift all the line that is out directly from
the water. *Palm* the line gently in until the fly is
well clear of the fish. It is not like fishing a stream
where you know the position of your feeding fish and
where the current carries your fly down past the fish
and out of its sight. The drag of the fly, gut, and
line when being lifted off the water from a long cast
is very apt to scare fish. Not much time is wasted
and the few false casts required in getting the palmed
line out dry the fly. Do not strike a fish quickly ;
these large fish often take slowly."

"When you find a rising fish, get quietly near it and
watch to see how it is feeding; you can generally see the
direction in which it is heading, and anchor so that you
are within fair casting distance of its beat and can cast
your fly so that it alights on the surface in front of the
fish on the course it is taking. Do not move the fly
until you are sure the fish has passed it. In casting to
a fish be careful not to rock the boat at each cast
by moving your whole body instead of only the arm.

The wave from a boat thus rocked reaches further than the fly can be cast. A brightly varnished rod when fished into the sun casts a glint like a helio-graph that can be seen over a mile across a lake. I think fish shy at this, but not as much as at the shadow cast by rod, fisherman, and boat, when they are between the fish and the setting sun. It is generally possible to avoid these troubles by fishing across the sun. I should not have thought it neces-sary to mention these errors, but I have seen them so constantly committed that it may be as well to draw attention to them. Overhead casts I only use when obliged to ; and I sit down in the boat to cast, as the more out of sight one can get the better."

" In the sheltered spots close in shore and when one is fishing from the shore the midges are sometimes very troublesome. The most effectual and pleasant *dope* to use is Betula Alba jelly, made up in tubes by Osborne, Bauer, and Cheeseman."

"A large gig or golfer's umbrella is a very useful thing, and takes up little room in a boat. I do not recommend its use out in the open lake in a breeze, but when on shore it keeps you and your lunch dry. You can sort flies, rig up tackle under it without everything getting wet. For wet weather in a boat I find a macintosh skirt and short coat best. You can keep thoroughly dry in this rig with the addition of a broad-brimmed hat. Damp double-faced Selvyts are useful in a boat for keeping fish or drinkables cool."

" The *dapper* and the dry-fly fisherman should not

interfere with each other's sport on a lake, as the former is said to delight in the strong breeze and the big rolling wave, and the latter only wants some quiet sheltered spot where flies collect and fish feed. If you anchor to fish close on a good dapping drift you and your fish will constantly be disturbed. The dapping-boat has often to pull back up wind to the head of a drift, and very naturally the boatman takes an inshore course to save labour, and you have no cause to blame him ; but if you are in some calm and sheltered spot away from any reasonable drift it alters the case, and the fishermen in the other boat should instruct their boatman not to pull close in to you and disturb any fish that you are watching or fishing. On lakes where there are clubs or associations strong enough to have rules and regulations carried out it would help to have a few simple ones drawn up, the fewer and simpler the better. On calm days especially (when dapping is useless), the draggers, i.e. boats dragging after them many baits (I have seen five rods out from one boat) disturb the fish feeding in shore a good deal, as they pull close along all reed beds on chance of a pike ; in most cases where you or your fish are disturbed it arises from ignorance or curiosity, seldom from *cussedness*."

"Some may consider fishing alone in a boat dull work. My own experience is that there is plenty to interest the dry-fly fisherman whilst waiting for a rise."

"The lough is an open book waiting for us to read

in it, the wind and sun often turning the pages, and as we read and begin to comprehend some of the things we see there the more engrossed we become in its contents and the more we realize how great is our ignorance and how much there is still to learn from the study of Nature's pages. With two in a boat there is sure to be a certain amount of talking, which, if it does not frighten the fish, certainly scares off many other interesting things. The younger you begin to read the book the better, and as you gradually begin to understand the more interesting will your fishing become. Bateman's 'Freshwater Aquaria' and Miall's 'Natural History of Aquatic Insects' have in many cases helped me."

" John Henderson."

CHAPTER IX

STRIKING AND HANDLING A HOOKED FISH

WE have now arrived at the point when all the conditions previously laid down have been satisfactorily accomplished, and the trout or grayling has been so thoroughly deceived by the imitation fly and the lifelike nature of its course down the stream that it has come up to it open-mouthed, and the disturbance on the surface leads us to believe that it has just sucked in the conglomeration of feathers and hook constituting the artificial fly. What now remains to be done is to drive the hook over the barb in the fish's mouth so that we can play it, exhaust it, and bring it safely to land in the net.

Striking. There is no occasion here to debate the vexed question of whether to strike or not to strike. Since the days when " Dry-Fly Fishing in Theory and Practice" was written, it has been conceded by all the best-known authorities that whether the action of forcing the hook-point into the mouth of the fish is called striking or designated by some other name it is, in effect, tightening on the fish and fixing the hook securely into one of its lips, the sides of its jaws, or its tongue.

The strike must be made with sufficient force and no more. If insufficient the hook will not penetrate far enough to hold the fish in its subsequent struggles, and if the force is excessive the gut will break at its weakest point, and leave the fly and possibly one or more strands of gut in the trout's jaws. The angler should acquire the habit of striking from the reel, i.e. without holding the line in the hand. Many old fishermen prefer holding the line when striking, but it is at best a risky proceeding, and too likely to result in a breakage of the gut.

Striking slowly or quickly. When a spectator sees a dry-fly man strike a fish and either just prick it or experience no resistance at all he is prone to say, "You struck too late." Now all the pastmasters agree that small fish rise quickly and eject the artificial fly quickly when they discover the fraud, while the monster comes up deliberately and sucks in the fly slowly. As a rule, if a large fish rises and takes the fly one can hardly be too slow in striking, and the angler in his haste is only too likely to pull his fly away and strike before the fish has got hold of the hook. Very often, too, the cause of the fisherman failing to hook his fish is that it has not actually taken the fly into its mouth at all and has come short.

Most of us have had the experience of hooking fish which have given sport out of all proportion to their actual size. When such a fish breaks, goes to

weed, shakes out the hold of the hook, or escapes in
some one of the many pos-
Hooked foul. sible ways, the beginner will
often persuade himself that he
has lost *the* fish of the season. The old hand will
generally turn to his companion or gillie, and dismiss
the episode laconically with the casual remark,
"Hooked foul, I suppose." When the fish is landed
no doubt can exist on the subject, because the weight
on the spring-balance and the fact of having to extract
the hook from some part of its external anatomy constitute conclusive evidence.

In some cases the foul-hooked trout is beyond
doubt a victim to a turn of real bad luck, having had
no intention of taking the artificial fly, in fact never
having risen to it. Many years ago such a case
occurred to me on the Anton. A fish was rising in
the upper part of a run of water from an open hatch,
and quite at the lower end of this run, another fish
was feeding with its head buried in the weeds and its
tail well above the surface of the stream. The rising
trout came short, and as I struck, the other fish below
went off with a rush making the reel sing merrily.
On my landing the trout, one of about $1\frac{1}{2}$ lb., the
hook was well home in the adipose fin.

I take it, however, that this was quite an exceptional
case, and that as a general rule a foul-hooked fish
is one which has risen to the fly and missed it, either
accidentally or intentionally. I once landed a Wandle
trout which had rolled the cast round its gills, the

gut being caught up in the bend of the hook, which was not fastened to the fish in any way. I take it that this fish was lightly hooked and in the first run the hook came away, caught the gut of the cast, thus running it up into a noose, and the trout in its struggles twisted itself up until it was literally suffocated in the tight turns of the gut collar. Trout have, in my own experience, been hooked outside between the nostrils, two in the anal fin, one with spent gnat in the right eye, the barb having penetrated the pupil, and one in the gills. This last does seem to me almost inexplicable, because the hook was fixed in the gills from the outside, and the only possible solution that occurs to me is that it came short, missed the fly, rolled over the gut, and the effect of striking was to drive the hook into the gills which were open at the moment for respiratory purposes. One large grayling which I killed was hooked in the dorsal fin, and cases of killing fish with the hook just outside and close to the mouth have not been uncommon.

As soon as the angler feels that he has fastened he should, without a moment's hesitation, put considerable strain on the fish and, if he can, turn its head downstream.

Procedure when the fish is hooked.

If he succeeds in doing this and at once starts walking or running down, towing the trout after him, it is astonishing how poor a chance the fish has. I know that this sounds a risky proceeding, but the moment after a fish is hooked it seems to take time to consider,

and if advantage is taken of this momentary pause
the odds are in favour of the fisherman. Big fish
when first hooked seem to be in this state of doubt
longer than small ones; possibly the larger the fish
the slower is the cerebration. The further down the
stream the fish is towed the less likely is it to go to
weed, and when swimming downstream head first with
its mouth open is unable to use its respiratory organs,
and is therefore quickly drowned.

Chalk-stream trout when hooked have a great
propensity to bury themselves
Fish going to weed. in the nearest weed-bed. It
is a good policy to try at
once, if possible, to prevent this, but if the fish succeeds in getting into the dense growth of weeds there
is no reason to despair. If it is well hooked you
ought to land it, and if not you are almost sure to lose
it under any circumstances. In 1889 I preached the
doctrine of slacking line to a weeded trout and
working it out by hand, and in each edition of " Dry-
Fly Fishing in Theory and Practice " published since
then I have renewed and amplified this device. I am
convinced that it has saved me the loss of an incalculable number of good trout, and I am gratified to hear
that a few of the dry-fly men adopt the plan nowadays.

The following advice is given on the subject in
the fourth and last (1902)
Handling a hooked
trout in the weeds.   edition of "Dry-Fly Fishing
in Theory and Practice."

" Thus when a hooked fish is well weeded the rod-point should be dropped and everything left slack ; to keep pulling is only to impel the trout to bury itself more deeply in the weeds, or even to wriggle in and out between the stems so as to escape the strain. Let out plenty of line well below the fish, then laying down, or spearing the rod, or holding it in one hand, if preferred, take the line between the thumb and forefinger of the other hand and apply a gentle strain accompanied by a backward and forward or swaying motion. After a time the presence of the fish will be evidenced by movement. If this movement is upstream, all must be left slack again, or the fish will only weed more deeply. If downstream, the line should be dropped, the rod resumed and the fish be reeled down to the net. If it weeds a second time the same tactics should again be pursued, and it may be laid down as a rule that a weeded trout firmly hooked will inevitably in time succumb to this treatment, while a lightly hooked one will, with this or any other procedure, probably escape."

When the fisherman has handed the trout out of the weeds, if he is in a hurry,

Hand-playing. or fears further entanglement, he can play the fish by hand. This means that with the line lightly held between the thumb and forefinger he can gather in the line quietly hand over hand, using very little force. The moment he experiences strong resistance, or if the fish makes a run, he slacks at once, and then commences once more to gather in the line by hand.

To my mind there is an absence of sport in this hand-playing, because the fish never seems to realize that it is in danger, and more often than not can be towed up or down to the net and lifted out without a kick. After playing a fish, and especially if the trout has gone to weed, it is well to examine and test the strength of the gut in any places where it has the appearance of being frayed.

It is probably the jarring of the reel or its click on the ratchet-wheel that terrifies a fish while it is being played. A curious outcome of this is that, in awkward places or in very heavy water where it is impossible to reel a hooked fish up, it is often quite easy to walk upstream and tow the fish after you. This is a principle which may be advantageously applied to many kinds of fish and under ever-varying conditions. I have tried it successfully with salmon and sea-trout as well as the ordinary *Salmo fario*, and I have almost invariably found it successful. In one instance, on the Spean, I worked a 14-lb. salmon up and away from a rough weir, where if the fish had once got into the pool below I could not have followed it, and it would have been inevitably lost.

Walking a hooked fish up or down-stream.

In any awkward position, such as above a bridge or hatch where trout generally make a bolt downstream, the policy of slacking the moment they are hooked is strongly advised. A hooked fish

Slacking in awkward places.

on a slack line will never travel far, but settles down to the bed of the river and lies there, so giving the angler plenty of time to get below, and consequently in the best position to prevent it from running down to or through the bridge below.

I would suggest that a hooked fish is very like a pig being driven to market. The farmer ties a cord to one of the pig's hind legs, and the harder he pulls the faster the pig runs in the opposite direction. So with the hooked trout, the more you try to pull it downstream the more anxious it is to run up. Do not let yourself be persuaded by any antiquated notions on this subject. Your old keeper will try to impress upon you the great fallacy that if you do not keep a strain on the fish's mouth it will get away. The hook which falls out when the line is slack is never home, and is in any case unlikely to hold while you play the fish.

The rod should be kept in an upright position while playing a fish under normal conditions, but when it is desired to exert any extra strain the rod-point should be lowered to an angle approximately of 30° to the horizontal. It is surprising how little strain the most powerful fly-rod can bring to bear. Many years ago, when I was talking over this with the late Thomas Andrews, the pisciculturist, he only half believed me. He put up his biggest salmon-rod, and was electrified to find that he could not lift a 2-lb. weight off the ground on his lawn with the rod in an upright position. Mr. Sheringham tells me that he has seen a 2-lb. weight lifted from the floor to a table with a 10-ft. split-cane rod, and candidly I am surprised to hear this.

When your fish is played out you should, if possible, keep below it, and **Landing the fish.** hold the landing-net in the water below. The landing-net must always be held in the lower hand, so that with a short line you can lead the fish into it. The correct position of the angler landing his fish is shown in the Frontispiece. When the fish is in the net draw it back and, as far as practicable, do not lift it; this for two reasons : (1) that the trout is very likely to jump out of the net if you do ; and (2) that raising the net with the trout in it places a dangerous and unnecessary strain on the handle. As you draw the net and fish back in one hand it is a good plan to take hold of the ring of the net as soon as you can reach it with the other hand, and thus steady the net and fish until it is safely on the land.

When the fish is landed, if it is not large enough to kill, hold it firmly without un-**Returning unsizable** due pressure, extract the hook **fish.** with care and return it to the river at once. Slide it in gently, and do not hurl it on the water and thus stun it. If it is inclined to be sick and turns on its side or back, nurse it with its head upstream in a place where the current is only moderately strong until it has re-covered its wind and can swim away. If you are fishing a friend's water, or are a member of a club, do not steer close to the regulation limit. A good plan is to have a number of marks cut on the handle of the landing-net, showing such lengths as 10, 11, 12, and 13 inches, which are the most usual size limits. A fish just up to the limit should invariably have the benefit of the doubt and be restored to its native element. Above all, do not listen to talk about fish being rendered preternaturally shy by being returned to the water. This is the stock argument of the pot-hunter, and I am more than surprised to find experts who should know better giving this theory the benefit of their support.

If your fish is sizable, give it a smart tap on the head just at the summit of the **Killing the sizable fish.** spinal column to put it out of pain. It is a true saying of non-sporting men that all sport is cruel, and the neglect of this humane action is an aggravation of the cruelty. Weigh your fish accurately on the spring-balance, register its weight in your diary, and here again do not be tempted to record it at an ounce or so above its real weight; rather call it a trifle under than the smallest fraction over the weight as registered on the spring-balance.

PART II

THE FISHERMAN'S ENTOMOLOGY

CHAPTER I

THE STUDY OF ENTOMOLOGY

ONE of the charges most persistently brought against modern dry-fly experts is that of overloading the subject with a quantity of scientific detail which is quite unnecessary for the fisherman at the river-bank. They are charged with running the risk of burying the sporting aspect of the question under a mass of crack-jaw Greek and Latin scientific names. My object here is to try to remove as many of these charges as can by any stretch of imagination be described as well-deserved. I therefore propose to avoid using as far as possible the scientific names of the insects referred to, but it is absolutely essential to set forth in this book the name appended by modern entomologists to each fly at least once besides the name which is given to it in the vernacular.

It is the more necessary because unfortunately different writers are prone to designate the same insect by different and distinct names. Too many of these write at great length, to try to prove that the name by which one common British insect is generally known should be applied to quite another genus or species. As an example of this the welshman's button can be fairly cited. This name

I have humbly ventured to suggest has nothing in common with the nation (Welsh), nor with that particular form of fastening (button) which is in modern times applied to a particular method of closing the garments we wear. Eminent and persistent angling writers have appealed to the authority of comparatively unknown fishermen, natives of or residing in Wales, to support the contention that it is in fact a beetle, and not *Sericostoma personatum*, one of the *Trichoptera* or caddis-flies, which has from times almost immemorial been designated a welshman's button by the Hampshire school of fly-fishers.

The reader must bear up bravely under the infliction of a small dose of **Description of** entomology. Insects or Hexa-**insects.** poda (six-footed) are divided into a number of orders and these orders again are subdivided into a number of families. The insects to which the dry-fly fisherman's attentions are devoted are comprised in six families : *Ephemeridæ*, or mayflies, duns and spinners ; *Trichoptera*, or caddis-flies ; *Perlidæ*, or stoneflies ; *Sialidæ*, the sole British example of which is the alder ; *Diptera*, which include the smuts or curses and the so-called black gnat ; and *Hymenoptera*, which are represented by the ants.

The chief characteristics of all insects are as follows : The body is divided into three regions— the head, thorax and abdomen. The thorax is divided into three segments called respectively the prothorax, mesothorax, and metathorax. The abdomen is composed usually of ten rings or segments, and has at the tail end various appendages such as the setæ or tails of the *Ephemeridæ* and the male genitalia in most insects.

Respiration takes place by means of tracheæ, a system of tubes distributed throughout the body, opening externally by orifices in the sides of the abdomen. There are invariably six legs attached in pairs to the under or ventral side of each segment of the thorax. A pair of antennæ are placed on the head. Some have four wings, some two, and some none; the wings are always attached to the upper or dorsal side of the thorax by strong muscles and ligaments. The wings, if there are two pairs, are attached, the fore wings to the mesothorax and the hind wings to the metathorax. If there should be only one pair of wings it is generally attached to the mesothorax.

The skin is the hardest and most solid portion of an insect's anatomy, and is composed of a substance called *chitin*, which is tough, flexible and horny. Some insects subsist on solid food and are called *mandibulata* (jawed), others live on fluids and are called *haustellata* (suckered).

Most insects can see, and have two kinds of eyes: *Ocelli* (single eyelets), three or a pair; and a pair of *oculi* (eyes), formed of eyelets touching one another in faceted or *compound* eyes but less

crowded in *clustered* eyes. *Mandibles* are the upper
or strong pair of jaws, and *maxillæ* the lower or
weaker, and the jaws of insects generally open and
close laterally. The upper lip is called the *labrum*
and the lower lip the *labium*. The feelers attached
to the jaws are called *palpi*. The maxillæ carry
feelers called the *maxillary palpi*, and the labium
other feelers known as the *labial palpi*.

The changes in outward form through which an
insect passes after its birth,
Incomplete prior to becoming an adult, are
metamorphosis. called *metamorphoses*. *Nymph*
is a term applicable to the
young of insects with incomplete metamorphosis.
Insects of which the immature forms nearly resemble
the adults, only differing from them in minor detail
and requiring such further development as the
unfolding of the wings or the loss of temporary
organs peculiar to early stages of life, are said to
undergo incomplete metamorphosis.

Complete metamorphosis is undergone by insects
when their form at birth bears
Complete meta- no appreciable likeness to
morphosis. their adult form. The young,
whether with complete or in-
complete metamorphosis, are generally voracious, and
grow rapidly, changing their skins from time to time
as their growth necessitates. In the former case a
rest stage then intervenes, during which there is
a total cessation of feeding. When the frame of the

perfect insect is fully developed the last change to the fly is effected. The first form of an insect having complete metamorphosis on emerging from the egg is called *larva*, the second *pupa*, and the third or complete insect *imago*. Those of my readers who, as boys, have kept and bred silkworms, will appreciate these terms by remembering that the silkworm is a larva, the chrysalis a pupa, and the moth an imago.

Subimago. The nymphs of the Ephemeridæ when full-grown rise to the surface, and winged flies emerge, leaving the shuck or outer skin from which they have disentangled themselves on the surface. They can fly, but are not the perfect insects, being covered by a thin, hairy integument, which is shed at the last stage. Before shedding this hairy integument the winged insect is called a dun or *subimago*, and after shedding it the perfect insect is styled a spinner or *imago*.

Collecting implements. The dry-fly man who wishes to identify the winged insects floating down or the immature forms in the water below the surface should provide himself with three nets. (1) An ordinary butterfly-net with short handle ; (2) a small net like a landing-net on a diminutive scale on a ring of, say, three inches in diameter ; and (3) a net for digging up larvæ, nymphs, etc., from the weeds or mud on the bed of the river. The butterfly-net is useful to collect insects in the air, sweep them from rushes, etc., or even held in the water to intercept any little insects or larvæ drifting down.

The best material for all these nets is cheese cloth, and for the miniature landing-net which is intended to take floating flies off the water the two top joints of an old pike-rod make the best handle. The dig-

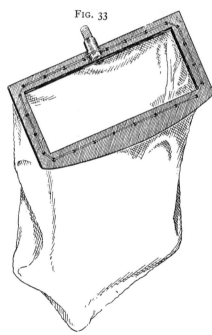

FIG. 33

ging-net should have a strong iron frame about 7 inches long and $3\frac{1}{2}$ wide of the form shown (Fig. 33). The net attached to this frame by string passed through the holes should be a long deep bag of cheese cloth, and a strong ash or bamboo staff four feet long should carry it.

For a rapid examination of the insects, and in many cases even for their identification, a pocket lens is all that is required. One of the modern aplanatic lenses made by Zeiss, Reichert, Baker, etc., with a linear magnification of ten diameters, and for examining mouth organs, male appendages, and such matters requiring a greater magnification, similar lenses × 20 or × 30 can be procured from all opticians.

If the student should wish to preserve any of the insects for future reference he

Preservation. should, when collecting, drop them into a tube containing what I call the collecting fluid, consisting of one part rectified spirits of wine, two parts 2 per cent formalin, and as many crystals of menthol as it will dissolve. This solution requires filtering before use. As soon as they are dead and have sunk in the collecting fluid they are transferred to the permanent preserving fluid, which is 2 per cent formalin. What is called 2 per cent formalin is made by adding 1 oz. of formalin to 19 oz. of water and filtering. It is an inaccuracy to call this a 2 per cent formalin solution, as it is in fact a 2 per cent solution of formic aldehyde. Formalin is the trade name given to a 40 per cent aqueous solution of formic aldehyde.

Entomologists generally collect and kill insects in an ordinary cyanide bottle, and pin or gum them on to cards after relaxing and arranging their parts. These are stored in boxes and cabinets, and kept for study and examination. Such insects as Trichoptera can be treated in this way, but the delicate Ephemeridæ become disintegrated in a very short time.

A sub-committee was formed some years ago of members of the Fly-Fishers'

Collection at the Fly-Fishers' Club. Club to collect and preserve the insects which are of special interest to all fly-fishermen. Most of the early specimens were collected and arranged by me, but when the time had arrived when I could not devote the necessary time to this work the Committee were very fortunate in finding a man at once capable and willing to continue the work of making this collection. My friend Martin E. Mosely, to whom these lines refer, has not only persevered himself in collecting, identifying and arranging the fly-fisherman's insects, but he has succeeded in enlisting the sympathy of anglers all over the country. In many cases not only has he enlisted the sympathy of fishermen, but he has persuaded them literally to take off their coats and collect a great number of specimens with such particulars as he has required in each case. If, as seems quite likely, this work continues on the same lines and under the same able supervision for a few years, I venture to predict that the collection in the cabinets at the Fly-Fishers' Club of the various insects in which we are interested will be the best in the world.

For the information of any fisherman desirous of collecting and preserving these insects for reference, the specimens in two of the three cabinets are mounted in the 2 per cent formalin solution referred to in what are called solid watch-glasses, i.e. slabs of plate-glass half an inch thick and about two and a quarter inches square, with a circular hollow cell about two inches in diameter worked in the centre of each. When the insect is in place, the solid watch-glass, brimful, is covered with a square of flat glass which is securely cemented to it.

I must apologize for having digressed from the immediate subject to refer to the question of permanent preservation of the insects and the grand collection which is progressing by leaps and bounds owing to the splendid efforts of brother anglers (both members and non-members of the Club). Nearly all the specimens in the cabinets have been set up and arranged by members of the Natural Fly Sub-committee of the Fly-Fishers' Club, and all credit is due to them for the success of the movement, and I know that the general body of members realize this and appreciate the quality of the work done.

Method of identification at the river-side. The fisherman is now equipped with the nets required for catching the insects and his lenses for careful examination and identification of them. He will place himself below a rising fish and proceed to collect some few of the flies floating down. In connection with this it should be remembered that the examination of one or two individual flies will not always warrant his arriving at the conclusion that he has determined the pattern of fly he should use. Of course, if the hatch is sparse he must perforce content himself with a comparatively small number, but if the flies are plentiful he should collect as many as he conveniently can.

The next step is for him to determine the family or families to which these flies belong. To assist him in this a set of drawings have been prepared, and

reproductions of them are reproduced here.   Fig. 34
is a march brown, one of the
Rough identification of Ephemeridæ, and is in the
family.   outline the type of all the
winged mayflies, duns and
spinners, varying in size and colouration   In the dun
or subimago stage they will all carry their wings in the
erect position shown on the block, but the spinners or

FIG. 34.   MARCH BROWN × 4

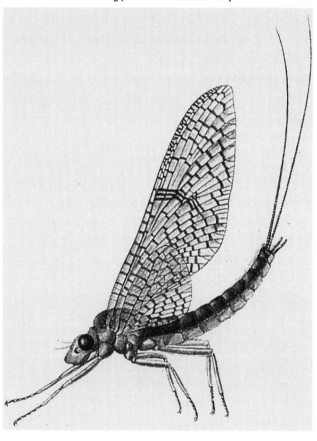

imagines spent, or after the work of procreation is complete, will have their wings flat on the water and approximately at right angles to the line of the body.

A casual examination will show the general outline, the taper and curve of the **Mayflies, duns and** body, and the assistance of **spinners.** the × 10 lens will also reveal the presence of two or three thread-like tails which are called whisks by the angler and *setæ* by the entomologist. Some genera have two and others three tails, and it often happens that one or more of these have been broken off, even after the most careful handling. It is for this reason that I advise the use of the lens, as with it the angler will in most cases be able to distinguish one or two joints of the tails close to the end of the body.

FIG. 35. CAPERER × 2

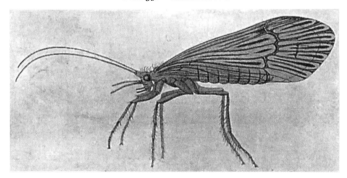

Fig. 35 is a caddis-fly called the caperer, showing the typical appearance of these **Caddis-flies.** insects in profile. The student will note the long multi-articulate antennæ and the four wings of nearly equal length, the hinder ones lying under the fore wings. The lens will further reveal maxillary palpi, i.e. feelers attached to the maxillæ, and labial palpi attached to the labium. In all the females he will find that the maxillary palpi are five-jointed, and in the males the number of joints varies from three to five, but the labial palpi are three-jointed in both sexes. The mandibles or upper jaws are atrophied, so that the mature insect is incapable of feeding. On the fourth joint of the legs, the tibia or shank, there are movable spurs in addition to hairs and strong spines, and the disposition and number of these spurs are important factors in classification. The wings are more or less covered by short hairs, and the remaining parts of the caddis-flies are also clothed more or less densely with hairs and spines.

FIG. 36. WILLOW-FLY × 3

The wings of butterflies and moths are covered with scales, and this is the feature by which the caddis-flies with hairs on their wings are distinguished. The position of the wings lying nearly flat will tell the fisherman at a glance that the fly is not one of the Ephemeridæ.

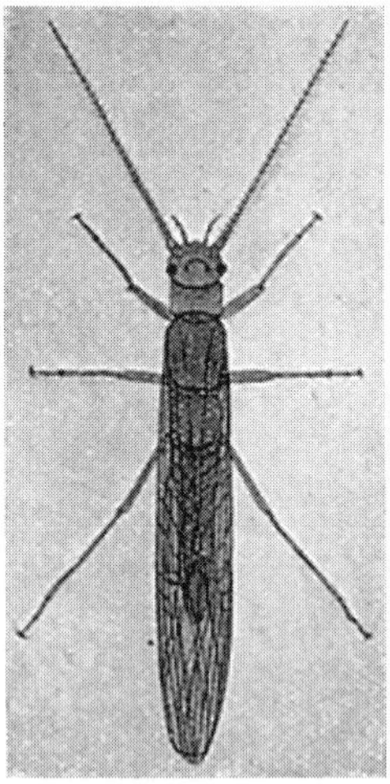

The accompanying, Fig. 36, shows the willow-fly, one of the

Stoneflies.

stoneflies or Perlidæ, in its normal position when at

rest. When flying the four wings are set out from the body, and very materially alter the appearance of the insect, and make it look far larger. The length and narrowness of the wings, their peculiar appearance when folded together, and their general characteristic shape will prevent the angler from confusing the stone-flies with the caddis-flies. In some species the wings of the males are so abnormally short—even reduced to mere scales—that the insects are incapable of flight. Some genera of Perlidæ have two ciliated, multi-articulate caudal setæ or tails.

FIG. 37. ALDER (FEMALE) × 3

Fig. 37 shows an alder in profile as it appears when crawling along on a post or rush. Although, as will be shown later on, it is not a fly which is often found on the water, still it is so plentiful on the banks of most of the rivers and streams in this country that the angler will see many specimens. Kingsley, in his " Chalk-Stream Studies," has brought it so prominently before his angling readers, and sur-rounded it with such an atmosphere of admiration, that it must be included in the list. It can be easily

Alder.

Q

distinguished from either of the orders previously referred to by its peculiar hunchback appearance, the shape and coarse nervures of its wings, the absence of hairs on the wings, and of spurs on the legs.

Fig. 38 represents the reed smut, one of the smuts or curses of which the larvæ **Smuts or curses.** and pupæ are generally found attached to reeds or ribbon weed. Like all the insects called by the angler smuts or curses, it is

FIG. 38. REED SMUT × 9

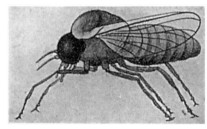

very much smaller than any of the orders previously referred to in this chapter, and cannot by any possibility be confused with any of them. It is one of the very numerous examples of genera and species belonging to the order of Diptera.

The last of our list of flies on which the fish are likely to be feeding is the **Winged ants.** winged ant. The form of the ant with its slender waist and enlarged lobe at the hinder part of the abdomen is so well known that the angler can have no difficulty in distinguishing it when it is present.

The foregoing hints are probably sufficient to enable the dry-fly man to determine the order under which the individuals he has collected should be classified. For further identification the student must refer to the following chapters of this part which treat of the generic and specific differences which will enable him to determine these points. I also propose to treat briefly of the larval, nymphal, and pupal stages of the various insects, so that the fisherman who wants to dive more deeply into the subject can obtain some notion of the nature of the immature insects he will find when collecting below the surface with the digging-net.

CHAPTER II

MAYFLIES, DUNS AND SPINNERS

THE insects designated by the fly-fisherman by the names comprised in the title of this chapter are all members of the family of Ephemeridæ. It will be noted that in " Modern Development of the Dry-Fly " no less than twenty-five of the thirty-three patterns in the series are classified as genera and species of this family. Hence no apology is needed for devoting a considerable space to the description of these insects, and it is obvious that they constitute the most important group for the dry-fly man.

Rev. A. E. Eaton, the leading modern authority on this family, says of the habits of the flies that "the popular supposition that they are strictly ephemeral is fallacious in most instances. It is true that the adult insect cannot eat owing to atrophy of its mouth organs and to the condition of its alimentary canal ; but provided that the air be not too dry the imagines of many genera can live without food several days." He goes on to explain that oviposition is usually performed in fresh water, and that while some species discharge the contents of their ovaries *en masse*, the majority extrude

Rev. A. E. Eaton on habits of the flies.

228

their eggs gradually part at a time in one of the following ways. The female either alights on the water to wash off the eggs which have issued from the oviducts during her flight, or else she creeps down into the water, enclosed within a film of air with wings collapsed so as to overlie the abdomen and, with her setæ close together, to lay the eggs in rounded patches on the underside of stones in a single layer evenly spread. She then floats up to the surface, where her wings are suddenly unfolded and erected and either flies away, or if her setæ have become wet she is detained by them, and is drowned on the surface of the water. He adds that "in some instances, however, the female dies under water beside her eggs."

The eggs hatch in due course, and the nymph, **Nymph.** which emerges from the eggs, is in shape very like the adult insect, but it has invariably three ciliated caudal setæ or tails, and the mouth organs are fully developed, as at this stage it requires a considerable quantity of food. The nymphs live, some on minute aquatic vegetation and some on mud, but judging from their powerful mandibles some species are probably carnivorous.

They all have tracheal branchiæ of various shapes, which are arranged in pairs on seven or fewer of the foremost segments of the abdomen ; and their function is considered to be the change of carbonic acid, introduced into the air contained within the tracheal system from the fluid which serves as blood, for oxygen held in solution in the surrounding water.

As they grow they shed their skins, and adolescence is evidenced by the advancement towards maturity of the reproductive organs internally and externally by the outgrowth of rudimentary wings from the hind borders of the proper segments.

In 1843 F. J. Pictet, Professeur de Zoologie et d'Anatomie Comparée à l'Aca-

Pictet's " Monograph." démie de Genève, published his great " Monograph " on the Ephemeridæ. He classified the nymphs in four divisions : Digging, flat, swimming and crawling—or in his own language—*Larves fouisseuses, Larves plattes, Larves nageuses* and *Larves rampantes.* In his time entomologists gave the name *larva* to the wingless, and the name *nympha* to the wing-budding grades of the immature insect. Modern entomologists desig-nate all the subaqueous stages in the development of the young Ephemeridæ after emergence from the eggs as *nymphæ.*

Very possibly, too, Pictet's classification of the nymphs may not be quite orthodox according to the ideas of the modern exponents of the science, but for the fisherman they are not only descriptive of their habits, but eminently useful for his rough-and-ready process of identification.

The digging nymphs, among which the immature mayflies are included, com-

Digging nymphs. mence digging out burrows or tunnels to form their habita-tions as soon as they are hatched. Plate XV shows

Mayfly Nymph

× 3

PLATE XV

Swan Electric Engraving Co. Ltd.

the general appearance of a mayfly nymph, and the student will notice that it is furnished with powerful mandibles and forelegs somewhat similar to those of the mole cricket. These are used for digging and making the tubular galleries in the clay, mud, or sandy grit on the bed of the river. The life of a mayfly from the egg to the perfect insect is computed at from two to three years.

The nymphs in this division have all parts of their bodies wide and flat. They **Flat nymphs.** are not shaped so as to be able to dig, and naturally do not hide in burrows like the immature mayflies. They are not rapid in their movements, and the small depth of their bodies is eminently fitted to their scheme of life as they pass the whole of the nymphal stage clinging to the underside of large stones. Their life from egg to imago is generally believed to extend to one year, but some species are believed to grow more rapidly and produce two broods in the

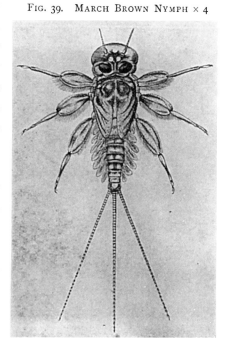

FIG. 39. MARCH BROWN NYMPH × 4

year. The type of the Ephemeridæ of this division is the march brown, and Fig. 39 gives a very good notion of the appearance of one of these flat nymphs.

The organization of the swimming nymphs differs greatly from the preceding **Swimming nymphs.** types. They are long, cylindrical in form, and have feeble legs. Perhaps the most remarkable and unmistakable feature about them is the close fringe of strong hairs placed horizontally on both sides of each of the three caudal setæ. They prefer water of only moderate pace, and are ever plentiful in the weeds of a chalk-stream which is free from pollution. Their duration of life is generally believed by modern entomologists in some species to extend to one year, and in others they are credited with producing two broods in the year. Thus in these species the nymphs hatched in the spring arrive at maturity and oviposit in the autumn, and the eggs of these imagines again hatch out in the following spring. Fig. 40 shows a

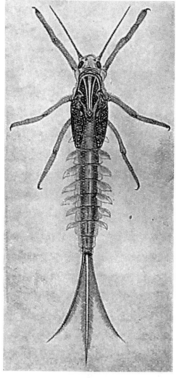

FIG. 40. BAËTIS NYMPH × 6

nymph of *Baëtis*, one of the genera with swimming nymphs.

According to Pictet the nymphs belonging to this division have been the worst **Crawling nymphs.** treated by nature. Not having powerful mandibles and muscular forelegs like the digging nymphs, having neither the strength of the flat nymphs, nor the fin-like tail of the swimming nymphs, they are slow in their movements, unable to dig, and thus escape from their numerous enemies, and could not well secure their prey if they did not make up by cunning for what is wanting in strength and agility. They live in parts of the stream where the flow is not very rapid, and are prone to shelter in gravelly places on the bed of the river. They envelop themselves with a thin coating of mud or other *detritus*, and are often almost invisible under such conditions. At the same time the small larvæ and other creatures on which they feed cannot distinguish these nymphs lying in ambush, and fall an easy prey to them. Fig. 41 shows a nymph of the blue-winged olive, which is the type of this division.

FIG. 41. BLUE-WINGED OLIVE NYMPH × 6

When the nymph is ready to undergo the change to a winged insect examin-**Subimago.** ation with a lens will show its wings folded up within the two dark excrescences or wing-covers on the back of the thorax. It will also be seen that inside the nymphal skin there is visible the form of the winged insect, its head, thorax, body, legs, and tail perceptibly of more slender proportions than in the nymph. The swimming nymph (Fig. 40) shows this very well.

The digging and swimming nymphs swim up through the water, arriving at the surface and there splitting open the outer skin at the back of the thorax. The thorax and head are first pushed up and out, then the legs struggle out, the body and setæ being partly worked out almost at the same time. Next the wings are unfolded and withdrawn from their covers one at a time, and, lastly, the body and setæ are drawn forth. The subimago then rests on the cast nymphal skin until its wings are dry, when it flies ashore to shelter on the grass, rushes or boughs. The crawling nymphs effect the change to the subimago in a similar manner, but the flat nymphs require a dry spot, to which they attach themselves for the process of metamorphosis to the subimago. Their nymphal shucks are often found adhering to the stones on the river-bank.

Subimago is the term applied by modern ento-mologists to this stage in the life of the Ephemeridæ, and the students of old books on the subject must not be surprised to find them called the *Pseudimago*—a name which has been condemned as etymologically incorrect, being compounded of two words, one Greek and the other Latin. Anglers call the sub-imago of the smaller Ephemeridæ a dun. The green drake is the subimago of the genus *Ephemera*, and the march brown the subimago of certain species of the genus *Ecdyurus*.

The subimago is not a perfect insect, its entire structure being enveloped in **Imago.** a thin skin and covered with a multitude of tiny hairs or ciliæ. Its movements are slow and its powers of flight very limited. It takes shelter until it is ready for the next change to the imago or perfect insect. Once more it distends and splits its skin, and the imago emerges, leaving behind a filmy envelope retaining the form of the subimago, except that the cast skins of the wings collapse. The imago is a much more elegant and delicate creature than the subimago; its wings are transparent and glossy, its body slender and tapering; it is altogether better able to fly than the comparatively heavy and ciliated insect in the subimago stage. The legs of the imago are longer than those of the subimago, as, too, are the setæ, and the forelegs and setæ of the male are much longer than those of the female.

The lapse of time between the assumption of the sub-imago or first winged form and the final metamorphosis to the imago is largely dependent on temperature; it may be a few hours (in some genera a few minutes) and it may take some days, and these questions are difficult if not impossible of solution from experiments with insects in captivity, because when we place the Ephemeridæ among artificial surroundings they do not implicitly follow the course pursued in a state of nature.

When the fly has once assumed the imago dress the behaviour of the two sexes **Male imago.** is in many ways diverse. The males congregate in great numbers, and are seen disporting themselves in the air, sometimes at a great altitude, and at other times only just above the bushes or trees at the river-bank. They seem to be continuously engaged in an aimless dance, rising swiftly and descending slowly. As soon as a female imago leaves the shelter of the rushes or boughs, the males in great numbers pursue her, two or more seizing her from below and one coupling in flight. The male then drops its wings, and the female not being generally able to support the weight of both with her wings, they descend, and by or before the time when they reach the ground, the connection is generally terminated. The male flies away to resume with his companions the *danse d'amour*, and, being addicted to polygamy, seeks a second mate.

After resting awhile, the female deposits her eggs in one of the ways previously **Female imago.** described in this chapter. The eggs sink to the bed of the river, hatch there in process of time, the nymph emerges, and the life history goes on as before. Some years since I counted under the microscope the number of eggs in six specimens of the mayfly, added these numbers together and dividing by six found that the average number laid by each female is approximately 6500.

After oviposition the female falls on the water with her wings flat and outstretched at right angles to the line of her abdomen. At this stage she is almost lifeless, floats down without a struggle, and falls an easy prey to the hungry trout. Anglers generally call the imago of the smaller Ephemeridæ—whether male or female—a spinner, and in the case of the mayfly the name applied by many anglers is *spent gnat*. The modern dry-fly man is, however, inclined to abandon this singularly inappropriate name and apply to the perfect mayfly its more correct appellation of *imago*.

The male imagines continue their dance long after their consorts have oviposited, and do not fall until probably the last brood of females of their own species during the season has also completed its share in the work of procreation. Some fall on the water, but many, and it is believed the vast majority, of the male imagines fall on the land wherever they may happen to be, or at the part to which they have been carried by the force of the wind. In all the Ephemeridæ the males are considerably smaller than the females, whether in the nymph, subimago, or imago stages.

The fisherman is now supposed to have caught a number of specimens of the **Identification of genus and species.** floating insect on which he believes the rising trout is feeding. He has decided that the insects belong to the family of Ephemeridæ, and he is now confronted by the difficulty of deciding which of the twenty-five patterns representing flies of this family in the new series—or of a far greater number, if he is a votary of the old standards—is the one to use as an imitation of the natural insect.

The mayflies are so much larger than any other of the British Ephemeridæ that **Mayflies.** even the fisherman who had never seen one before could scarcely fail to identify them. There are three British species of true mayflies—*Ephemera danica, Ephemera vulgata* and *Ephemera lineata*. These three species can be identified by the difference in the dorsal markings on the abdomen of the imago.

Eaton describes the markings of the male thus : "*E. vulgata*. The dorsal markings are a pair of curvilinear triangles, broadest at the base of the segments and ending abruptly at its thickened hinder margin, and a pair of fine curved longitudinal lines interposed between them, which are often effaced." Of *E. danica* imago male he says : " Abdomen with the foremost four or five dorsal segments ivory white, with a pale cinereous broad triangular blotch at their base on each side pointing backwards ; the hinder segments varied with pitch-brown or very deep brown-ochre, instead of with cinereous, their markings sometimes confluent (leaving in the middle an ivory-white triangle upon the hind margin of the segment

FIG. 42. DORSAL MARKINGS × 7

E. vulgata   E. lineata   E. danica

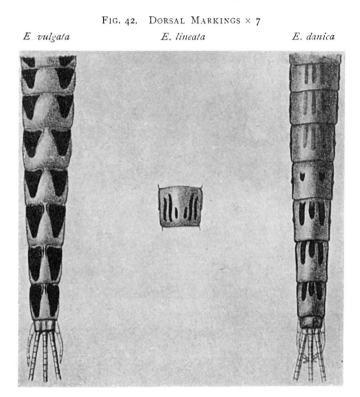

pointing forwards) sometimes differentiated into an abbreviated thin streak on each side of the dorsal vessel at the base of the segment, flanked by a longer and broader tapering streak which falls short of the hind margin of the segment and does not extend to the side. The larger of these streaks are represented sometimes by triangular spots in some of the more forward segments ; last segment altogether dark above. The spiracular region is edged with an irregular dark line above and an abbreviated line from the base below, in every segment."

Of *E. lineata* imago male he says : " The segments marked with longitudinal curved or slightly sinuous black streaks tapering at the ends, the anterior segments having each two long streaks on each side of the middle of the back and the posterior segments two short lines from the base between the two pairs of streaks."

Fig. 42 represents these markings on *E. vulgata*, *E. danica*, and *E. lineata*.[1] It is probable that the angler will be able to identify these species from the markings, and it may also assist him to know that the subimago of *E. danica* is of a greener tint in the wings and generally paler than the other two species. *E. vulgata* and *E. lineata* in the subimago stage are almost identical in colouring, slightly browner in the wings and generally darker and slightly larger than *E. danica*.

I have given here two plates of the winged mayflies : the first, the subimago male, in Plate XVI, and the imago female in Plate XVII. Both of these were drawn from specimens of *E. danica*, but with the exception of the colouration in the subimago and the markings before referred to, the species are so similar as to

[1] I am indebted to the Rev. A. E. Eaton for his kind permission to reproduce his drawing of the markings of *E. lineata*.

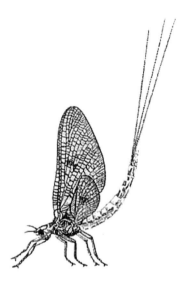

Mayfly - Subimago Male

× 2

PLATE XVI

Swan Electric Engraving C.Ld

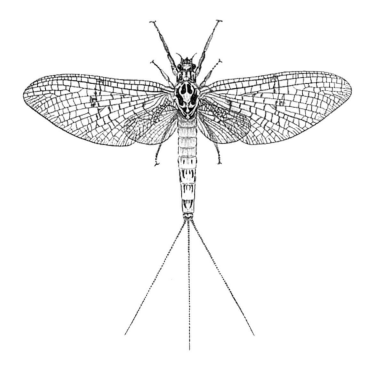

Mayfly Imago Female

X 2

PLATE XVII

Im. Stone Engraving Co.

be almost identical. The angler should at once realize from the colour of the wings whether the specimen he is examining is a green-winged one, *E. danica*, or a brown-winged one, *E. vulgata* or *E. lineata*. The four patterns of mayfly in the new series consist of Nos. 1 and 2 male and female green mayflies which represent *E. danica*, and Nos. 3 and 4 the male and female brown mayflies or imitations of *E. vulgata* or *E. lineata*.

The imagines of the three species are so nearly alike that I have only included in the patterns of the imago or spent gnat Nos. 5 and 6, the male and female respectively. As previously remarked in the chapter on "Choice of Pattern," Marryat's old standard pattern is an imitation of the female.

If the insect under examination is not a mayfly it will in the south-country chalk-**Duns and spinners.** streams probably be if comparatively large either the turkey brown or yellow may dun, and if small one of the duns or spinners designated by fly-fishermen by the names of *olive, pale watery, iron-blue,* or *blue-winged olive,* and the next task is to give the angler the necessary information to enable him to differentiate these insects. The olive, pale watery, and iron-blue duns and spinners have two tails or caudal setæ, while the blue-winged olive has three, and in most rivers this latter fly is not generally present before the middle of June, and does not hatch in great numbers before July. When I fished the

R

Kennet at Ramsbury the blue-winged olive was often found at the commencement of the trout season in April, and continued to show up to the end of October. Probably it was present even later in the year, but I had no opportunity of proving this by the positive evidence of observation, not being at the river-side during the late autumn and winter.

The olive and the dark olive dun are the names applied by all fly-fishermen to

Olive dun.

five species of the genus *Baëtis*. Three of these are comparatively rare, and may therefore be excluded from our list. The other two, *B. rhodani* and *B. vernus*, are found in most English streams, and are very plentiful in the south-country chalk-streams during the months of April, May, June, September, October and even later in the winter. Being very similar in appearance the species are not easily determined, and from the fisherman's point of view may be treated here as one.

They may be described generally as having smoky or mousy-grey wings. The legs are in some portions greenish grey, in others sepia-grey, and the setæ are described by Eaton as greenish grey with reddish or warm sepia joinings. The effect of this colouring is that the body, legs, and setæ give the appearance, when viewed with a hand magnifier, of being olive of a more or less bronze shade in some and green in others.

In the new list of patterns Nos. 7 and 8 are the

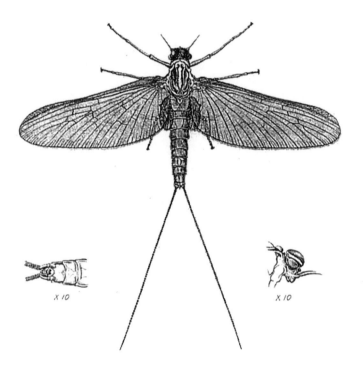

X 10   X 10

Olive Dun Male

X 5

PLATE XVIII

Swan Process Engraving Co Ltd

male and female olive duns, and 9 and 10 the two sexes of the dark olive dun. I am inclined to think that the two flies are varieties of the same species, but at the same time I shall not be astonished if entomologists at some future date give different specific names to these two varieties of the olive. It is not unusual to see one hatching out exclusively on one day and the other on a second day, and possibly on a third day the two mixed up indiscriminately.

The male olive dun is figured in Plate XVIII, and on the same page a drawing is

Male olive. given to a larger scale of the head in profile, and the ventral view of the tail end of the abdomen. All the plates of insects excepting the mayfly are shown with their wings flat, because entomologists usually figure them in this attitude as giving a better opportunity of displaying their parts for identification. The male olive, pale watery, iron-blue, and blue-winged olive (duns as well as spinners) are distinguished from the female by the presence of what appears to be a turbinate cap on the top of. the head. Of this Eaton says :—

"The *oculi*, always much larger in the male than in the other sex, are in him, in some genera, divided each into two parts transversely ; the upper portion has larger facets than the lower, and is sometimes differently coloured. The division between these segments of the oculus may amount to nothing more than a mere superficial furrow or impressed line traversing the faceted surface horizontally ; but when it is deeper the upper part of the oculus (always much the larger of the two), assumes a short subcylindrical or turbinate form, faceted only on its summit, and supports on its outer base the smaller division, which is oval and faceted all over."

Another distinctive mark of a male of any of the Ephemeridæ is the presence of a pair of forceps or claspers on the lower side of the body at the hinder end of it.   These turbinate eyes and abdominal forceps are not present in the females.   The forceps are generally referred to by modern entomologists because the variations in their form, etc., are largely used in determining the species when the insects are very similar.

The differences in the arrangement of the nervures of the hind wings are **Hind wings of olive.**   most valuable indications of species.   I will therefore, in the cases of the three insects—olive, pale watery, and iron - blue — give figures showing their hind wings magnified to such an extent as to be easily distinguishable.   Fig. 43 shows one of the hind wings of an olive × 30.

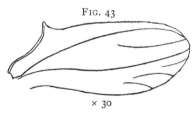

Fig. 43

× 30

The fisherman will not have any great difficulty in recognizing the spinners of the olive and other duns. The glossy transparent wings and the absence of the

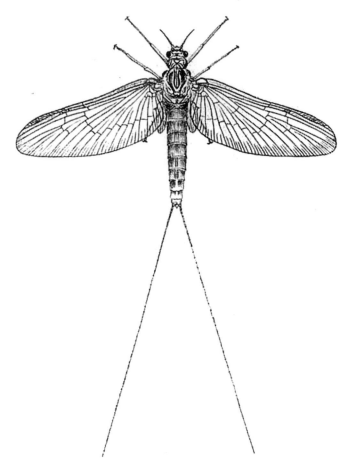

Olive Spinner Female

PLATE XIX

X 5

ciliæ or short hairs on the surface and at the margins
of the wings of the spinners
Male olive spinner. are by themselves sufficiently
remarkable to bring home to
the student the difference between the two stages
of subimago and imago. The male olive spinner
has a nearly black head and thorax and brown-red
turbinate eyes. The first six segments of the body
are pale green-grey and transparent, and the remaining four segments at the tail end of the body are
a rich brown. The legs and setæ are pale·grey-olive.
No. 11 in the new set of patterns is the imitation of
this insect.

The female spinner, apart from the difference of
colour of body, is distinguished
Female olive spinner. from the male by the absence
of the turbinate eyes and of
the abdominal forceps. The fisherman will notice
that I have given two patterns of this fly, No. 12 olive
spinner female and No. 13 olive (red) spinner female.
The former of these is an imitation of the spinner
when depositing its eggs, and has a golden bronze-
green body with some of the segments on the ventral
side at the tail end of primrose-yellow. No. 13 is an
imitation of a female olive spinner after depositing its
eggs, and being what fishermen often call *spent* or
burnt, and its body is a dark dead-leaf colour. I have
added the word (red) to the name of this fly to distinguish it from the olive-bodied spinner, and also because, to my mind, this insect is the prototype of the

old *red spinner* so well known to the fly-fisherman.
Plate XIX shows this insect.

The name pale watery dun is applied by fishermen
to four natural insects, two
Pale watery duns. species of the genus Baëtis—
B. binoculatus and *B. scambus;*
and two of the genus Centroptilum—*C. luteolum* and
C. pennulatum. They are so similar in appearance

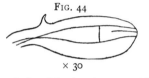
FIG. 44
× 30

that for all practical angling purposes they may be taken as identical. It is, however, quite easy
to differentiate them by the shape
of the hind wings. The hind wings of *B. binoculatus*
are as shown in Fig. 44, and the hind wings of
C. luteolum and *C. pennulatum* are given in Figs. 45
and 46 respectively. The angler will never forget the

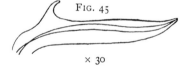
FIG. 45
× 30

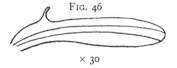
FIG. 46
× 30

difference in shape between the hind wings of *Centroptilum* and *Baëtis* if he will just consider that the derivation of the word *Centroptilum* is from the Greek κέντρον,
a spur, and πτίλον, a wing. He can distinguish the olive
dun from *Baëtis binoculatus* by the nervure of the hind
wing, and also by the fact that the pale watery is a much
smaller and generally paler coloured insect than the olive
dun. Plate XX shows a female pale watery dun, *B. binoculatus.* Nos. 14 and 15 in the new set of patterns are
the male and female pale watery dun respectively.

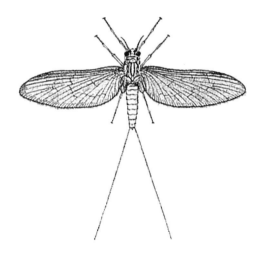

Pale Watery Dun Female
X 5

PLATE XX

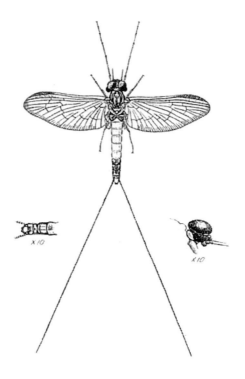

Pale Watery Spinner Male

PLATE XXI

X 5

Swan Electric Engraving Co. Ltd

The pale watery spinners can be identified by the hind wings, and Plate XXI **Pale watery spinners.** shows a male spinner with the head in profile on a larger scale to show the turbinate eyes and a ventral view of the hinder end of the body, on the same scale to show the abdominal forceps of the male. The turbinate eyes of the male pale watery spinner vary considerably in the different genera and species generally designated by this name. Eaton gives them in describing *B. binoculatus*, *B. scambus*, *C. luteolum* and *C. pennulatum*, respectively, as lemon or bright yellow, clove or warm sepia brown, bright light red, and light cadmium orange. The patterns of the male and female pale watery spinners are Nos. 16 and 17 respectively.

Under the fisherman's name of iron-blue two species of the genus Baëtis are in- **Iron-blue duns.** cluded—*B. pumilus* and *B. niger*; they are both fairly plentiful, and it is not easy even for experts to distinguish between them. Plate XXII shows the female, and Nos. 18 and 19 in the new set of patterns are imitations of the two sexes. Fig. 47 shows the hind wing, and the student should note that it differs from that of the other duns in the shape of the intermediate nervure, which is forked. The smoky

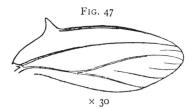

FIG. 47

× 30

blue colour of the wings is unmistakable, and will serve to distinguish the iron-blue from the olive (which, too, is much larger) and from the pale watery dun, which is approximately the same size.

The imagines of this species are both very striking —the female is a small spinner **Iron-blue spinners.** with brilliant glossy and transparent wings and body of a dark maroon shade. The male is the jenny-spinner of the old-fashioned fisherman, with a deep brown thorax, the fore segments of the body a translucent white, and the three hind segments a deep red-brown. This insect is shown at Plate XXIII, and the turbinate eyes and abdominal forceps are depicted on the same plate drawn to a greater magnification. In the new set of patterns Nos. 20 and 21 are imitations of the two sexes of the imago of this insect.

The blue-winged olive (called by entomologists *Ephemerella ignita*) is an in- **Ephemerella ignita.** sect found very plentifully in the majority of British streams. In reference to some of the details of its life history I am able to speak with more certainty than I can of other genera and species of the Ephemeridæ. With the collaboration of Mr. T. P. Hawksley I collected the eggs, and he hatched them in captivity, and positively succeeded in raising one individual to the subimago stage in a London greenhouse. The life of this particular specimen from egg to imago was approximately one year.

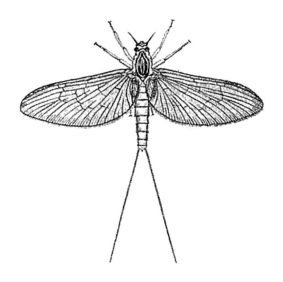

Iron-Blue Dun Female

× 5

PLATE XXII

Swan Electric Engraver Co Ld

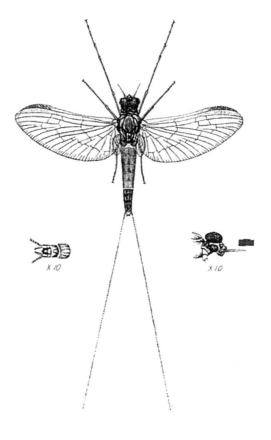

Iron Blue Spinner Male

X 5

PLATE XXIII

Swan Electric Engraving Co Ltd

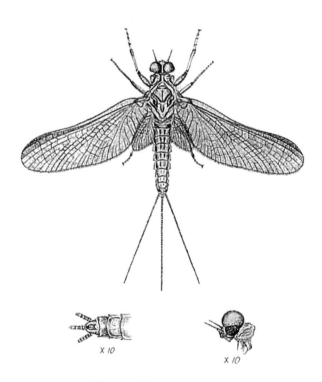

X 10

X 10

Blue-Winged Olive Male
X 5

PLATE XXIV

Swan Electric Engraving C.º

The nymph of the blue-winged olive is included by

Nymph of blue-winged olive. Pictet under the heading of *larves rampantes* or crawling nymphs, and is drawn in Fig. 41 on page 233, and there given as the type of nymphs of this class. It is so different in marking and form that any student can, at a glance, distinguish it from the digging mayfly nymph, the flat march brown nymph, or the swimming nymph, in which class are included the immature forms of the olive, iron-blue, and pale watery duns, the latter whether *Baëtis binoculatus*, *B. scambus*, *Centroptilum luteolum*, or *C. pennulatum*.

The male blue-winged olive is shown in Plate XXIV,

Blue-winged olive. and the head of the male and ventral view of abdominal forceps are also, in the same plate, drawn to a greater degree of magnification. The features by which it can be readily distinguished from either of the other duns are the presence of three setæ, the numerous cross veinlets on the wings, and the shape of the hind wings, It will be seen, too, that the wings are somewhat longer in proportion to the length of the body than in any of the preceding species of Ephemeridæ. Nos. 22 and 23 in the new patterns represent the male and female respectively.

The spinners of the blue-winged olive are called sherry spinners, and their habits in reference to oviposition are quite different from those of the other

duns and spinners treated here. The female sherry
spinner in some way expresses

Sherry spinner. her eggs and rolls them up into
a small ball, carrying this ball
against the ventral side of her body on the penultimate
segment of the abdomen. These eggs, blue-green in
colour, are enveloped in a sac in some mucous fluid,
and when deposited in the water this sac expands, and
the eggs soon lose their striking colouration and
become a dull brown. The female sherry spinner is
seen at Plate XXV, and the drawing to a larger magnification of the lower side of the hinder ends of the body
reveals the presence of lobes which, with the assistance
of the setæ turned under against the body, serve to
keep the little ball of eggs in position when the insect
is in flight. The eggs are deposited by the female
turning the setæ outwards when close to the surface,
and allowing the egg mass to fall into the water.
Like the eggs of all water-bred insects they are
specifically heavy and sink to the bottom. The
patterns of the two sexes of sherry spinner in the
new series are Nos. 24 and 25.

The march brown (*Ecdyurus venosus*) is shown in
outline at Fig. 34, and the

March brown. nymph at Fig. 39, as the type
of the flat nymphs. I have
never secured a single specimen of the fly on the Test
or Itchen, but it must be present, because on both
these rivers I have quite exceptionally found nymphs,
and they were in some cases verified by the Rev.

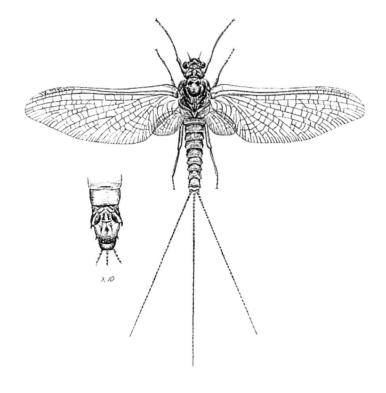

Sherry Spinner Female

× 5

× 10

PLATE XXV

Lown Electric Engraving Co

A. E. Eaton. On many rivers it is most plentiful, and is taken freely by the trout. It is essentially an inhabitant of rapid streams, and even to this day few fishermen on this class of river are votaries of the dry-fly. It is larger than any of the Ephemeridæ referred to herein with the exception of the mayfly.

In " Dry-Fly Entomology " I say of it : "It is a large fly of the usual form of the Ephemeridæ, the wings of the female measuring about ·55 and of the male ·50 of an inch ; the body of the female about ·65 and of the male ·60 of an inch. It has two dark brown setæ, a reddish-brown thorax, and body of reddish brown with light fawn-coloured joinings. The wings are a faint brown colour with strong brown nervures, and the legs more or less dark brown in colour. The nymph of Pictet's *larves plattes* can be identified from the plate. The imago of the march brown is the great red spinner of Ronalds."

The yellow may dun is an insect often seen on the chalk-streams from June through **Yellow may dun.** the summer until October. It generally hatches out in the evenings, and many of my friends have declared that the trout feed on it ravenously. At one time Marryat and I dressed imitations of it with upright hackle point wings dyed a sulphur-yellow, hackle and whisk dyed a greenish yellow, and a quill body dyed lemon-yellow. We never killed a sizable trout with the pattern, and in many hundreds of autopsies found only one solitary specimen. Still it is said that in some parts of Ireland, where I believe it is called the *yellow hawk*, it kills well, and Mr. M. E. Mosely tells me that he has found it in autopsies from rivers and streams in Co. Cork. The scientific names of two insects to which anglers attached the name yellow may dun are *Heptagenia sulphurea* and *H. flavipennis*, the difference between these two species being only microscopically distinguishable. The nymph of the yellow may dun is another of Pictet's *larves plattes*.

Turkey brown. The turkey brown is a fly which is plentiful on the chalk-streams in the spring, and, like the last fly referred to herein, does not appear to be taken by the trout, as in the numerous autopsies made I have only found one single example of this insect. It is somewhat similar in colouration to the march brown, but is much smaller and besides has three caudal setæ, while the march brown has only two. The scientific name of the turkey brown is *Leptophlebia submarginata*.

Claret dun. Another member of this family is known in Ireland as the claret dun, and is very plentiful on some of the Irish loughs, notably Lough Arrow. Like the turkey brown, this insect is furnished with three setæ. The subimago will be readily distinguished by its smoky, blue-black wings and the deep claret colour of the body. The imago is very similar to that of the turkey brown, the differences in structure being so minute that they may well be ignored by the fly-fisherman. The scientific name of this fly is *Leptophlebia vespertina*.

Rhithrogena semicolorata is another fly which is

Rhithrogena semicolorata. found at times on the chalk-streams, and although I have never found it in an autopsy it is quite possible that the trout feed on it. In the north country, moreover, it is one of the most abundant of the Ephemeridæ and has been frequently found in autopsies.

In the dun stage the fore-wings are light grey and the legs greenish or brownish grey. The spinner is very similar in appearance to that of the yellow may dun, with which insect

Yellow upright. it shares the popular name of yellow upright. It is, however, smaller in size, and may always be distinguished by a triangular dark streak in the middle of the thigh.

The smallest of all the Ephemeridæ called *Cænis rivulorum*, is figured in Fig. 48. It is seen in great numbers on the chalk-streams on warm summer evenings, and some fishermen are quite convinced that the trout take it well at times.

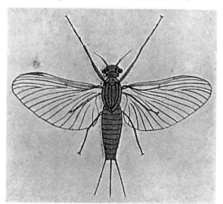

FIG. 48. CÆNIS RIVULORUM × 6

Continual observation of

autopsy spread over more than a quarter of a century
has failed to produce any of these insects in the autopsies made. At the same time
Cænis. it may well be possible that at
times, under different condi-
tions and in other streams, it is a favourite kind of
food for the trout. In the new set of patterns, No. 20,
the male spinner of the iron-blue, is the best imitation,
but it is far larger than the natural insect.

Periodically this insect is referred to in the sporting press as the *little white curse,* and we are
solemnly assured that when the clouds of this fly
are in the air they settle on the fisherman and
sting or bite him. In "Dry-Fly Entomology" I
have tried to answer all these points in the following paragraph :—

"To answer these points : Firstly, the flies that
fishermen call curses are Diptera, but this is one of
the Ephemeridæ. Secondly, in many hundreds of
autopsies I have never found a single Cænis in a
trout or grayling. Thirdly, Cænis has no sting and
the mouth organs are so aborted that it is incapable
of biting. The tiny insects usually appear in countless numbers on hot calm evenings when the fish
are likely to be rising freely at various other flies
on the water ; they settle down on the clothes, the
hands, face or any other part of the fisherman only
because they require some firm object to stand
upon while casting their subimago skin and emerging as the imago or perfect insect."

CHAPTER III

CADDIS-FLIES

THE caddis-flies, which are called Trichoptera by modern entomologists, comprise a number of aquatic insects of which the larvæ make either movable cases which they drag about, or fixed ones that they anchor to heavy stones, going in and out of them according to their inclination. The caddis, sometimes most incorrectly called caddis-worms, are plentiful in the majority of rivers in Great Britain and abroad. Every observant fisherman has seen those with movable cases literally in hundreds on the bed of the stream or of a carrier, and until he had examined them has wondered how the solid-looking structure of stone or of twigs and other vegetable matter could move about. When a specimen has once been taken in the hand, the sight of the head, thorax, and legs protruding in front and crawling along towing the case behind has elucidated this mystery.

The caddis-flies undergo complete metamorphosis, and the various stages of their existence after emerging from the egg therefore are *larva*, *pupa*, and *imago*. The eggs of some are carried in ovoid masses on the ventral

Life history of caddis-flies.

side of the females' bodies, and are either deposited on leaves, stems of aquatic plants, or dropped by the insect fluttering and dipping on the surface, and sink to the bed of the river. Some species descend into the water, like a few individual Ephemeridæ, and selecting a favourable spot among stones in the bed of the river, there deposit their eggs.

As before noted, the larvæ are divided into two well-marked divisions: (1) larvæ

Larvæ. making portable cases which they drag about wherever they go, and (2) larvæ making fixed cases, sometimes of small stones, which are generally attached to larger stones, issuing from them to roam in quest of food, and returning when alarmed or for repose. Occasionally these larvæ construct their cases of vegetable or other *débris* fastened together with silk in a loose and irregular mass, only forming solid cases when about to change to pupæ.

The larvæ begin to construct their cases almost immediately after they have emerged from the eggs and the jelly-like mass with which the eggs are covered. In the cabinet of the Fly-Fishers' Club one drawer is devoted to the life history of the welshman's button bred in captivity for the club collection to the order and instruction of Mr. Arthur N. Gilbey. In this collection it may be seen that the larva at five days old had constructed a perfect case of minute dimensions to contain it. The movable cases of larvæ vary much in shape and in the materials used for their construction. Some use sand, small stones, shells, and other mineral matter, while others build with vegetable matter such as leaves, twigs, reeds, and any stray particles of plants. Some, again, use partly vegetable and partly mineral matter as their building materials.

The larva invariably spins a silken cylindrical tubular case, on the exterior of which the stones or other materials used to build the case are fixed.

The distribution of the materials used in the construction of the movable cases is made with great care. The case must be light enough for the larva to be able to drag it along, and yet heavy enough to withstand the strength of the stream, and at the same time well balanced. When crawling along, the head, thorax, and legs are protruding beyond the case, and the abdomen inside the case is provided with two hooks at the tail end with which the larva holds on to the inside of the case and drags it along. As the larva grows it cuts away part of the case at the smaller end and constructs new segments as required of dimensions to suit its increased size.

The full-grown larva closes the ends of the case as a preparation for the rest stage **Preparation for the** during which it effects the **change to pupa.** gradual metamorphosis to the pupa. The closing of the ends is effected by a grating; this is differently formed by different genera and species, but is invariably constructed so as to allow free ingress and egress of water

s

from which the oxygen for respiratory purposes is extracted. In some cases the entrance is closed by small pieces of wood, leaves or stones fastened obliquely across, but never so closely as to render it impervious to water. Larvæ inhabiting rapid water fasten the cases to weeds, heavy stones, or other solid bodies to prevent them from being carried adrift by the current.

Larvæ with fixed cases. Larvæ of the family of the Rhyacophilidæ which make fixed cases commence by selecting a heavy stone and attaching to the lower side of it by means of the silk a number of small stones, and thus constructing a closed-in house, leaving only a small irregular-shaped door for ingress and egress. When full grown they close up the case, leaving spaces between the stones used for this purpose, so that the water so necessary for respiratory purposes can flow freely into or out of the little house. They then become covered with a brown, hard cocoon, in which they pass the rest stage while effecting the change to a pupa. Larvæ belonging to the family of the Hydropsychidæ also make fixed cases. They, however, make no cocoon, the pupæ merely lying in the closed-up case. In Plate XXVI Fig. 1 is the larva, Fig. 2 the larva enclosed in the cocoon, and Fig. 3 the pupa of *Rhyacophila dorsalis*.

The larva, whether one of the movable or fixed type, then effects the metamorphosis to the pupa, and Fig. 3 of Plate XXVI shows the general appearance

Rhyacophila Dorsalis - Larva - Case and Pupa

× 4

PLATE XXVI

Swan Electric Engraving Co.

of pupæ of both of these types. The wings are folded

Pupa.

up, the legs and antennæ against the body, but not enveloped in the same skin as with the chrysalis of the butterfly or moth, and there is a beak-shaped projection at the mouth. This beak-shaped projection is, in fact, a pair of powerful jaws or mandibles, and its function is to force or tear open the grating at the fore end of the movable case or to break away the stones from the entrance of the fixed case. The legs are furnished with heavy fringes, which act as paddles when subsequently the pupa requires to swim to the surface of the water. The pupa, enveloped in a thin skin, crawls out of the case, swims up through the water on its back, and finds a convenient and dry place on stones or weeds, where it makes its last change to the winged insect or imago. The time elapsing between the emergence of the imago and the swimming to the surface of the pupa is probably in some species considerably longer than in the corresponding change in the Ephemeridæ. Bred in captivity, the imago frequently occupied some hours in breaking through the pupal skin after having emerged from the caddis case.

The imago immediately after the metamorphosis is

Imago.

pale in colour and generally soft in consistency, but rapidly assumes its full colouration. It can fly fairly well, but remains generally hidden in the grass or among the sedges in daylight, emerging only at or after sunset. The life of these caddis-flies is usually one year from egg to imago, and this has been fully verified from the life-history specimens of the welshman's button presented to the Fly-Fishers' Club by Mr. Arthur N. Gilbey, as stated in a previous page. Mr. Mosely has also confirmed this in the case of *Notidobia ciliaris*.

The type of the largest of the Trichoptera, the large red sedge (*Phryganea striata*), is given in Plate XXVII.

The reader who has studied "Modern Development of the Dry-Fly" will

Patterns of sedge-flies.

see that I have departed from my ordinary routine in reference to the imitations of sedge-flies. Instead of matching from nature the great number of British genera and species frequenting the chalk-streams and other rivers, I have selected three types of colouration and size only. I am quite conscious of the fact that I may be accused at once of inconsistency and possibly, too, of indolence, but if a reference is made to McLachlan's "Monographic Revision and Synopsis of the Trichoptera of the European Fauna," published 1874–1880, it will be seen that he there computed the total number of species (then existing in collections) as between 250 and 300, and he fore-shadows a considerable increase in these numbers. Some years since Rev. A. E. Eaton examined a few specimens from the Test, and found twenty-three different species; and Mr. Mosely, who has for some

Large Red Sedge Male
× 3

PLATE XXVII

Welshmans Button Male

× 4

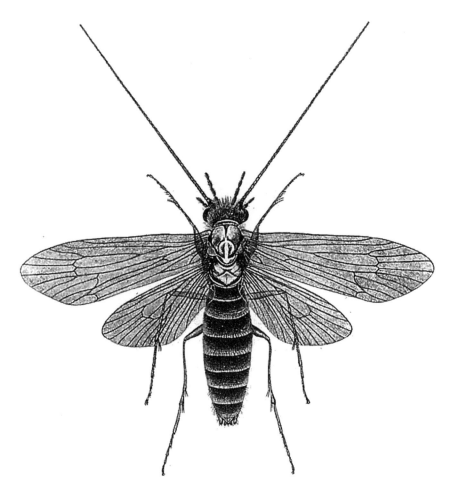

Welshman's Button Female

PLATE XXIX

× 4

Swan Electric Engraving C.

years collected a great number, tells me that there are 174 known British species, and of these nearly half are or will shortly be arranged in cabinets at the Fly-Fishers' Club.

The variations among these insects are generally in size and colour, in minor details, such as length of antennæ, the number and disposition of spurs on the tibiæ, the wing neuration, the form of the palpi, etc.; all these last matters, which would not concern the practical fly-dresser in reference to making patterns for the dry-fly man, are, however, of the utmost importance to the entomologist in determining the species. It would, to my mind, have been absurd to work out something like twenty patterns of sedge-flies and expect even the most enthusiastic fisherman to carry all of these, especially as the rise at sedge-flies takes place usually just at or after dark, when presumably slight variations of shade or colour could not well be visible to the fish.

The welshman's button I treated independently,

Welshman's button. because since the gradual disappearance of the mayfly it has become the fly-fisherman's sheet-anchor during, perhaps, the very best of the season, from the latter end of May to the end of June. To assist the fisherman in identifying the natural insect, I have given in Plate XXVIII a drawing of the male in profile, and in Plate XXIX the female. Nos. 29 and 30 in the set of patterns are imitations of the male and female respectively.

With reference to the remaining sedge-flies, I worked out with great care a **Three typical patterns of sedges.** colour scheme, and have, I think, succeeded in producing three typical patterns of sedges which should be sufficient for any fly-fisherman's box or book on any of the south-country chalk-streams. In other parts he might require other patterns. No. 31 is a dark-coloured fly of a dusky brown hue dressed on a No. 1 hook, and is called the *small dark sedge*. No. 32, paler, slightly more ruddy and larger, is called the *medium sedge*, and is dressed on a No. 2 hook, and No. 33, the largest of the three, has mottled wings of a cinnamon tint, a dull yellow-green body and brown ginger legs ; it is dressed on a No. 3 hook, and is called the *cinnamon sedge.*

These were all matched from the types of natural insects selected for the purpose, and one of the leading entomologists of the day named these insects independently and confirmed my identification. The small dark sedge was a male *Goëra pilosa,* the medium sedge a female of the same species, and the cinnamon sedge a male *Limnophilus lunatus.*

The grannom (*Brachycentrus subnubilus*) is a fly **Grannom.** which thirty years ago was most plentiful on the Test, and it was always welcomed by the old school of dry-fly men in the spring, because many of the large fish were killed by it, and it certainly was an insect which seemed to bring the trout rapidly into condition. Unfortunately, it has almost disappeared from this river, and, as stated in an earlier chapter, all efforts have failed so far to reintroduce it. The following is a description of it in brief :—

Larva, slender and subcylindrical. *Case*, a four-sided tube of vegetable matter tapering slightly towards the tail (shown in Fig. 49). *Pupa*, similar to *Rhyacophila dorsalis*, but with a dull blue-green body. When the pupa is rising in the

FIG. 49. GRANNOM CADDIS × 3

water to assume the imago stage it usually spins round and round on the surface as the thin pupal shuck distends and splits, allowing the perfect insect to emerge. The fly is only of moderate size, the wings a pale smoky grey membrane marked with yellowish or fawn-coloured hairs or spots and with whitish fringes. Its body immediately after its change from the pupa is a yellowish grey-green colour. The female subsequently carries an enormous oval mass of blue-green eggs at the tail end of the abdomen.

Notidobia ciliaris. *Notidobia ciliaris* is the scientific name in " Dry-Fly Entomology" I have given to the brown silverhorns. This I must confess is a mistake, as I am convinced that the brown silverhorns of the Hampshire fishermen is *Leptocerus cinereus*. Fig. 50 is a drawing of the male *Notidobia ciliaris*. It is a fly which is very plentiful on chalk-streams and other rivers, and is best imitated by the small dark sedge, No. 31.

FIG. 50. NOTIDOBIA CILIARIS. MALE × 4

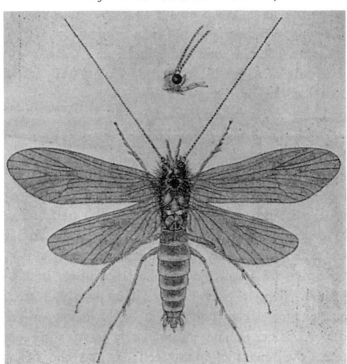

Rhyacophila dorsalis, which is shown in Plate XXX, is one of the Trichoptera, the **Rhyacophila dorsalis.** larva of which makes a fixed case as previously stated, and the larva is figured in the paragraph referring to caddis belonging to this division. It is very numerous on most rivers, and is very fairly imitated by the medium sedge, No. 32.

Rhyacophila Dorsalis Male

X 4

PLATE XXX

Swan Electric Engraving Co. Ltd

Limnophilus rhombicus is somewhat larger than

Limnophilus rhombicus.

L. lunatus, and has a snuff-brown coloured body and well-marked brownish wings. The same pattern, No. 33, will serve for both of these species. The larva of *L. rhombicus* makes a quadrilateral case of vegetable matter or of shells, sometimes of both ; it is shown at Fig. 51.

FIG. 51.   LIMNOPHILUS RHOMBICUS × 3 (CADDIS)

The black silverhorns (*Mystacides nigra* or *M.*

Black silverhorns.

azurea) are seen in great numbers over the surface of the stream on warm calm evenings. No doubt the fish feed on them at times, and although they are much darker and blacker than the small dark sedge, No. 31, I think the pattern would be successful in the dusk or half-light. A marked peculiarity of all the Mystacides is that the fore and hind wings are hooked together in flight. The hooks for this purpose, placed towards the extremity of the anterior margin of the hinder wings, are curiously shaped at the tips, and fit into a narrow fold on the inner margin of the fore wings.

The student who wishes to be able to identify more
of the caddis-flies which may
Identification of other Trichoptera.
be found on the banks of the
river, will have to devote some
time to the consideration of a little more science and
put up with more Greek and Latin names. I will try
as briefly as possible to set out the points to which
he must give his best attention.

The Trichoptera are divided into two divisions :
(1) Inæquipalpia or caddis-flies
Inæquipalpia and Æquipalpia.
with the maxillary palpi (the
longer and upper pair) with
fewer than five joints in the male and five in the
female; and (2) Æquipalpia, in which the maxillary palpi
are five-jointed, and generally similar in both sexes.

The following is McLachlan's tabulation of the
families :—

DIVISION I

INÆQUIPALPIA

Phryganeidæ.—Maxillary palpi of the male four-jointed,
only slightly pubescent, their form similar in both
sexes.

Limnophilidæ.—Maxillary palpi of the male three-
jointed, scarcely pubescent, their form similar
in both sexes.

Sericostomatidæ.—Maxillary palpi of the male two or
three-jointed, ordinarily very pubescent or pilose,
and always formed in quite a different manner
from those of the female ; varying very greatly
according to the genus.

DIVISION II

ÆQUIPALPIA

Maxillary palpi always five-jointed, and with few exceptions similar in form in both sexes.

Leptoceridæ.—Palpi (maxillary understood) strongly hairy, ordinarily ascending, and with the last joint usually long, but simple, although often flexible. Wings very pubescent, and for the most part narrow. Antennæ, as a rule, very long and slender. The case of the larva tubular, and free.

Hydropsychidæ.—Palpi long, and more or less deflexed, the last joint whip-shaped, and composed of numerous minute jointlets, slightly pubescent, wings pubescent. Antennæ variable. Case of the larva fixed ; the pupa not enveloped in a special cocoon.

Rhyacophilidæ.—Palpi deflexed, joints cylindrical, rarely hairy, the last joint similar in form to the others. Wings variable in amount of pubescence. Case of the larva fixed; the pupa enveloped in a cocoon.

Hydroptilidæ.—Insects very minute, and simulating *Micro-Lepidoptera;* very strongly pubescent and hairy, the wings with numerous erect hairs. Palpi very hairy, simple in structure. Antennæ short and stout. Case of the larva free, membraneous and seed-like.

The student should be able to identify the family from the foregoing tables.

PHRYGANEIDÆ

The following insects of this family are likely to be found and are fairly plentiful. Advisedly, I omit those which are comparatively rare, because they are of little or no importance to the fisherman.

This is the largest of the British Trichoptera.

Phryganea grandis.

Large red sedge.

It is very similar to *P. striata*, but is a trifle larger and the body paler. Experts differentiate the male from the male of *P. striata* by the difference in shape of the genitalia. It may for all practical purposes be considered as identical with *P. striata*, and both species are known by the popular name of large red sedge, the female being the *Murragh* of Irish lakes.

Phryganea striata.

The male is figured in Plate XXVII.

Phryganea varia.

Mosely has found this on Lough Arrow in Ireland. The fly is a smaller insect than either of the two aforementioned species; has grey wings strongly marked with dark patches. It is a striking and handsome-looking insect.

Phryganea obsoleta.

Phryganea obsoleta, another species, is larger than *P. varia*, but not so large as *P. grandis* or *P. striata*. It is found plentifully on the lakes in the neighbourhood of Blaenau-Festiniog in Wales, and no doubt elsewhere.

The number of the spurs on the tibiæ is deemed
of great importance in deter-

Spurs on tibiæ. mining the family and genus of
the Trichoptera, and I propose
in each case giving what is called the spur formula.
The spur formula for all the Phryganeidæ is 2, 4, 4,
which means that there are two spurs on the tibiæ of
each of the fore-legs, four on each of the medial legs,
and four on each of the hind-legs.

LIMNOPHILIDÆ

Of this family in the genus *Limnophilus, Anabolia,*
and *Stenophylax* the spur formula for both sexes is
1, 3, 4.

The following may be taken as fairly plentiful of
the British insects belonging to these genera :—

Limnophilus. *Limnophilus rhombicus,* referred to at page 265.

Limnophilus flavicornis, very similar to *L. rhombicus,* but not so well marked. The caddis case has

Fig. 52. LIMNOPHILUS FLAVICORNIS × 2 (CADDIS)

a curious round brush-like appearance, and is shown
in Fig. 52.

Limnophilus marmoratus.—Very similar in appearance to *L. lunatus*, but larger and without the lunate marking characteristic of the latter insect.

Limnophilus lunatus.—The type of the sedge pattern, No. 33. McLachlan describes it as a reddish or reddish-fuscous insect, but even if less scientific I prefer the word *cinnamon* as defining its general colouration. The body of the male is greenish, and there is a distinct lunate marking at the tips of the fore-wings.

Limnophilus affinis is very common in Britain from April to October, and is frequently found at great distances from its breeding-ground. A specimen was recently captured in a London dwelling, and it has been recorded from light-houses far out at sea. About the same size as *L. lunatus*, and very varied in its brown markings.

Limnophilus sparsus is a common British sedge, with broad rounded wings, thickly covered with dark hairs. It is a summer and autumn fly and very variable in its colour.

Anabolia nervosa is the only British species of this genus, and is exceptionally **Anabolia.** common in our chalk-streams. It is a dark sedge, with narrow fore-wings, nearly or quite self-coloured. McLachlan says that when handled it has a strong odour, which has been compared by some entomologists to that of the *Pelargonium*. It appears to have what may be called a *forma minor*, not aberrantly but constantly. The small form may, I think, be considered a variety. The larva and case are shown in Fig. 53.

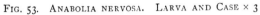
FIG. 53. ANABOLIA NERVOSA. LARVA AND CASE × 3

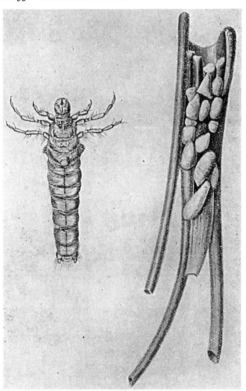

Stenophylax stellatus. A large insect, with broad grey fore-wings marked with pale **Stenophylax.** elongated streaks in most of the areas and cellules and with a large bilobate pale spot beyond the middle.

Very plentiful in July and August, and appears just at dusk in great quantities along the river-banks.

Stenophylax latipennis.—McLachlan says, " I know of no general characters whereby to separate this from the large-sized individuals of *stellatus ;* the colours are possibly slightly paler (more testaceous) on an average." Mr. John Henderson has found it on the Dove in the early spring, and date of its appearance is perhaps the best indication of its species.

The spur formula for both sexes of the genus *Halesus* is 1, 3, 3.

Halesus. *Halesus radiatus* is the well-known caperer shown at Fig. 35. It has broad fore-wings, parabolic at the tip and of a yellow grey colour streaked longitudinally with darker grey in most of the areas and cellules. It is a large insect.

Halesus digitatus. Very similar to the foregoing species and plentiful in the South of England. It has also been found in Scotland in the Clyde district. Rather larger and paler than *H. radiatus*.

In this genus the spur formula of both male and female is 1, 3, 3.

Drusus. *Drusus annulatus* is a medium-sized brownish sedge-fly, of which McLachlan says that it is not uncommon in rocky and mountainous districts of England and Scotland in summer and early autumn.

The spur formula for both sexes of this genus is 1, 2, 3.

Ecclisopteryx. *Ecclisopteryx guttulata.* The general characters of the flies of this genus are similar to those of *Drusus*, but of course the difference in the spur formula will at once enable the student to separate these two genera. It is said to be widely distributed, appearing in May, June and July in the North of England, Scotland, etc. A specimen was sent to Mosely for the Fly-Fishers' Club cabinet by Mr. John Henderson, jun., from the River Neath, and the fly is found quite plentifully on the Dove towards the end of May.

In this genus of the Limnophilidæ the spur formula for the male is 0, 3, 3, and for **Chætopteryx.** the female 1, 3, 3.

Chætopteryx villosa. This is a most unmistakable insect when once it has been seen. The derivation of its scientific name—χαίτη, a mane, and πτέρυξ, a wing—indicates at once the nature of the fly. Its wings are short and broad, with long, erect hairs inserted partly upon the nervures and, to a large extent, upon granulation scattered over the membrane. This gives a fairly good representation of a mane on the wings. It is a moderately small insect of a medium-sedge colour, and is covered with pubescence and hairs. It is fairly plentiful on the Test, Itchen, Kennet and other rivers.

T

SERICOSTOMATIDÆ

The spur formula for both sexes of *Sericostoma* and *Notidobia* is 2, 2, 4.

Sericostoma personatum is the welshman's button of the Hampshire fisherman. The **Sericostoma personatum.** difference between the sexes is marked not only in the size but in the great disparity between the maxillary palpi. In the male the palpi at the first glance are not always easily distinguished be-

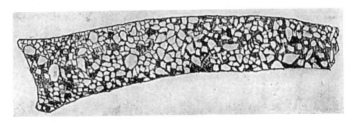

cause they are turned back, masking the face. They are covered with silky hairs, hence the name *Sericostoma* (σηρικός, silky; στόμα, mouth). The palpi of the female are very long, strong and hairy, the basal joint short, second longer and stouter than any succeeding, third, fourth and fifth thinner and sub-equal. I have given at Fig. 54 a drawing of the case of the larva, and at Plate XXVIII a male imago in profile. Plate XXIX shows the female imago.

Notidobia ciliaris, of which a male is shown in Fig. 50, although similar in many respects to the

welshman's button, is altogether a darker fly. Mc-
Lachlan says : " The living
Notidobia ciliaris. insect is entirely very deep
black (with a slight steel-blue
reflection) excepting the legs, the posterior tibiæ and
tarsi being yellowish or testaceous, the anterior and
intermediate less decidedly so, more dusky ; but the
expanded posterior wings are paler and more transparent than the anterior. After death the colour
becomes gradually less intensely black (more
brownish)." The female may frequently be observed
carrying a yellowish mass of eggs at the extremity of
the abdomen, and these eggs, when deposited in the
water, open out into two thick flat plates, joined by
an intervening thickened ridge.

The spur formula of the two succeeding genera—
Goëra and *Silo*—is for both sexes 2, 4, 4.

Goëra pilosa. The palpi of the male are very
striking. Like those of
Goëra pilosa. *S. personatum* they are very
closely pressed against the
front, and scarcely distinguishable in a state of rest ;
they are three-jointed, the two basal joints very short,
and the third large, apparently subcylindrical and
curved. If the living insect is pressed between the
fingers these palpi become greatly elongated. It is then
seen that there is an apical portion which is ordinarily
concealed in the cavity and the basal portion is attenu-
ate and curved at the extremity, and that the whole
inner surface is covered with small blackish tubercles.

The maxillary palpi of the female are slender, the two basal joints short, the others long, but the fourth slightly shorter than either the third or fifth.

Of the imagines McLachlan says: "Body fuscescent in the male, ochreous in the female; antennæ brown in the male, ochreous in the female." This difference of colour between the sexes continues throughout his description, the male colouration being fuscous or smoky, and the female ochreous or yellowish brown. Now the two patterns of the new

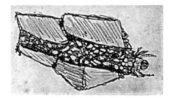

FIG. 55. GOËRA PILOSA CADDIS × 3

series, No. 31 small dark sedge and No. 32 medium sedge, were matched from the male and female respectively of *Goëra pilosa*, and, I venture to suggest, accurately reproduce their colours and general appearance. Fig. 55 shows the peculiar caddis of this genus.

Silo pallipes is a small black sedge having a very triangular appearance when at rest. Like the other genera of the Sericostomatidæ the male has maxillary palpi of abnormal shape, closely pressed upwards against the face, and clothed with elongate clavate hairs. It appears towards the end of spring, and lasts on through the summer.

Silo.

Silo nigricornis is very similar in general characteristics to the last-named species, but is of a slightly larger size. For angling purposes the two species may be considered as one.

The grannom (*Brachycentrus subnubilus*) has a spur formula for both sexes of 2, 3, 3. The name is derived from two Greek words (βραχύς, short ; κέντρον, a spur) referring to the shortness of the two spurs on the tibiæ of each of the fore-legs as compared with those on the medial and hind legs. The fly is well known to many anglers, and the case of the larva is quadrangular, of vegetable matter, and is figured at Fig. 49. The grannom is one of the earliest of the sedges, appearing in extraordinary numbers about mid-April on the rivers which it frequents. On the Kennet, during a good hatch, the fly has been observed like a grey mist across the river, and the water itself has been covered from bank to bank with a scum of cast-off pupal shucks.

Brachycentrus subnubilus.

Lepidostoma hirtum is an insect in some ways resembling the grannom, inasmuch as the egg sac is of a very similar blue-green colour. It can be readily distinguished from the grannom, as its spur formula is 2, 4, 4. It can also be separated from others of this group and family by the presence of black scales on the palpi and the basal joint of the antennæ of the male. The name is derived from λέπις, -ίδος, a scale ; and στόμα, a mouth. It appears generally about August, while the grannom is essen-

Lepidostoma hirtum.

tially a spring fly. The larva also resembles that of the grannom in making a quadrilateral case which may be distinguished by its greater length and more gradual taper.

DIVISION II

ÆQUIPALPIA

Trichoptera which in both sexes have five-jointed maxillary palpi.

LEPTOCERIDÆ

Molanna angustata. Spur formula 2, 4, 4.

This insect may be identified by its long narrow straw-coloured wings project-
Molanna angustata. ing some distance beyond the body. It has long sprawling legs and a general characteristic appearance. The larva makes a very curious case, consisting of a central tube surrounded by a mass of sand and fragments of silex, so arranged as to give a very broad and flattened external aspect. The case is shown at Fig. 56.

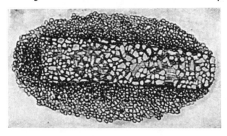

FIG. 56. MOLANNA ANGUSTATA CADDIS × 4

The mature fly is nocturnal in its habits, and is only seen by day when accidentally disturbed from the reeds or foliage in which it finds a refuge.

Odontocerum albicorne, spur formula 2, 4, 4. A very handsome grey sedge with dark markings.

Odontocerum albicorne. When at rest the long white antennæ are pressed closely together and project straight in front, continuing the line of the body. The generic name is derived from the Greek ὀδούς, a tooth; and κεραία, a horn; and the specific name emphasizes the white colour of the antennæ, and is taken from the Latin *albus,* white; and *cornus,* a horn. The Greek generic derivation describes the curious toothed appearance of the antennæ, which can be observed under a glass of quite low magnification. There appears to be only one species in the whole genus.

Leptocerus. The spur formula for both sexes and all species of the genus Leptocerus is 2, 2, 2. *Leptocerus nigro-nervosus.* A large, strong-flying sedge with long dark antennæ. As may be inferred from the Latin derivation of the specific name, the wings are very strongly marked with heavy black neuration. This fly is fairly general, and has been observed in large quantities along the shores of Lough Arrow.

Leptocerus aterrimus. A very common form, similar to the black silverhorns of the angler. It is distinguished from it by the two spurs on the fore-legs, the true black silverhorns having none.

Leptocerus cinereus. A very common and plentiful species, and is probably the insect referred to by fishermen as the brown silverhorns. Very common on the Thames and its tributaries.

Leptocerus albifrons. A chocolate-brown silverhorns, with white markings on its wings. Very common on certain portions of the Test and other rivers.

The Mystacides, or black silverhorns, have a spur formula of 0, 2, 2.

Mystacides. *Mystacides nigra.* The wings are black, the hind ones a trifle paler than the fore-wings, and in the fore-wings a metallic purple lustre may be observed.

Mystacides azurea is distinguished from *M. nigra* by its more slender form and narrower wings of a steel-blue colour.

Mystacides longicornis. This fly is the grouse wing of the North, and the popular name exactly describes the mottled brown patches on the wings. It differs from the two above-named species in its general brown appearance. The Mystacides are referred to in more detail at page 265, under the marginal heading of black silverhorns.

HYDROPSYCHIDÆ

The spur formula for both sexes is 2, 4, 4. The genus is peculiar in having a

Hydropsyche. slightly elevated and blackened ridge winding round the antennæ in a loose spiral, described by McLachlan. The species are difficult to separate and many of them appear in bright sunshine.

Hydropsyche pellucida. A large yellow-grey sedge fairly common on the Test, and appearing usually on sunny days.

Hydropsyche guttata. A smaller fly than the above, very variable in its markings, and appearing in clouds on hot days throughout the summer, apparently preferring sunny places.

Hydropsyche instabilis. A very handsome medium-sized sedge with strong markings on the wings. Female insects are more abundantly captured than the males.

Philopotamos.   Spurs 2, 4, 4.

Philopotamos montanus. A very beautiful insect, slightly resembling *Phryganea varia* in the markings of its wings, which are mottled with varying shades of brown. It may be identified by two lobster-claw-like appendages at the extremity of the abdomen of the male.

Polycentropus.   Spurs 3, 4, 4.

Polycentropus flavo-maculatus. πολύ, many, κέντρον, spur, referring to the number of spurs ; and *flavo-maculatus*, spotted with gold, referring to the markings on the wings.

This insect is a small brown sedge found in nearly all British rivers in considerable abundance. The general markings of the wings are similar to some of the species of *Hydropsyche*, but the fly is of much smaller size. Like Hydropsyche it appears to have no objection to the sunlight, and may often be seen flying about from one resting-place to another along the river-bank.

Tinodes.   Spurs 2, 4, 4.

Tinodes wæneri. A small light-brown sedge with reddish body. Found on many British rivers, but particularly plentiful on Lough Arrow, where the boats are occasionally completely covered with many thousands of these little insects.

Psychomyia.   Spurs 2, 4, 4.

Psychomyia pusilla. A very small yellow-brown coloured sedge, appearing on most rivers during the summer, but taking shelter under the leaves of trees and bushes during the day. A slight tap on a branch by the river-side will usually disturb a considerable number of these small flies.

Chimarrha.   Spurs 1, 4, 4.

Chimarrha marginata.—A plentiful small dark sedge with dark-brown wings edged with a golden-yellow outer margin. The larvæ have a preference for portions of the river where the flow is fast and mossy boulders abound.

RHYACOPHILIDÆ

Rhyacophila.   Spurs 3, 4, 4.

Rhyacophila dorsalis.—Described on page 264, the larva, case, cocoon and pupa shown in Plate XXVI, and the male imago in Plate XXX.

Glossosoma.   Spurs 2, 4, 4.

Glossosoma vernale.—A small brown sedge with a curious cup-shaped indentation on the inner margin of the anterior wings of the male.

HYDROPTILIDÆ

The Hydroptilidæ are minute insects, of which McLachlan says that they "may be justly termed *Micro-Trichoptera*, for the largest European form expands to no more than 10 mm. and the smallest to only $3\frac{1}{2}$ mm." I do not think that a family, the largest members of which measure across their outstretched wings no more than 10 mm. or approximately ·4 of an inch, is of any great interest to the fisherman.

CHAPTER IV

STONEFLIES, ALDER, SMUTS, ETC.

THE stoneflies or Perlidæ are most important on the north-country, midland, and **Stoneflies.** other rapid rivers, where the sunk-fly fisherman is more often seen than the dry-fly man.

Hints for identifying an insect as belonging to this family are given in page 224, and it may be well to add here that the genera and species vary considerably in size. The largest of the stoneflies are among the giants of British insects, and small ones like the willow-fly when at rest are comparatively small and attenuated flies, although these when in flight with their four long and narrow fluttering wings convey to the student the impression of far larger insects than one really sees.

The eggs are ovoid and generally dark in hue, and are packed in a bunch covered **Life history.** by a thin integument and enclosed in the tail end of the body. When detached they are not surrounded by any gelatinous envelope, and are deposited by the female while flying at some height above the water. As they fall they separate and sink at once to the bed

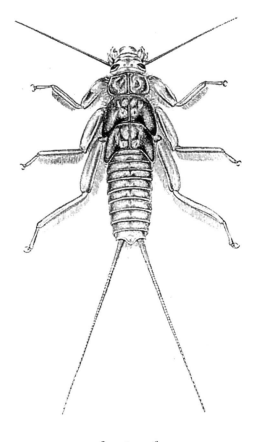

Stonefly Larva
X 3

PLATE XXXI

Sun Electric Engraving Co.

Stonefly Imago Female
× 2

Louis Stacie Engraving Co.

PLATE XXXII

of the river, and it is said that the females do not crawl down under the water to oviposit like some of the Ephemeridæ and Trichoptera.

The nymphs of the genus Perla are invariably found in rapid parts of the stream, while of the genus Nemoura, according to Pictet (who wrote an admirable monograph of the family), some frequent fast-running, and others calm, quiet, and in some cases even stagnant water. The nymphs are very similar in appearance to the mature insect, but at the early stages the wing-covers are scarcely visible. As the nymphs grow the four wing-covers gradually develop until near the next change, when they are quite prominent dark ovoid protuberances in which the wings are beautifully folded up. The mouth organs of the nymphs are fully developed, mandibles, maxillæ, labrum, labium, etc. The legs are ciliated; the fore and medial ones very short, and the hind-legs powerful, all armed with two strong curved claws. All the nymphs of the Perlidæ are provided with two caudal setæ, and even at the earliest stages this will serve to differentiate them from nymphs of the Ephemeridæ, of which all the genera and species referred to here have three caudal setæ.

Nymphs.

When the nymph is ready to change to the imago or winged and perfect insect it crawls up out of the water, and selecting a heavy stone, reed-stem, or other comparatively solid body with a rough

Imago.

surface on the bank, fixes its claws therein, and proceeds to the next metamorphosis.

The change is effected very much in the same way as in the Ephemeridæ, the thorax, head, and antennæ appearing first, and then the wings and legs, followed by the abdomen, and lastly the caudal setæ, if the imago has any, and it flutters away leaving the nymphal shuck adhering to the resting-place of the nymph.

At first the fly which has just issued forth in the winged form is flaccid and **Imago.** pallid, but in time it acquires its full strength and colour. It is not an insect which is strong on the wing, and hence keeps in the vicinity of the river until sexual intercourse has taken place. This is never attempted in the air.

Among the giants of the British Perlidæ is the large stonefly, which is one of three **Perla cephalotes.** species of the genus *Perla*, and the one I have generally found on the chalk-streams is *P. cephalotes.* Other large species are *Perla marginata, Perla maxima. Dictyopteryx microcephala*, another large stonefly, is quite plentiful on the Kennet. These large stoneflies, excepting the last-named on the Kennet, are not plentiful on the south-country chalk-streams, and are seldom present in sufficient numbers to tempt the rising trout. Up north they are plentiful, and the nymph form (generally called a *creeper*), as well as the winged insect, are among the very best flies to fatten

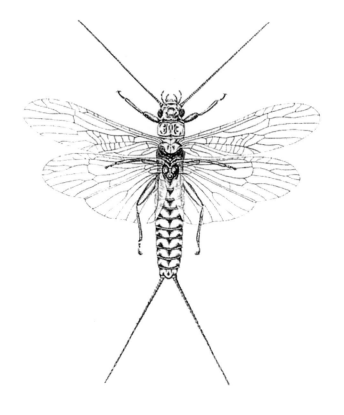

Yellow Sally Imago Female

PLATE XXXIII

X.S

The Electric Company eng Co.

the fish, and consequently very killing, either the artificial or the living creature. Of course, it is understood by my readers that on the north-country rivers the natural insect and the creeper in its immature form are not *taboo* as baits. The appearance of this larva and general characteristics can be seen by reference to Plate XXXI.

The female imago of the stonefly (*Perla cephalotes*) is a very large and handsome insect, and the drawing of it from which the figure, Plate XXXII, was reproduced is very true to nature. The male is a much smaller insect, measuring across its outstretched wings about ·8 of an inch, while the spread of the wings of the female is approximately 2 inches. The wings of the male are quite rudimentary, and not at all adapted for flying. When they are folded in repose they do not extend as far as the end of the body.

The yellow sally (*Chloroperla grammatica*), a female of which is shown in Plate **The yellow sally.** XXXIII, is often seen on the south - country chalk - streams during the early summer. It is generally of a greenish yellow colour, and is another of the flies which I have never seen in an autopsy. Some of the old writers on the subject have suggested that it has a bitter flavour, and that for this reason is not appreciated by the fish. The female measures about 1 inch across its outspread wings, and the body is approximately half an inch in length.

A similar but smaller fly (*Isopteryx torrentium*) has

been found in autopsies of trout sent to Mr. Mosely from Ireland and also from Lancashire.

Another of the Perlidæ, the february red (*Tæniopteryx nebulosa*), is taken **February red.** freely by the fish in rivers where it is plentiful, and in these parts is in great repute.

Nemoura meyeri. A very common member of the family, often mistaken for the **Nemoura meyeri.** february red. The whole of this genus may be identified by a curious X-like configuration of the nervures towards the costal margin of both anterior and posterior wings.

The willow-fly, needle-brown, or spanish needle (*Leuctra geniculata*) is very **Willow-fly.** plentiful on most of the British rivers. It makes its appearance generally in the late summer and continues in evidence throughout the autumn. Its appearance when in repose or crawling about is shown in Fig. 36, given in Chapter I of this part, as the type of the stoneflies or Perlidæ. As remarked there, when fluttering with its four long and narrow wings moving in the air it looks quite a large insect, while at rest it resembles nothing more than what is suggested by its two popular names, a *needle*, but of an unduly thickened description. I have on one occasion found a considerable number of these insects in an autopsy of a large grayling killed at

Houghton on the Test. I do not think, however, that it is at all well taken generally on that river. On some north-country streams I am told that an imitation of it is quite a useful pattern. A moderately good imitation is given in " Dry-Fly Entomology," but I think the colouration generally is too orange in hue.

SIALIDÆ

One genus only is comprised among the British Sialidæ and this the well-known

Alder. alder (*Sialis lutaria*) is one of the commonest of insects seen at the river-side from the middle of May to the middle or the latter part of June. There is a second species called *S. fuliginosa*, and McLachlan, writing on it in the " Transactions of the Entomological Society " in 1868, says that these two species (*S. lutaria* and *S. fuliginosa*) can only be distinguished by the presence in the latter species of one transverse nervule in the anterior wings.

Angling writers have so glorified the alder that one is almost compelled to give some space to it, although, as will be seen by the following brief sketch of its life history, it is at no time during its life in the winged stage voluntarily on the water, and therefore is not likely to form an important part of the food of the rising fish. I do not want to exaggerate this statement in any way. If it is by chance blown on to the water and comes down over a feeding fish struggling on the surface, it will of course be taken,

U

but it is only an occasional specimen on the wild or windy day which is so blown *nolens volens* on to the stream.

The female alder when ready to oviposit selects a flat sedge or rush generally **Life history.** overhanging or close to the edge of the stream. She commences methodically from one side to deposit her eggs singly touching one another in a convex line, the

convex side uppermost. If by chance she misses a space she will later deposit an egg out of the usual course to fill up the gap. She always works backwards, crawling over the eggs already deposited and covering them throughout with the wings laid flat in pent-house shape. The eggs in a cluster as laid are shown in Fig. 57, and in Fig. 58 single eggs are shown to a larger magnification. They are of long ovoid shape, and each with a small projection or stem on top, and are arranged in a series of rows on the sedge or rank grass, each female laying about 2000 to 3000.

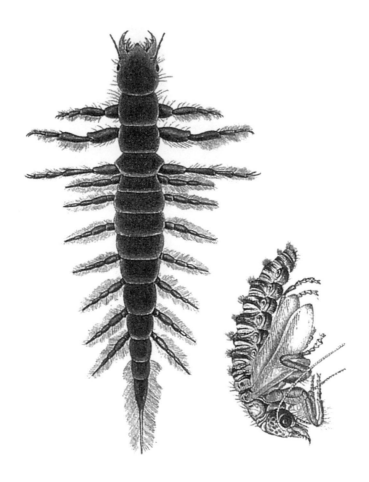

Alder Larva and Pupa
× 5

PLATE XXXIV

Swan Electric Engraving Co. Ltd.

In eight or ten days, the time varying according to temperature, the eggs open near the top end, and a tiny larva creeps out and makes its way as soon as possible to the water. The young larva, which is very similar in form to the full-grown one, dives down and burrows into the mud, where it passes the greater part of its larval existence, living chiefly on small aquatic larvæ, feeding voraciously and growing rapidly, and within less than a year from the date of oviposition is fully grown and ready for the next metamorphosis. The full-grown larva is shown at Plate XXXIV.

It then crawls ashore, digs an oval cavity in the ground at a depth of some six or eight inches, and retires into this for the brief resting stage preparatory to the next change to the pupa. It gradually develops into a soft motionless pupa, also shown in Plate XXXIV. This pupa is curiously curved in the cavity, the head bent down and against the thorax. The tail end of the body is bent downwards and the wing-covers, legs, and antennæ are lying near and parallel to the abdomen. In a few days the pupa within the cavity gradually develops into the winged insect, which breaks through the thin envelope and makes its way to the surface of the ground and flies away.

The outward appearance of the imago is described at page 225 and figured in Fig. 37. This life history I can describe without fear of inaccuracy, having made a long series of observations with my late friend Marryat when rearing the alder in captivity. In the same way I am able to assert as a fact that the duration of the life of the insect from the egg to the imago is approximately one year.

It will be seen from the foregoing life history that at no time during its winged existence has the alder any occasion to be on or near the water. The eggs are laid on the sedge, the baby larva crawls into the water, lives until it is full grown in the mud, and makes its way ashore before pupating. The pupa develops into an imago in the ground, the imago emerges and oviposits on the sedges, rushes, or coarse grass.

In all sincerity no doubt angling writers have for generations averred that they have seen alders in great numbers on the surface of the stream, but evidently they are in error. As before stated, individuals may be forced on to the water by a hurricane or heavy thunderstorm, but these are only rare cases, and brought about by pure accident. Any observer who doubts these assertions can prove or disprove them himself. The next time he thinks he sees great numbers of alders on the water, let him catch, say, twenty specimens in one of the three collecting nets, and I venture to prophesy that at the outside two may possibly be alders and the remaining eighteen will be caddis-flies, and in all human probability he will find these eighteen are all specimens of the welshman's button (*Sericostoma personatum*).

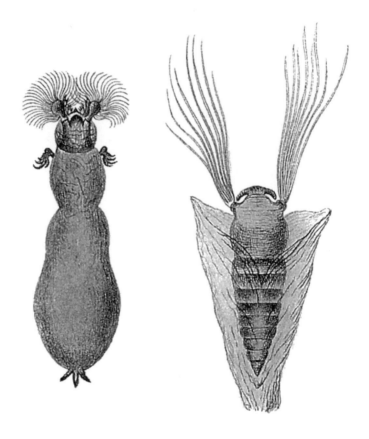

Reed Smut. Larva and Pupa

SMUTS OR CURSES

The smuts or curses (in which the black gnat of the angler is included) are small black or dark brown flies belonging to the great order of the Diptera. I do not propose troubling the reader with much dissertation on the Diptera generally, and as in 1888 the late Mr. G. H. Verrall in "A List of British Diptera" included about 2500 species and foreshadowed further additions, it is perhaps as well if the length of this book is to be kept within any ordinary limits.

Fisherman's curse. The fisherman's curse (a name given nearly half a century ago) is one of the genus *Hilara*, which belongs to the family of the Empidæ. It is believed that the larva is aquatic, and the winged insect is described as being small, and of a grey-black colour, sparsely covered with hairs. Palpi three-jointed, proboscis prominent, antennæ curved upwards. Eyes separated in both sexes, ocelli three, abdomen brown in colour, slender in the male and broad in the female.

Reed smut. Reed smut was a name given by Marryat to the smuts, of which the larvæ and pupæ pass their lives attached to reeds or ribbon weed (*Sparganium ramosum*). In Plate XXXV are shown the larva and pupa, and the insect itself is referred to at page 226 and drawn in Fig. 38.

The name black gnat applied by anglers for many generations to this insect is

Black gnat. a most inaccurate one. The fly is scarcely black, and certainly is not a gnat. It is one of the family *Bibionidæ*, genus *Bibio*, and species *johannis*. The larvæ are cylindrical maggots living underground, feeding on the roots of plants and destroying the vegetation. They are whitish brown in colour, with brown head and two biting mandibles. The pupa is dark brown, of shrivelled appearance, and the wing cases are small. The male black gnat (*Bibio johannis*) is shown in Plate XXXVI. The female is broader and shorter in the body than the male. In the new set of patterns the imitations of them are Nos. 26 and 27, the male and female respectively.

This insect, one of the Chironomidæ, must be described here. In the chapter

Chironomus tentans. on "Dry-Fly on Lochs and Lakes" my friend Sheringham has referred to its abundance in the Blagdon Lake, and also to the fact that it is well taken by the trout there. He submitted specimens to Mr. Mosely, who identified them without much difficulty, and later contributed an excellent article to the "Field" on the subject. This, by the kind permission of the proprietors and editor, I am allowed to reproduce wholly or in part here. I will give copious extracts from it.

"A brief description of an insect, *Chironomus*

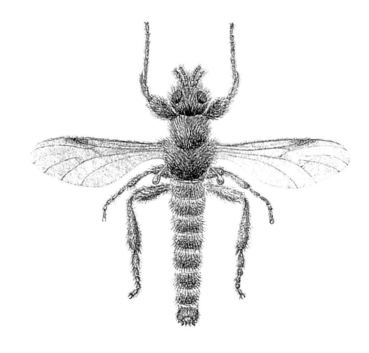

Black Gnat Male.
×8

PLATE XXXVI

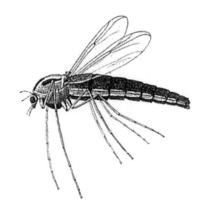

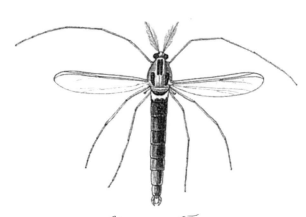

Chironomus Tentans
Male and Female
X 4

PLATE XXXVII

C. C. Knight ad nat del

tentans, which occurs at times in great quantities on many of our lakes and reservoirs, may perhaps be of interest to the angler. When a really good hatch is in progress this fly is taken greedily by the trout, and there ensues a quite phenomenal rise of fish. The actual specimens I am describing were collected at Blagdon Reservoir, but very closely allied species have also been seen and captured on Lake Killarney, Lough Arrow, Loch Leven, and many other still waters."

"*Chironomus tentans* is one of the many harmless midges which are so often confused with gnats or other blood-suckers. It is, however, quite innocent of spears and lancets or any weapons of offence. In the male the colour of the body is a rich deep green-olive, the legs being of a bright green-olive hue. The body is about $\frac{5}{12}$ths of an inch long, and each wing $\frac{1}{4}$-inch, but these measurements vary slightly according to the individual fly selected. The female insect has a body of a much darker colour, deep shagreen verging on brown, and about $\frac{1}{2}$-inch in length, each wing being about $\frac{7}{12}$-inch. The sex is easily distinguished, as the male, in addition to a pair of claspers at the extremity of the abdomen, is furnished with large and feathery antennæ, which form a very striking characteristic of the male members of this family. The female is somewhat larger and clumsier in build, has no claspers, and no specially distinctive antennæ." Plate XXXVII shows the appearance of the insects.

" The larvæ of various species of *Chironomus* are popularly called 'blood-worms' owing to their colour. They frequent muddy ditches, sluggish rivers, lakes, and ponds. Very often they may be seen in water-butts or wooden cattle-troughs. Their food consists of dead leaves or other vegetable refuse, and when the mud is of sufficient depth they make therein a shelter in the form of a nearly vertical tube, with the mouth opening out on to the surface. Miall, in his work on this genus, states that 'If a larva be placed in a saucer with a few bits of dead leaves it will gather them about its body, weaving them together with viscid threads passed out from its mouth. In a quarter of an hour it will be completely concealed by a rude sheath, which is not easily distinguished from the similar objects which lie around."

" In course of time the blood-worm undergoes a metamorphosis, becoming a pupa. The head-end becomes much enlarged, and the swathed wings, limbs, and antennæ of the perfect insect show through the thin skin. Two feathery branchiæ project beyond the head, enabling the pupa to maintain its supply of oxygen as it lies at the bottom of the water with its tail buried in the mud and its head just projecting above the surface. In due course this pupa comes up to the top of the water by means of a series of jerks, splits open its skin, and the perfect fly emerges."

" The female insect, after impregnation, expresses

her eggs gradually in a dark gelatinous string. As the end of this string touches the water it swells up, and the egg mass eventually assumes the form of a cylinder of jelly, the end of which is firmly attached to some fixed object close to the water's edge. The larvæ hatch out within three to six days, and then follows a rapid succession of broods from the beginning of spring to the late autumn, though such larvæ as are alive during the winter continue in the larval and pupal stages until the following spring. An interesting fact concerning the reproduction of species in this genus is noted by Darwin, namely, that pupæ of either sex of certain species of *Chironomus* produce larvæ which finally develop into males and females reproducing their species by depositing eggs in the ordinary manner."

Winged ants. The appearance of winged ants is probably so well known that it is unnecessary to describe them. When they are on the water the fish take them in great numbers, and the pattern in the new series, the brown ant, No. 28, may be tried with fair prospects of success.

Other insects taken by rising trout. Any insect floating down over a feeding fish in position will most probably be taken, and hence, of course, in autopsies a great number of single specimens, or perhaps three or four of a sort, are found in the trout. Perhaps, too, this may account in a degree for the success of some of the awful monstrosities called fancy flies, which are prescribed as infallible because on some happening-day a feeding fish took one and was duly landed.

There are, of course, great differences of opinion on all questions appertaining to the art of the fly-fisherman, and I am the last to wish in any way to exhibit a spirit of intolerance. Every well-considered opinion, every well-thought-out pattern of artificial, every detail of rod or tackle, every worked-out theory of cheating the wind or of casting against it, in fact, every conceivable theory which is the result of study or observation is worth a prolonged series of trials and experiments before adopting or condemning it.

It is, above all, however, necessary for a writer to express his own opinions clearly, openly, and without reserve. I believe that a dry-fly man who is equipped with the rod, tackle, and gear described in a previous part of this book, and with the thirty-three patterns correctly and well dressed in accordance with the details set forth in "Modern Development of the Dry-Fly," is in a position to cope with the shyest and most educated trout of the clearest of chalk-streams if he will read, learn, and inwardly digest the advice given as to how, when, and where he should cast his fly. In some rivers where other insects prevail he may have to make a few (but very few) additions to the number of patterns; but, above all, I must once more recapitulate the dictum

that I have so often uttered, namely, that no fisherman can hope to succeed when using gear or patterns
in which he has no confidence, and as a natural
sequence that the more confidence he feels in his
gear and his patterns of artificial flies, the more likely
he is to rise, hook, and kill his trout under all circumstances and every conceivable condition.

PART III

THE MAKING AND MANAGEMENT OF A FISHERY

CHAPTER I

SELECTION OF A WATER

THE word "selection" seems to point to a choice of one among several waters which are offered to the prospective lessee. Possibly my readers' experience may not tally with my own, but during the last forty years, although it has often been my fate to be looking out for fishing, it has seldom, if ever, fallen to my lot to have an opportunity of selecting from two or more the particular fishery which, from its description, would seem to be the most suitable. Usually a rod on, or possibly a stretch of what may perhaps be styled a second-rate chalk-stream, is offered at what appears to be a very heavy price. As a rule we have to say *Yea* or *Nay* very quickly, and if our answer is in the negative, it is safe to predict that the fishery will be snapped up with little delay by some other ardent votary of the craft.

For the sake of argument let it, however, be conceded that there is a *bona fide* offer at what one does not, at the first glance, consider an absolutely prohibitive rental, and that the refusal is given for a space of time long enough to enable one at least to consider and possibly inspect the water. If it should be a length of one of the well-known Hampshire rivers, like the Test or Itchen, it is well to settle and take it at once, even if it does not seem to have yielded very good sport in the immediate past, provided the tenure is for a fairly long term of years, and there are no very inconvenient restrictions in the conditions of tenancy.

One of the most objectionable conditions which the lessor loves to introduce **Reservation of rod by** is the reservation of a rod, **lessor.** either for himself personally or for any friend staying with him or delegated to use it for a day or longer time. The agent will, in all probability, strive to minimize the importance of this reservation by volunteering the information that his principal does not often fish, and is not keen on giving his friends leave. The fishery has probably been neglected for years, weeds cut anyhow or not at all, banks rotten and overgrown with rank rushes and sedges, and in some cases filling up a considerable portion of what ought to be the stream with a tangle of coarse vegetation. Very possibly, too, the river teems with pike, perch, roach, dace, chub, and other coarse fish. Under these conditions the proprietor neither cares to fish often, nor do his friends even take the trouble to ask for leave.

Wait a couple of years and see what happens when the tenant has at great expense improved the water, trimmed the banks, cut the weeds systematically, killed down the pike and other vermin, and last, but not least, introduced a considerable number of trout,

many of which are by this time sizable. The sport
is then so good that the freeholder is either out himself or represented by a friend on nearly every favourable day during the season.   If the prospective tenant
finds that it is imperative for him either to make some
concession as to the lessor's right of fishing, or to lose
the chance of securing a desirable piece of water, he
should in his negotiations stipulate that there must be
some limitation of this right.   If he can do so it is a
good plan to agree that the landlord's right is to be a
strictly personal one, and whether it is strictly personal,
or can be used by a friend either staying at the house
or delegated by the lessor, it is wise to have it stated
in the agreement of tenancy that the landlord's fishing
right cannot be exercised for more than a limited
number of days in any one season, and that no two
of these days should be in the same week.

When considering whether it is worth his while
to enter into negotiations in
Reputation of the respect to a fishery, the pro-
river. spective tenant should as a preliminary devote himself to ob-
taining reliable information in respect to the reputation of the river, and particularly as to the stretch
offered, or other stretches in its immediate vicinity.
If the stream is considered a *dour* one, in which trout
do not take surface food well, he had better at once
decide not to entertain the offer.   If he allows himself to
be persuaded that by introducing a good stock of sizable
fish he will revolutionize the character of the trout

x

in the stream, he is courting disaster. On this point I can speak feelingly. Four of us took a twenty-one-year lease of some miles of fishing on a river in which the trout were said only to rise well during the mayfly. We killed down pike and coarse fish in great numbers, stocked with the very best two-year-olds we could grow in a stew, and after great expenditure and four years of disappointment we were glad to surrender our lease and seek our sport elsewhere.

Where possible, too, it is well to find out what is the reputation of the particular length of the river offered. There are stretches even on the very best of south-country chalk-streams, on which the fish seldom take surface food, and these fisheries are of little or no value to the dry-fly man who is a purist and does not affect the methods of the wet-fly man.

I can give an example of a length of something short of one and a-half miles of a first-class chalk-stream of which I have heard some particulars from time to time since it was offered to me more than a quarter of a century ago. I did not entertain it then because I did not care to go to the expense of making a water which had been neglected for many years, and would not, in my opinion, ever be anything better than third-rate. The greater part of this fishery is deep and sluggish, affording congenial quarters for numbers of large and small pike and other coarse fish, while the trout are generally large in average size, but very few in numbers.

Since then very little improvement has been attempted until within the last few years, but it has been let generally for single seasons at rents varying from the original figure asked twenty-five years ago to as much as five or six times this amount. Latterly, as the result of the policy referred to in a later chapter of this part of the book on "Stocking," a number of the degenerate, stew-fed, overgrown, unhealthy trout have been introduced. A few more fish have since been landed each season, but it can hardly be considered as sport by the dry-fly man to rise and hook these with any fly, to tow them into the landing-net and to find them repulsive, loathsome, lanky, black specimens, unfit for the table, long enough to weigh 3 lb., but registering on the spring-balance perhaps no more than $1\frac{1}{4}$ to $1\frac{1}{2}$ lb.

The prudent man, before taking a piece of water, should make a careful and prolonged inspection of it himself.

Character of water.

The ideal stretch of a chalk-stream contains both deep and shallow parts, swift runs and quiet deep reaches. The shallows ought to be of a nature to enable the trout to spawn. If the inspection takes place in January or February the presence of spawning fish will be most evident, and later than this, even well into the spring, an observant man will detect the heaps of clean gravel or *redds* where the ova have been deposited by the trout during the spawning season. If there are salmon in the river, their redds too will be visible, and except for their generally greater size they are very similar in character and appearance to those of the trout.

The presence of salmon in a trout-stream is to be deplored. It sounds in some **Salmon in a trout-** ways curious, but I am firmly **stream.** convinced that the extermination of every salmon in a Hampshire chalk-stream would be of incalculable advantage. Conversely, the interests of every preserver of salmon would be served by the removal of every trout from the river in which his work of preservation is being carried on. Each disturbs the other on the redds, and the trout certainly devour when they can get them the fertilized or non-fertilized eggs of the salmon. The opposition of all the Test and Itchen trout fishermen to the suggested inclusion of a large part of these streams in the Avon and Stour Conservancy was due to an intimate knowledge on their part of the impossibility of preserving both efficiently.

The best of the chalk-streams always contain a luxuriant growth of weeds of **Weeds.** the kinds in which the food of the trout and grayling delights to live. When inspecting a water special attention should be paid to this point. Water celery (*Apium inundatum*), water crowfoot (*Ranunculus aquatilis*), and starwort (*Callitriche vernus* or *C. autumnalis*) are the forms of weed in which the nymphs of the small Ephemeridæ, the caddis, or larvæ of the Trichoptera, as well as crustaceans, such as *Gammarus pulex*, the fresh-water shrimp, and various mollusks, such as snails, are most abundant. The ribbon-weed (*Sparganium ramosum*) is generally covered with great numbers of larvæ and pupæ of *Simulium* and other smuts.

Many other aquatic plants may be found, such as the so-called American weed (*Elodea canadense*), the various water-lilies, hornwort (*Ceratophyllum demersum*), which is commonly called squirrel's tail, but the majority of these do not contain any great quantity of the various forms of subaqueous animal life on which the trout and grayling subsist.   One of the water-mosses (*Fontinalis antipyretica*) establishes itself on boulders in rapid parts of some chalk-streams.   It harbours a considerable number of fresh-water shrimps and insect larvæ, but trout generally do not care to lie on it, so that it is often desirable, although expensive, to remove it forcibly.

Some quantity of mud will always be found in comparatively still and deep

Mud.   reaches, but the foul, black foetid sort which is the ultimate product of the decomposition of vegetable matter (usually more or less polluted by sewage), beyond holding a few water woodlice (*Asellus*), blood-worms, which are the larvæ of *Chironomus*, water-bugs, such as *Corixæ*, and alder larvæ (*Sialis lutaria*), is not of much use in respect to harbouring food for the fish. The pale-coloured, sandy, gritty mud found in parts of the chalk-streams is the home of the mayfly nymphs, and an examination of it will generally convey some idea of the quantity of mayfly to be expected. It should be remembered that the colder the weather the deeper down the nymphs of the *Ephemera* will burrow, and hence to find them in cold weather the digging down may well be a heavy and laborious process.

Food supply generally in a fishery is, as before mentioned, chiefly dependent on the presence of the weeds in which the best forms of food for the fish are found. The most important for the dry-fly man are the duns and spinners (*Ephemeridæ*) at the nymphal stage and the caddis or larvæ of the *Trichoptera*. I class these as the most important, because when in their winged states they are more or less on the top of the water, and are, in fact, the inducement to the trout to come to the surface and feed there. It must not, however, be forgotten that in poor Marryat's own terse words, "while floating food is *caviare*, sunk or mid-water food is *beef* to the fish." Hence when engaged in his examination of the weeds and the animal life contained therein the fisherman should remember that he can only expect well-fed, good-conditioned, healthy and consequently game trout in a river which contains a bountiful supply of crustaceans, such as fresh-water shrimps, and mollusks, such as snails of the genera *Limnæa*, *Planorbis*, etc. etc. The presence of the crayfish (*Astacus fluviatilis*) may also be hailed as of good omen as indicating at

Food supply.

once comparative purity of the water and a welcome source of food for the fish in it.

It is well to ascertain at the preliminary stage what extent of fishing the lessor **Extent of the fishery.** claims to own. In reference to this branch of the subject it must be noted that agents often measure both banks, so that the right of fishing from both sides of half a mile of the stream is described as one mile of fishing. I do not suggest that this is a misrepresentation, but I would respectfully urge that it is a most misleading method of measurement. When the land owned by the lessor includes a number of carriers and irrigation channels the combined lengths of all these carriers and channels are by some included in the total length of water offered. This may be a fair estimate of the length of the fishery in cases where the flow of water through these carriers is fairly constant, but where, as well may happen, many of these are dried up during a good part of the season they can scarcely be described as fishing water. In a water-meadow country the lessee should, if he can, ascertain not only which of the carriers are constant in their flow, but also what are the water rights. Neglect of this preliminary information may land him in considerable expense to compensate tenants for waiving their rights to water for irrigation purposes, or the alternative of finding his fishing considerably curtailed by the diversion of the stream during the best of the fishing season.

Millers' rights are at times very prejudicial to those
of the fisherman, and millers,
Millers' rights. as a class, are rather prone to
claim more than their strictly
legal rights. In the absence of any specific grant, a
miller is entitled to the natural free and unimpeded
flow of the stream, and may cut himself or require
to be cut for his convenience any weeds which create
an obstruction to such flow. If a tenant finds himself
likely to be landed in a difficulty on such a point,
he must do all in his power to settle the question
amicably. Lawsuits are proverbially expensive, and
the result even of a successful lawsuit is apt to be
unsatisfactory. Then, too, to get at loggerheads with
a local miller or a local farmer or your landlord and
his agent, or even with the humblest of farm labourers
on the estate, often lowers the fishing tenant in the
estimation of the locals generally, and brands him
as a cantankerous and undesirable addition to the
amenities of the district. When once he is locally
considered in this light it is safe to predict that his
life at the river-side will not be a happy one, and
somehow the fishing will not turn out as good or
as pleasant as it should. The motto of a sensible fishing tenant in dealing with his neighbours
should be *suaviter in modo sed fortiter in re*,
by which I mean that, except for the strongest
reasons and in reference to the most serious in-
fringements of his rights, he must try to smooth
over difficulties. If perchance he is forced to show

fight it must be a case of *war to the knife* and no quarter.

If the water has been let before, it is always well to communicate with the pre-
Advice to communicate with previous tenant. vious tenant and obtain from him all available information in reference to his sport, the average size of the trout, their condition, and any other particulars of the fishery. It is better, if possible, to have a personal interview, because we are all prone to being careful and even reticent when reducing our opinions to writing. At the same time the intending lessee should learn what he can as to the accessibility of the water, the accommodation to be obtained, and if he has any idea of letting his wife and children spend part of their holidays with him at the river-side, he must ascertain whether it is a healthy and bracing place. Many of the valleys through which our chalk-streams flow are very re-laxing and quite unfit for children who require good and bracing air.

Many landowners object to letting their fishing for a term of years, and insist
Tenure. on the agreement being one from year to year. Their view of the question is that when once the tenant has a lease the control of the water passes out of their hands, and to some extent one can sympathize with them. Cases are not infrequent of so-called sports-men taking a fishery on lease and proceeding to let

a number of rods for the season or sometimes even for single days. The meadows are then overrun with fishermen, the tenants' grass is trodden down, the banks are injured, the fishermen do not always confine themselves to the fly or dry-fly, and undersized fish are killed.

I quite advocate a freeholder protecting himself on these points by laying down stringent conditions as to the number of rods on the water, the limit of size, the necessity for the fishing being pursued in a sportsmanlike manner, the seasons during which the tenant and his friends may fish, etc. etc. The lessor must remember, however, that with an agreement requiring renewal from year to year a tenant cannot afford to make permanent improvements in the fishery nor to stock properly with the view of ensuring good sport in years to come. If the lessee goes to heavy expense in reference to these and similar matters he runs a great risk of finding his rent raised in subsequent seasons.

For myself, I should not care to embark on the venture of making a fishery with a tenure of less than seven years, and even then I believe the landlord would find his property greatly enhanced in value at the termination of the lease. The ideal tenure for a true sportsman is a lease of twenty-one years, terminable at the tenant's option by giving six months' notice to determine at the end of the seventh or fourteenth year. It is even worth while for the sake of obtaining a longer lease to offer a small increase in the rent payable during the second and third terms of seven years.

Before finally entering into a contract the lessee must satisfy himself that he has **Form of agreement.** a right of access to the water and a right-of-way along the banks. It is well to stipulate that rates and taxes should be paid by the landlord, who should also keep the banks, planks, hatches, etc., in proper repair. A formal agreement should be drawn up by the lessor's solicitors and submitted for approval to the lessee's solicitors. The last chapter of " Fishing" in the "Country Life Library of Sport," written by Mr. G Willis Bund, should be carefully read, and the parts referring to angling agreements require close study on the part of anyone intending to take a lease of dry-fly water.

It is clearly and correctly laid down by Mr. Willis Bund that a right of fishing being an incorporeal hereditament can only be conveyed by deed under seal and not under an agreement by hand. It is well for the tenant to see that his lease or agreement is drafted in accordance with this legal maxim. It was, however, pointed out to me by an eminent Chancery barrister that in an agreement under hand, purporting to convey a right of fishing, a clause could be inserted stating that, if required by either party to the agreement, a proper lease must be drawn and executed by both parties. He told me that in equity such a clause would be held to compel either the landlord or tenant to execute a binding lease under seal.

The following statement of the desirable covenants of both lessee and lessor was **Lessees' and lessors'** given in " Making a Fishery," **covenants in a lease.** and as it was carefully considered by my late friend Basil Field, whose knowledge and experience of the law on the subject were very great, I feel I cannot do better than repeat it here :—

"After naming the parties to the lease it should specify whether the sole and exclusive right of fishing is let, and whether the taking of eels is also included. The name of the river should be given, and it should be stated that the right extends to carriers and ditches, and reference should be made to a plan to be a portion of the lease. As before remarked, it is desirable that this plan should be one of the Ordnance maps. The numbers of the plots (as on the Ordnance map) over which the fishing extends should be enumerated, and it should be stated that all the lessor's rights of fishing on the property are included, excepting such as are specially excepted in subsequent clauses."

" It should set forth that the lessee has the right to cut weeds, clear away mud or soil and deposit them on the banks, and generally do any work deemed desirable for the improvement of the fishery ; and it should further recite description or position of any house or keepers' cottages covered by the lease, any right-of-way required by the lessee to gain access to any portion of the fishing, the term for which, and the date from which the right is let, the amount of rent, and how payable. The rights, if any, excepted or reserved for the lessor on any portion of the river over which the lessee should not have the right of fishing should be detailed, as well as the right of the lessor, or his servants to enter for the purpose of repairing banks, cutting down or planting trees or bushes, or to raise or lower the level of the water to enable him to carry out any work required in the interests of the property."

"The lessee's covenants should follow: To pay rent, keep a good stock of fish, and leave the same at the expiration of tenancy, to keep houses or cottages in repair (if this is one of the lessee's obligations), to cut and clear away weeds, to make good any damage occurring to other tenants' land by negligence or wilful act on the part of the lessee or his keepers, and not to underlet or assign without assent of lessor, such assent not to be withheld without just and reasonable cause. The lessee should undertake to provide keeper or keepers, to prevent poaching, to fish in a fair and sportsmanlike manner with rod and line only (except in the case of pike, eels, or other coarse fish), to make proper rules for the regulation of the fishery, such rules to be applicable to himself and his friends, and to specify any limits of size or number of Salmonidæ to be killed in one day as well as the seasons during which they can be taken."

"The lessor's covenants should set forth that he

should pay all rates. This is a moot point and one that sometimes leads to long discussion. It is, however, desirable that the rent should be fixed at a figure sufficiently high to warrant the lessor in doing so. If the lessee has to pay rates the local authorities are prone to assess the sporting rights at an excessive sum, as they argue that the London gentlemen coming down there to fish should be made to contribute liberally towards the rates. If the rates are paid by the landlord they do not seem to realize that they are included in the rent, and are apt to consider that their own neighbour, as lord of the manor, should not be bled as freely as a stranger. There are other reasons, such as the liability to be summoned on juries, etc., why the tenant should, if possible, try and be exempt from assessment."

"The lessor must undertake to lower and regulate the water-level as required by the lessee for the purpose of weed-cutting and netting. This is necessary, because the regulation of hatches in such cases is usually in the discretion of the millers and farmers. They may or may not be on good terms with the fishing tenant. If he is a man of sense and judgment he will do all in his power to be friendly with them ; but occasionally there are millers and farmers who resent the intrusion of any so-called stranger, and who might refuse to raise or lower hatches, and thus effectually prevent the tenant from carrying out his obligations to cut and remove weeds, net, etc."

"The lessor should further undertake to keep in repair all banks, hatches, sluices, carriers, and this is not unreasonable, seeing that he has already either agreed with his farmer and miller tenants to do so or has contracted himself to effect these repairs for them. He should also be required to abstain on behalf of himself, his agents or tenants, from boating on the water or from any act which would tend to prejudicially affect the fishing rights he has let."

"The usual lessor's covenants should follow as to peaceable possession so long as the rent is paid and the conditions of the lease duly observed, with the usual provisos as to recovery of rent and re-entry if necessary."

CHAPTER II

GENERAL MANAGEMENT

THIS chapter is intended to cover more ground than would be conveyed in the ordinary course to the reader by the term *management*. The work of making and improving a fishery is so intimately connected with the general management that I think it should be described here in general terms, and the details of such special work as weeds, weed-cutting, dealing with poachers and other enemies of the trout, and the all-important question of stocking should be treated under their respective headings.

Making a fishery in the sense of starting with a **Making a fishery.** length of a suitable stream in which there are few or no trout or other Salmonidæ has been seldom attempted. It would, I think, be a most fascinating undertaking. If only one could find a stretch in a promising river and begin at the very beginning by introducing the weeds and the insects, crustaceans, etc., which would serve as food for the trout, stocking with eyed ova, alevins, or healthy yearlings raised from a good strain of wild fish, it would be a most interesting experiment for a young man who could afford to wait patiently for the results.

Most of us are, however, too old to be able to regard with equanimity the prospect of watching the growth and development of the fish and their food supply for, say, three or four years before attempting to cast a fly or kill a trout.   Hence we must be content to make our fishery only in the sense of assisting nature, taking the stream as it is and devoting all our best attention to the necessary operations of making improvements by stimulating the production of the food supply, introducing new stock and waging war on pike, coarse fish, and all the other creatures which prey on the young or adult trout.

When a length of water is leased by a number of rods one of the fishermen **Supervision.** should be selected to take the general management.   I would suggest that if the other rods on the water are desirous of having good sport and at the same time keeping on friendly terms with the one designated to supervise the fishery they must be prepared to defer to his judgment, especially in matters of detail, and the less they interfere with him the more agreeably will the joint occupation and sport proceed.   He himself must not be too autocratic, and should as far as he can consult the men fishing with him even on matters of detail—needless to say, on larger questions of policy, expense, etc.   If he is fit for the work he will get his friends together on convenient occasions, and while making his own suggestions must listen and be guided by the voice of the majority.   Provided all

Y

the fishermen are sportsmen, unselfish, and companionable, the arrangements are likely to work smoothly and amicably, but the presence of a greedy fisherman or a pot-hunter will infallibly tend to break up the pleasant *coterie*.

Proper accounts must be kept; where practicable it is a wise plan to open a separate banking account for the fishery, and it is generally a convenience to arrange that all cheques should be signed by the manager and one other member. At the end of each year detailed statements and analysis of receipts and expenditure should be prepared and submitted to the members at an annual meeting, where, too, some kind of a report of the sport, etc., should also be rendered.

Keeping accounts.

Personally, I think it most important to have correct records for each season of the number and weights of fish killed, the number returned, the results of wiring, netting, or trimmering for pike and any other particulars available. Some of my friends do not agree with me in this, and are loth to keep their own diaries, from which the general records must be compiled.

The first step to be taken when once the fishery lease is completed is to find one or more competent keepers. If one cannot hear of a suitable man seeking a situation the only available plan is to advertise. The answers to an announcement of this

Keepers.

kind are not generally numerous, and a goodly proportion of these answers are usually from men who
have neither knowledge nor experience of the work.
Men trained as gamekeepers are as a rule quite useless.   The fact that in addition to looking after the
pheasants, the man in his previous place had to watch
and preserve a salmon pool or some length of a brook
containing trout of the average herring size is no recommendation.   An honest, sober, hard-working, intelligent man who starts with the intention of devoting
himself to the fishery will generally in a few years
gain enough information and experience to be quite a
good keeper.   If one has the good luck to find a suitable man or to train one who can learn, he must be
paid liberal wages and have a comfortable cottage
near the stream.   Obviously such a keeper must be
treated with courtesy and consideration, and every
effort should be used to retain his services as long as
possible.

If two are required, the under-keeper should be
under the control of the head-keeper, and all orders
should be issued to the head-keeper, who should communicate them to the under-keeper.   A thoroughly
reliable head-keeper should receive his own and the
under-keeper's wages, handing over to the under-
keeper the amount due to him each week.

During the fishing season, while the fishermen are
at the river-side, the keeper is very much in evidence ;
but in the early autumn, when the trout fishing is
over, the anglers who do not care for grayling fishing

generally bid farewell to the keeper, and do not as a rule revisit the water before **Keepers' work in autumn and winter.** the following spring. Anglers should know that their sport in the coming season is largely dependent on the quantity and quality of the work done by the keepers during the short days of the fall and winter. Here and there are to be found keepers who can be relied upon to work with the same zeal and the same intelligence in their master's absence as in his presence, but such keepers are unfortunately the exceptions which go to prove the rule.

With every desire to do his duty, it is, after all, only human nature for the keeper to be depressed by the lonely life on the river-banks and to be attracted from his monotonous work by the congenial society of his fellow-men in the nearest village inn. When once he has acquired the habit of frequenting the tap-room the seeds of intemperance are only too likely to be sown, with the inevitable result of undermining his constitution and eventually causing him to lose his situation and become a loafer or worse, perhaps even a poacher. Without any desire to palliate the offence, it is yet a moot point whether the employer is not often in a great degree to blame for the degeneration of his *employé*. A sportsman who is really interested in the work of maintaining and improving the stream he fishes would certainly not be bored if he made it a rule to spend one day in each month of the close time at the river-side with his keeper. Such a course might not commend itself to the pot-hunter or to the fisherman desirous of establishing records in the number or size of the trout and grayling he kills.

The task of getting the water into the most favourable condition for the natural **Preparation for the** reproduction of the trout on **spawning season.** the spawning-beds should be started as soon as the fishing season is over. Generally even where continuous warfare has been waged on the pike it is necessary to net the water during the autumn. This work will be described in detail in a subsequent chapter. For successful netting the weeds must be cut ruthlessly ; the chain scythes worked up and down the stream will clear the middle of the river, while the hand scythes are used to cut the sides clear of weeds and rushes on the bank. Harrowing is sometimes recommended, but although it is a most efficient means of clearing the river-bed, especially where thick mud-beds accumulate, it requires to be undertaken with some caution and consideration. It is apt to tear out the roots of the weeds, and for quite two years after its use the absence of subaqueous vegetation will often cause the migration of the trout to other parts of the stream. When the work is done by the scythes, many of the roots are untouched, and the weeds will make vigorous and healthy growth in the next spring, and provide the shelter so necessary for the fish in the hot weather.

Spawning shallows cannot be too clean. In addition to the severe weed-cutting **Spawning shallows.** they should be well raked over to remove any vestige of mud, and leave the gravel clean and bright. A fairly heavy iron rake, worked easily or forcibly according to the depth of the water, should be used for this purpose, and some care is required to avoid tearing up the roots of water celery, water crowfoot, and other weeds which are the home of the nymphs and larvæ of the water-bred insects and of the crustaceans and mollusks, so necessary to get fish into condition. Wherever there is a ford which is frequented by the cattle and horses walking in and feeding on any weeds growing there the gravel will always be hard and bright. The fisherman may object to the disturbance caused by the traffic, but he must remember that these fords are ideal shallows for fry and yearlings, and as a rule, too, are natural spawning-beds.

On this subject Mr. Corrie is of opinion that he can point to many fords on the Itchen, all of which attract large numbers of good fish, and adds that he can instance cases where the number and condition of the trout have rapidly deteriorated when the river crossings were abolished. He says, too, that he hardly knows of a ford in a moderately well-stocked water open to light farm traffic (milk-cart traffic for choice) where an extra fine class of trout is not present on the ford or in its immediate vicinity.

Although, as remarked in a previous chapter, it should be the business of the **Repairs to banks, etc.** lessor to keep in repair banks, stiles, planks, etc., it is not a good policy to worry him or his agent about every little blow-hole in the bank or other minor matters. During the winter months a really good keeper can frequently find time to look after such points as these. Generally the estate will be willing to provide any planks, piles, chalk, or other material required, and the keeper can do part of the work himself, or, better still, give an occasional week's work to any unemployed labourers, selecting the most respectable and sober ones. I take it, too, that finding such work locally is a far better form of charity than distributing alms, and thus tending to pauperize men who are willing to work when they can find work to do.

Permanent improvements should as a rule be undertaken in the close season. **Improvements to the fishery.** One of the most important is the removal of mud, which always accumulates in the deeper and slower reaches. A great cause of the thick mud-beds in some parts is that our neighbours often neglect the proper cutting of the weeds. Another fertile source of this trouble is that a plan has been advocated of cutting down each bank and leaving a forest of vegetable growth in the middle of the river. This vegetation dies down, decomposes, and the ultimate residue of decomposed vegetation in the water is mud, generally black or dark in colour, fœtid, and foul-smelling. This treatment is the worst possible one for any fishery, and wherever it is indulged in the trout are certain to be scarce. All the stocking in the world will not cure this, because well-fed healthy trout will not remain in such water, but migrate to more favourable stretches above or below.

Some of the accumulations of mud are caused by the wilful act of those who ought to know that it is at once illegal and unsportsmanlike. They are, however, persuaded by keepers, and in some cases even by so-called experts, to rake up the mud and let it flow down to the next fishery. The unfortunate tenant of the water below may stir it up and send it down, increased in volume by his own accumulations, to another length below, and thus in his turn commit an illegal and an unsportsmanlike act. There is only one right and proper method to deal with heavy mud-banks, and that is to remove as much as possible by panning it out and distributing it on the bank. It serves too to help in the upkeep of the banks, because they always tend to sink in level, and the deposition of the mud is a means of restoring them to their proper height above the surface of the stream. Even with the greatest care some of this mud is driven down to one's neighbours, who will soon complain if the volume of it is to their minds unreasonably great.

For shifting mud from one part to another part of the same fishery the use of hurdles is recommended. With a few piles and hurdles a temporary obstruction can be constructed across the river. By removing one or two hurdles at the part where the mud is too thick the force of the current will dash through the opening and wash the mud down. This plan works very well on some shallows, but when the mud has been driven into slow, deep water below it must be panned out and laid on the bank. Hurdles, too, are useful to make up banks when they are very rotten. The hurdles are laid flat and pegged down in place, chalk or mud is spread over them, and over this again it is well to lay some rough turf, thus making a fairly good path where before it may have been impossible to get along the side of the river. A hurdle fixed in the stream in deep water will in some cases deflect the flow, and leave a quiet place in which a large trout is certain to take up its position. Sometimes, too, a judiciously placed hurdle will enable a keeper to set a trimmer in a place where without it the stream would be too strong for the live bait to work about, and thus attract the attention of any pike in the vicinity.

Use of hurdles.

There are often parts of a fishery which have every appearance of being most favourable for large trout, yet in some of them the number, even in a well-stocked stream, is quite in-

Weirs.

significant, and in others, although the fish are present, they do not seem to rise or take well. In the water I have rented for some years there is a stretch which is so emblematic of this, and which has been so greatly improved by the work carried out there, that I am tempted to describe it in some detail.

Below the footbridge shown in Plate X the stream runs at a great pace for about 150 yards, and when I first fished the water we seldom saw a trout rising in it. At first the theory was promulgated that this particular stretch for some reason did not contain a large head of trout, but one day, when the water was abnormally low, I made a very careful and prolonged inspection of it. It was somewhat surprising to see a very large number of trout, some of quite heavy weight, lying in this part. After some consideration and consultation the keeper, Mr. E. Valentine Corrie and I arrived at the conclusion that if somewhere near the lower end a rough weir were constructed, it would steady the flow of water from the footbridge to the weir, and probably the trout would rise in this comparatively steady length. The water flowing over the weir would certainly make a deepish hole below into which the turbulent stream would empty itself, and thus make a weir pool which might or might not be a favourable place for the dry-fly.

A place where the water was shallow having been selected, the next point to consider was the least expensive method of building up an efficient weir. It is probably known to some of my readers that for many years past the Thames Conservancy have effected repairs to parts of the river where the banks and towpath are likely to be injured by the wash of the numerous launches and motor-boats by means of rough walls constructed with bags of dry concrete deposited *in situ.* The water sets the concrete until it is as solid as a rock, and in time the canvas of the bags rots away. As these bags are simply laid in place dry, they at once adapt themselves to the contour of the land on which they are placed, and if the lowest tiers are arranged, say, with three bags side by side, the next tier with two, and the next with one, a solid wall is made which will withstand the action of water for many years.

Every local adviser warned me that to try to build a weir after this plan would end in failure, and I was told on all sides that the first winter flood would wash it away. The weir was constructed nearly seven years ago and to-day it is stronger than ever. Probably it will outlast the lives of every one of us who assisted in the work. The expense was infinitesimally small—a few sacks of good Portland cement, a few loads of clean, sharp gravel, and a few old sacks and sugar-bags.

The concrete was mixed in the proportion of three parts of gravel to one of cement. I am told by competent engineers that a very much smaller proportion of cement is required if only it is fresh and of the very best quality, but I think that in a remote Hampshire village one is not certain to get really good cement, and hence I would advise it being mixed in these proportions.

Sack after sack was filled with the concrete, the mouth of each securely tied up, the sacks were laid diagonally across the stream one at a time, and the structure raised until at a level where the stream at its usual summer height was about six inches above the topmost tier of bags of concrete. By the same evening the concrete had set, and the next morning I had the gratification of walking across the stream on the bags, and found everything firmly set. If I were to try to give some idea of the number of trout, large and small, landed on that length during the last six years I should probably be accused of the angler's proverbial deviation from the strict truth.

It will be noted that on the plan of a shallow, given in Plate X, there are a **Piles on shallows** number of piles placed in different positions. This piling of a shallow is a most important part of the work of maintaining and improving a fishery. The piles serve a number of purposes, each of which is of the greatest benefit to the sport. The first and perhaps most obvious service rendered by the presence of piles is that it makes the work of anything like systematic netting very difficult and especially at night, and it is invariably after dark that the poachers pay their visits to the river. Of course they are at the same time impediments which interfere with the netting of the shallows for pike. It is well to draw the piles early in the morning before commencing the netting, and to replace them as soon as the day's netting is finished. I know of a shallow on the Test which was studded with great numbers of piles. The lessee, wishing to net for coarse fish, had them removed, and arranged to have them replaced the following day. The poachers, who were evidently aware of this, took the opportunity of sweeping this shallow down with silk nets during the night, and the lessee found it bare of fish the next morning.

Piles on a shallow serve another purpose which is an invaluable aid to fishery management. Wherever a pile is driven the cut weeds hang up and the masses of floating vegetation form most effectual hides for the trout, besides diverting the current and making a slack place immediately below the pile. What with the shelter from the sun's rays given by the weed masses and the quiet water just below them, it is safe to predict that there will be at least one large trout lying under each mass of weeds and rising at the flies floating down slowly in the slack water. Another favourite position for a big fish is just ahead of the pile, with its tail almost touching the pile itself.

Then, too, consider for a moment the effect of the diversion of the current caused by the weeds in contact with the pile. The flow of water is forced downwards, and will in a few weeks wash out even the roots of the weeds and leave a bare, clear gravel patch. The favourite position for a rising trout is over a clear gravel patch among the weeds, and any number of these favourable feeding-places can be made by occasionally shifting the piles. Of course, a hooked fish will at times hang up the line by getting round the pile, and thus break the gut or work out the hold of the hook. Surely, however, it is worth while for a true sportsman to run the risk of losing an odd fish here and there when, by running this risk, he is producing a great number of places where he can be quite sure of finding a feeding fish whenever there is a good hatch of fly.

Pollution. An incalculable amount of injury to all trout-streams is wrought by pollution of various kinds. No doubt under the Rivers Pollution Act this is quite illegal, but the law must be set in action by the County Council, Rural Council, or other public body, and from their general constitution these bodies are not likely to go out of their way to take action which will entail expense on the rate-payers.

Sewage is fatal to the ova, alevins, and young trout generally, but many of the largest and apparently best-conditioned trout are found in parts of streams where the crude sewage of villages and small towns flows directly into the river. Chemicals and so-called disinfectants are frequently used to counteract the fœtid odour and generally disguise the presence of fœcal matter. These disinfectants are generally poisonous and kill the fish, and this notwithstanding the blatant advertisements of their harmless character.

To turn into a stream any waste products is so easy and so inexpensive a method of dealing with them that the volume of pollution in most of our streams is far larger than any of us realize. A steam laundry is established on the bank of a river, and as a matter of course when once the chemicals have done their cleansing work they are sent into the stream and disappear. A mill for preparing hides or tanning leather requires a flow of water to remove the superfluous chemicals, and as a matter of course these chemicals go into the stream. A garage on the banks of the stream will in all human probability be the means of adding the accumulations of the foul lubricating fluid and oils, etc., used in cleaning the machinery to the pollution of the river. Fear of detection by the authorities will in many cases impel the offending parties to take advantage of the hours of darkness to carry out their nefarious practices.

Road-tarring. The general practice of treating the surface of main roads with various tar products is one which has done so much to allay the intolerable dust nuisance caused by the great increase of motor traffic that no efforts of fishermen or others interested in sport can hope to do anything to prevent it or delay its further use. It is, however, not unreasonable to hope that local authorities generally will adopt such tar products as will do the least possible harm to the trout and other fish in the streams.

Mr. Corrie, who has had great experience in investigating and reporting on cases of fish poisoning, alleged to be caused by the light oils in the tar being carried down into the rivers by rain or street washings, writes me as follows :—

" I have no doubt that the great rush of flood water which at or near Winchester drained into the Itchen was responsible for the destruction of nearly all the fish (trout, grayling, pike, eels and smaller fry) from Winchester down to, and half a mile below, Twyford. I do not say that the poisonous matter washed into the river was only tar products, for I have a suspicion that motor oils, etc., may help to form a very evil slimy sediment and liquor when the waterproofing of the surface of the road caused by tar allows nothing objectionable to soak away. All pollution is swept away to the lower levels almost as it might be off the slated roof of a house."

" In the Darenth (Sevenoaks district) some fifteen miles of trout-water was completely poisoned when flood-water off tarred roads swept into that stream. Even the weeds were killed, and the trout, when dead, had precisely the same appearance as our Itchen fish below Winchester. Fishery owners and lessees might approach the road authorities with advantage to persuade them to construct filtration beds at dangerous points."

Successful fishery management may, in fact, be summed up as an intelligent appreciation of a few leading points which must ever be kept prominently before the minds of both master or manager and keepers. Over and above the points previously referred to in this chapter, the general features of the work to be done may be classified under three headings: (1) Keeping down the enemies of the trout, (2) the cultivation of suitable weeds in the river, and (3) stocking. These questions will be treated in full detail in the three subsequent chapters of this book.

Whether the fishery is leased by an angler for his own and his friends' sport, or **Rules and regulations.** whether it is fished by a number of men as a club or subscription water, it is necessary to have a set of rules properly drawn up. Preferably these rules should be printed on cards issued to friends or to each member of a club or subscription water, as it is not fair on any sportsman to leave him in doubt as to what the practice is on the water he is fishing.

I do not suggest a cut-and-dried formula, because conditions are not identical on all rivers or even all parts of the same river, and everyone has his own ideas of the ethics of the sport. I, therefore, propose setting out the points to be considered, and what, from my own experience of the Test, Itchen, and other south-country chalk-streams, should be the provisos applicable to each branch of the subject.

z

The first point to deal with is the dates at which the season should commence

Season. and finish. My own idea is that for trout the season should commence on the 1st of April and terminate, say, on the 15th September, or in the case of a late river like the Itchen on the 30th September. If it is desired to preserve the grayling, they should not be killed before the 15th July, or, better still, the 1st of August, while the termination of their season may be any date not later than, say, the end of February.

The limit of size must vary according to the average size of the fish in the river. I

Limits of size. think that no trout under $\frac{3}{4}$-lb. should be killed on any chalk-stream. It is better to prescribe a length below which all fish are to be returned and a perfect trout of 11 in. should weigh $\frac{3}{4}$-lb., and this I would suggest as the minimum limit of size. On the Test no trout under 13 in. should be killed, and on the lower reaches of this river 14, 15, or even 16 in. is not too large a limit for killable trout.

In poorly stocked fisheries, or where there are a considerable number of rods in

Limit of number. proportion to the length of the water, it is often wise to limit the number of fish to be killed on any one day. I am, perhaps, more conservative than many of my brother anglers on this point, and on a club water I should feel perfectly satisfied with two brace of good-conditioned sizable trout as the result of any day's fishing.

Probably more ill-considered advice has been proffered in respect of the question **Returning undersized fish.** of returning undersized fish than on any other branch of the subject. Writers who should know better have asserted that hooking and returning the young trout has done more to render them shy than any other treatment by the angler. It is true that for a short time the yearling that has been pricked or landed and restored to its native element is not disposed to feed, but this is merely a passing mood. The alternative of killing every fish landed without regard to its size as compared with the average of the river is too terrible to contemplate. Many years ago a *soi-disant* sportsman promulgated the theory that every trout large enough to take a fly is big enough for the basket, and this was his defence to a keeper on a chalk-stream, who searched his basket and pockets to find them crammed with trout of $\frac{1}{4}$-lb., or even less, in weight. Let there be no mistake about it! The pot-hunter wishes to kill all he can, regardless of size, and the sportsman is not only willing to return any below the legal limit of the water, but exercises the greatest care both in extracting the hook and in returning the fish to the water. A small net bag is useful for weighing fish when in doubt as to their being sizable.

Every set of rules for a fly-fishing club or private

water preserved for fly-fishing should contain a very
distinctly worded clause to the effect
Fly. that fly-fishing only is permitted.
When the use of salmon flies,
Alexandras or silver-bodied patterns is prohibited,
this should also be succinctly stated. On an essentially
dry-fly water, I think that a short note should be
added to the effect that fishing with floating fly only
is allowed

It is well in the case of a club water to add a
request that all gates should be closed and that fishermen must take care not to trample down or injure
fences, stiles, standing crops, or grass in the meadows.
It is a prudent course to enact that no dogs are
allowed to accompany the fishermen, because farmers,
gamekeepers, and others object to their presence. In
the case of a water preserved by the lessee for his own
and friends' fishing, it should not be necessary to
insert these rules in reference to gates, fences, stiles,
crops, grass, or the presence of dogs.

CHAPTER III

WEEDS AND WEED-CUTTING

No apology is needed for devoting an entire chapter to the all-important question of weeds and weed-cutting. The presence of weeds in a chalk-stream is an absolute necessity, because all the insects in their immature forms and the crustaceans and mollusks which constitute the chief food supply of the fish live and flourish in the subaqueous vegetation. The fish, too, require beds of weed to shelter them from the rays of the sun in hot weather, and as a refuge from their numerous enemies. When scared by the sudden and unexpected appearance of the fisherman on the bank, when it has come short to his fly, and has been pricked and alarmed by the sharp point of the hook, often, too, when hooked and trying to escape from the restraint of the rod, the trout naturally looks for a hiding-place. If there are no weed-beds in the immediate vicinity it will make its way up or down the stream for a great distance when frightened, and this engenders an increase in the natural shyness of its fellows.

I do not suggest that the weed-beds are of any great benefit to the angler when dealing with a hooked trout, but I have attempted to show in a previous chapter the most efficacious method of defeating the fish's object in going to weed and trying to entangle the line among the stems of the weeds. We are thus confronted with a more or less complex problem. The fewer the weeds the more shy and unapproachable are the trout. The greater the quantity of weeds the more abundant are the various forms of animal life on which the trout subsists but the better chance it has of getting rid of the angler's painful hook.

Many years ago the theory was broached that if for a few years no weeds were cut on a length of one of our chalk-streams the action of the water would gradually undermine the roots in some places and in time wash the weeds away, leaving clean gravel patches and beautiful natural runs between the weed-masses. Theoretically such a course of procedure would produce ideal fishing water, but practically it is impossible. The weeds if uncut would by, say, the beginning of July, grow to such luxuriance that they would choke up the river, raise the level above, and cause serious overflowing and consequent undermining and destruction of the banks. The result would in all probability be that the lessee of the water would soon find himself the defendant in an action for damages, and his solicitors would, if they were honourable and straightforward, advise him to agree to pay some sum as damages and consent to an injunc-

Necessity for weed-cutting.

tion restraining him from repeating the offence in the future.

Recognizing the strength of this position, it is customary for all fishing leases **Weed-cutting** or agreements to contain a **by the lessor.** clause regulating the weed-cutting. In some instances the lessor undertakes to cut weeds, and as a rule carries out this duty in the most economical way he can. Generally he will let the weeds flourish until the stream is quite unfishable and then set to work and mow away every vestige of vegetation with the chain-scythes. The result on the season's sport can be well imagined. As the season advances and as the growth progresses the poor tenant finds himself continually thwarted by the profusion of the weeds. With the advent of hot weather when the shelter is a necessity for the fish the weeds are generally shorn away and the few trout which do not migrate to more favourable parts are quite unapproachable.

Where in his lease the tenant has to cut the weeds the usual proviso is that this **Weed-cutting** must be done twice a year. **by the lessee.** This suggests a very similar treatment of the river to what takes place when the landlord undertakes weed-cutting. The principles of scientific weed-cutting can be laid down in a very few words. Seeing that the presence of a considerable quantity of weeds is, as shown before, necessary at once for the well-being of the trout and for the sport of the fisherman, the scheme must be such as to leave sufficient weeds. Seeing that clean bare gravel patches among the weeds are always favourable places for the trout to lie on and to feed in, plenty of these clear spaces must be provided. Seeing that the young growth is more frequented by the nymphs, larvæ, and other forms of food than the old growths, the efficient keeper's efforts must ever be directed to cutting away and even rooting up the old or darker-coloured growths and leaving the tender young light-coloured growths to grow and flourish.

Proceeding on these lines the keeper can find continuous work in weed-cutting during the entire season. In the early part of it he will have far less to do than later on when the warmth of the sun has raised the temperature of the water and stimulated the rate of growth of the weeds. No cut-and-dried scheme of leaving masses at one time and ruthlessly sweeping them away at another time will produce a satisfactory result. It requires continuous and intelligent application of the knowledge conveyed by a due and proper comprehension of the principles first laid down.

An old hand-scythe blade fixed to a long ash-pole is the best tool for the majority of the work. It is necessary to have two of these, one right- and the other left-handed, and when the blades are being ground it is an advantage to remove the sharp point at the end of the scythe

Implements for weed-cutting.

and work it down to a rounded blunt end. When the ordinary sharp-pointed scythe is used it is found in practice that a number of trout lying in the weeds are wounded and sometimes killed while the scythes are being used. A small scythe fixed to a light bamboo-handle, about 16 feet long, is a handy tool for cutting out small weed patches or for getting rid of the rushes which grow in great profusion, especially at the end of the summer and during the early autumn.

Chain-scythes or, as the Hampshire keepers generally call them, *gang-scythes*, are necessary for the thorough weed-cutting required at the end of the fishing season and at any time when a wholesale clearance of any part of the river is desirable. The chain-scythe consists of a number of blades bolted together. At each end of the chain of scythes there is an iron ring about three inches in diameter, and to these rings ropes are fastened. To work the chain-scythes one or two men on each bank working in time draw the rope backwards and forwards, at the same time moving slowly along the banks. If the chain-scythes are worked downstream they will as a rule only cut the tops of the weeds, but if it is desired to cut them very short, each length of the fishery should be cut first downstream and then upstream, and these operations should be repeated as often as is necessary to complete the work. The chain-scythes, especially when worked upstream, are most efficacious in moving some of the mud. It must, however, be remembered that this action only shifts the mud from one part to another below it, and, as noted in a previous chapter, the only sensible method of removing the mud is by panning it out and distributing it on the river-bank.

When the weeds are cut the next point is to consider what is to be done with them. While the cutting is in progress they are gradually floating down and masses accumulating against every post, every projection on the bank, every bridge and every weed-rack. The usual custom is to let them down and clear from time to time every accumulation and get rid of these masses of floating weeds in the easiest possible way by letting them drift down from one's own fishery to the next one below. The keepers on this length in turn send them on with the addition of those they have cut themselves. This goes on from reach to reach, and each set of keepers has to deal with an ever-increasing quantity of cut weeds until at the mouth of the river they amount in the aggregate to an enormous and unmanageable mass.

Disposal of the cut weeds.

I have high legal authority for the statement that all this is quite illegal. Some of the advocates of the plan have urged that it has become legalized by custom, but again I am assured by the same counsel that an illegal action of this description cannot be rendered legal by custom. I am further told that every lessee or lessor could on application to the

Chancery Division obtain an injunction to restrain his neighbour from sending down these accumulations of floating cut weeds.

Some few years since a number of owners and tenants of fisheries on the two **Test and Itchen Asso-** rivers instituted the Test and **ciation.** Itchen Trout Fishing Association for the purpose of safeguarding the interests of the streams in question. The most influential men interested in the matter at once joined it, and a representative committee was appointed. All of us had hopes of their achieving good results.

One of the first questions to be considered by their committee was that of trying to propound a scheme which on their recommendation lessors and lessees should adopt voluntarily for the weed-cutting and disposal of the cut weeds. The recommendation adopted by the Association on the advice of the committee was to ask all who owned or leased fisheries to refrain from cutting weeds between some such dates as the 22nd May and 22nd June.

With every desire to support their action and with extreme reluctance to criticize the conclusions arrived at on the advice of the experts whom the committee had presumably consulted, I can only say that the suggested scheme was utterly impracticable. To leave the weeds uncut for an entire month during the time of the year when their growth is most rapid would be simply suicidal to chances of good sport.

In my own case it would undoubtedly have landed me in a lawsuit which in all human probability I should have lost. Later on a slight revision of dates was attempted, but the same idea prevailed that during the time the mayfly should be up the weeds should be severely let alone. For the last seven years the mayfly has been almost non-existent on the Test, and the experts who advised the committee in such a sense must have been quite out of touch with the present-day conditions, and thus led the Association astray.

A meeting was held at Stockbridge in February, 1912, of lessees of Test fisheries to consider the weed-cutting question. Being absent abroad I could not attend, and so far I have no idea what conclusions the meeting arrived at, nor what course they have suggested. The only solution which appears to me practicable is to give effect to the legal position. If there is any doubt about it one of these wealthy clubs could bring a test action to decide it. Personally, I am quite clear that if properly argued in court by competent counsel the judgment would be in accordance with the legal opinion given in a previous paragraph.

As far as the Test and Itchen are concerned the continuance of the present plan must in time infallibly force the Southampton Harbour authorities to take some drastic step to prevent it. The deposits of mud, the ultimate residue of the decomposition of these weeds, is constantly adding to the heavy accumulations already in Southampton Water. This must greatly increase the expense of dredging the channel to a depth sufficient for the large ocean-going steamers of the present day. The weed-masses floating down too are found fouling the screws of the large liners, and in some cases even causing delay in the commencement of their voyages. Many years ago the Thames Conservancy had a clause in their Act of Parliament in pursuance of which they have ever since prevented cut weeds from being sent down not only in the Thames itself, but even in the smallest tributary of it. Throughout the lengths of water controlled by the Thames Conservancy all cut weeds are taken out of the river, and on every dry-fly stream in the United Kingdom the same rule would apply if only steps were taken to enforce the fishery lessees' rights on the subject.

Systems of weed-cutting. The side and bar system which I have continually advocated for many years wherever carried out intelligently has not only improved the sport, but in addition has greatly decreased the labour of the keepers in cutting the weeds during the season. Briefly, it is to *bar* the shallows and *side* the deeps.

How to bar a shallow. The meaning of the expression to bar a shallow is that transversely across the stream a number of clean, bright gravel-bars are to be formed by rooting up, as far as possible, the weeds growing on it. These gravel-bars should be from, say, five to twelve yards in width, and the intervening weed-bars should be approximately of the same or a little less width. Thus, at this stage the shallow would appear as alternate bars of dense weed and clean gravel.

It will probably be found that in this state the water will be penned back too much, and possibly even land above the shallow may be flooded. To counteract this it is only necessary to cut here and there narrow longitudinal cuts through the weed-bars in the middle, or at the sides of the stream, and let the water down. It is often a good policy to arrange these cuts alternately on either side of the stream. Care and attention in carrying out this work will enable an efficient keeper to arrange the flow of water over a shallow so as to content the farmers and other tenants, and at the same time give fishermen the best chance of sport.

The exact arrangement of the bars should be thoroughly thought out and their positions should be marked by stakes on the bank before the work is commenced. The places in which the growth of weed is most luxuriant are evidently those designed by nature for weed-bars, and conversely wherever there are natural clean gravel-patches these are the parts designed for the gravel-bars. Every advantage must be taken of the natural set of the stream to provide desirable holts for the fish, and the classes of weeds which usually contain the largest supply of food should be preserved, while those which do not usually hold any great number of nymphs, shrimps, etc., should be ruthlessly cut away.

It might be convenient here to set out for the information of the reader the **Suitable and unsuit-** weeds among those generally **able weeds.** present which are most favourable and those which are less favourable.   Probably the best of all the usual chalk-stream weeds is the water celery (*Apium inundatum*), as it always contains great numbers of dun nymphs, shrimps, caddis, and other forms of animal life.   The water starwort (*Callitriche vernus* or *C. autumnalis*) is a weed usually containing a fair quantity of food for the fish.   The water crowfoot (*Ranunculus aqua-tilis*) is a very prominent water-weed, and generally holds a considerable quantity of caddis and a few Ephemeridæ nymphs.   It is a somewhat curious circumstance that in an aquarium used for observing the habits of these insect larvæ and nymphs the presence of water crowfoot in any great quantity is, as a rule, fatal to the dun nymphs.   The so-called American weed (*Elodea canadense*) is not good for any stream. It tends to choke up the water, and does not seem favourable for the food affected by the fish.   Ribbon-weed (*Sparganium ramosum*) is the home of the larvæ and pupæ of *Simulium* and other smuts in the chalk-streams.

When dealing with comparatively deep and slow water it is advisable to adopt the system of weed-

cutting known as the *side* plan. The meaning of this
should be quite clear to the

How to side a deep stretch. operator before he commences
the work. It is in effect that
as far as a man can reach
with his hand-scythe the weeds against either bank
are cut quite clean right down to the bed of the
stream. Over the remainder of the stream the weeds
are kept well topped, but are not cut down to the
bottom of the river.

It must be understood that it is not intended to
advise the cutting away at the bank and leaving the
weeds elsewhere uncut. Some admirers of the system
who have failed to grasp its real meaning have carried
out what they deemed to be the principle of it to an
exaggerated extent. True, they have cut out the
sides, but they have allowed a forest of tangled luxuriant vegetation to stand up above the surface of the
water down the centre of the stream, and thus made
the deep reaches most difficult, if not impossible, for
the fisherman. Besides these, gross and luxuriant
weed-beds are not favourite places for the trout.
When in the autumn they die down and decompose,
a deep bed of black fœtid mud is deposited on the
bottom of the river, and if not removed by panning
out or sent down the river to foul one's neighbour's
water below this will infallibly leave the stretch in such
a state that no self-respecting trout will take up their
positions on it. The rushes and sedges at the margin
of the river should be cut as little as possible. Of

course if they are very thick and abnormally high it may be absolutely necessary to trim them in places, but nothing tends more to render the fish shy than the absence of rushes, and conversely they are most useful in making a hide for the fisherman when stalking his fish.

The weeds in a fishery having been once cut on the side and bar system will **Trimming the weeds.** require very little further attention during the season. From day to day the keeper should walk along with his hand-scythe and trim away here and there weeds where they are growing too luxuriantly, and he should, as before remarked, invariably cut out the old growths and leave the young weeds uncut. This daily work should be carried out quite early in the morning, and long before the angler appears on the scene the keeper should have taken out his few cut weeds and laid them on the bank. If in a deep stretch the growth of the weeds in the centre of the stream should have become too dense, he and an assistant can draw the chain-scythes down fairly quickly and only take the tops off the weeds. This, again, if carried out in the small hours, will in no way inconvenience the fisherman. The notion that weed-cutting puts trout off the feed or makes them shy is only true to the extent that for perhaps an hour after cutting the weeds they will not be seen in position, but they may and at times do rise well a few minutes after the chain-scythes have been passed over them.

2 A

When the fishing season is approaching its end, say, the third or last week in September, the weeds and the rushes, etc., on the banks

Autumn cutting.

should be cut away as closely as possible. This is desirable, not only in preparation for the autumn netting, but also to clean the bed of the river, and thus encourage the fish to work up on to the shallows, there to deposit their eggs and perform the duty of propagating the species.

CHAPTER IV

KILLING DOWN THE TROUT'S ENEMIES

THE enemies of the trout are very numerous, and may for convenience' sake be roughly classified here under the headings of men, birds, otters, fish, and even some larvæ of insects. Of these the insect larvæ preying on trout are not numerous, nor are their depredations of a very serious character. It is true that many years ago an enthusiastic fishing friend sent me a bottle containing a larva of the large water beetle (*Dytiscus marginalis*) and a small trout. When secured the unfortunate little trout was dead, and on the lower side of its abdomen the voracious larva had inflicted fatal wounds with its powerful mandibles. Some authorities state that some of the larger caddis attack and devour the trout ova and alevins, but the evidence on this point is not, to my mind, altogether conclusive.

Poachers. Unfortunately there is no possible doubt on the score of man taking a prominent place in the list of the trout's enemies, and I hope our humanitarian friends will not take exception to the words "killing down" in the title of this chapter, and try to brand me with the stigma of advocating manslaughter as a remedy for their depredations. The sportsman who, in a sort of joke, has declared that every one of his fellow-sportsmen is at heart a bit of a poacher, is responsible in some degree for the glamour with which the village poacher is surrounded in the village inn. Let us for once "call a spade a spade"! The ordinary village poacher is an idle, dissolute vagabond, who will not work, does not dare to commit larceny, and is, above all, desirous of passing his life in a moderate degree of comfort at somebody else's expense.

He poaches fish in preference to game, because while magistrates, unless deterred by a wholesome fear of being pilloried in "Truth," pass severe sentences on game-poachers they generally err on the side of leniency in cases of fish-poaching. If only the *soi-disant* respectable tradesman who is willing to purchase, at a price considerably below their market value, trout or other fish which have obviously been obtained by unfair means could be successfully prosecuted as a receiver, much of this class of poaching would be effectually stopped.

The law on the subject is in some respects most unjust. The man who takes a trout off a fishmonger's slab can be prosecuted and imprisoned for theft, while the one who wires or nets similar fish from a chalk-stream shallow is not technically a thief, because the trout in the river are by a legal fiction styled *feræ naturæ*, and are nobody's property. The only preventive is a good keeper, and he is often discouraged by the absurdly small amount of the fine imposed by the magistrates for fish-poaching. Some keepers have a happy knack of impressing on the poachers the policy of abstaining from visiting their particular preserves, and these are far more useful keepers than those whose only resource is to bring the poacher up before the bench and get a small fine imposed. Nowadays, however, I think that poaching is not nearly as prevalent as it was a quarter of a century ago.

The chief factors which have tended to decrease poaching in country villages are: (1) that the standard of education has been raised by modern legislation, and the effect of this has been to engender a feeling of disgrace at being brought up before the magistrates; (2) that owing to his scale of living having generally improved, the villager is a more self-respecting man than his forbears; and (3) that the labouring classes are more abstemious and less inclined to indulge in alcoholic excess, and much of the old-fashioned poaching was undertaken as a means of earning money which was squandered in the village inn. As time goes on all these inducements to make him a better member of society are likely to continue and increase, so that in a few years anything like systematic poaching may be a thing of the past.

Many of the water-birds are dreadful poachers. Swans and ducks, as well as **Birds as poachers.** moorhens and dabchicks, prey on the ova, alevins, and even young fry. Kingfishers are deadly enemies of the trout fry and smaller yearlings. Herons are most destructive, and will stalk and kill even the largest trout in comparatively shallow water. I have been charged with gross inhumanity in advising keepers and others to use all legitimate means to keep down these birds, but, candidly, I do not see what other advice I could give to the lessees or keepers of good trout-streams.

Otters.

Otters have been cited by many authorities as most destructive of the Salmonidæ. It is, however, a moot point whether they do not prefer eels, pike and frogs to any of the salmon family. They may be shot or trapped, and if there should be a pack of otterhounds anywhere in the district the master will generally arrange a meet on any stream where the otters are present in any numbers. I fear, however, that a day's hunt over a short stretch of a chalk-stream with dogs and men on the banks and in the water in great numbers is likely to make the trout very shy for some days afterwards.

Fish.

Chub, perch, eels, and large overgrown ill-conditioned trout (especially males) are perfect sharks. Bullheads, and sticklebacks, are deadly enemies of trout alevins or young fry, and even roach, dace, and minnows compete with the trout for the food in the river. The chief enemy among the fish of the lessee of a trout-stream is decidedly the pike, and, although all the before-mentioned fish should be killed down where possible, the case of the pike is far more serious, and the war to be waged on them must be carried out on well-defined lines. I propose devoting some considerable space to this branch of the subject, and invite my readers to study carefully the suggestions made here as to the best methods of dealing with the pike.

The late Francis Francis placed the pike at the head of his list of poachers

Francis Francis on the pike. on a trout-stream. In conversation with the proprietor of a well-known chalk-stream fishery he held forth, in reference to one of those fresh-water sharks that he had wired, in some such language as the following: "Look here, you let a certain number of rods on your water at £30 a season; that brute would kill more trout during the year than any of your rods—*ergo*, its destruction is worth more than £30 per annum to you." History relateth not whether he proceeded to capitalize the yearly rental on a 5 per cent basis, and show his friend that the death of a 2-lb. pike was equivalent to putting £600 into his pocket. If he had, it could hardly have been deemed an exaggeration. This insistence on the importance of the pike question may lay me open to a chance of repeating myself; but in the opinion of all the best judges among modern authorities it is the paramount duty of every proprietor or manager of a stretch of the Test or Itchen to din into the ears of his keeper, daily and hourly, in season and out of season, the necessity of killing down pike by every available means and on every available day during the year.

When the enthusiastic dry-fly man has hardened his heart to agree to pay the exor-bitant rent asked, and has thus managed to get a lease of a length of a good chalk-stream, his first step generally is to find a keeper and install him as soon as possible after he gets possession of the fishery. If he is well advised he will then proceed to make a careful and exhaustive survey with the view of ascertaining the capabilities of the water he has taken, and he should begin without delay the work of trying to exterminate the ubiquitous pike. At first he will probably be surprised at the number killed, and very likely he will soon get keen himself on wiring them or spinning for them.

General considerations on the pike question.

At this stage his keeper, if one of the right sort, will be as keen as he is himself, and during the second season the bag of trout will probably show a better result than that of the previous year, and the number and usually the average size of the pike will show a marked decrease. This is the critical time. If he or his keeper gets slack in the work those that escape the nets, wire, baits, etc., will increase in weight only too rapidly, and the little pikelets which are always present will grow to such dimensions as to be able to levy a heavy toll on the trout fry, yearlings and even larger fish in the stream.

Besides the pike in his own reaches and their numerous progeny, the lessee of the fishery has to reckon with the vagaries and suffer from the *laches* of his neighbours. There have been cases of owners of chalk-stream fisheries who have preserved and even stocked with pike, but I am not here contemplating such a dire state. Probably there is no means of preventing any freeholder in this country from doing this on his own water, but fortunately, with all their faults, landowners generally are sane, and do not contemplate such suicidal policy as this to reduce the value of their own property. If the river above or below is not efficiently keepered, and the war against the jack is not waged relentlessly and continuously, a goodly proportion are certain to migrate to adjoining water, where, in consequence of the comparative scarcity of the genus *Esox*, or the liberal stocking with young trout, the pike will find abundance of palatable food ready to satisfy his appetite.

An ounce of fact is worth a ton of theory, so let me give some figures. Early in 1903, my friend Corrie took something over a mile of water, a small proportion on one side of the main Test and the remainder on a by-stream. This fishery had been utterly neglected for years, and contained a few, very few, large trout and a great number of pike. In September of the same year he put on a first-rate keeper, who for two years devoted the greater portion of his time to the slaughter of the jack.

Stocking on an exceptionally liberal scale with two-year-olds, yearlings, and alevins was begun and has been continued to the present time. I joined my friend and made one of three rods pledged to fish the water very lightly in 1905. At my friend's suggestion I took over his lease in the spring of 1906, and have since then kept the fishery entirely in my own hands.

Up to the end of 1905 the keeper had killed approximately 800 pike, including many large ones of 13 lb., 12 lb., 11 lb., 10½ lb., and so on, down to, say, 3 lb., and of course a great number of 1 lb. and less. In 1906, 155; in 1907, 65; in 1908, 68; in 1909, 60; in 1910, 53; and in 1911, 51 pike were killed; or an aggregate of 1252 pike from September, 1903, to the end of 1911. Just imagine the effect of any relaxation of our efforts, by which any great proportion of the pike might have been left in the river in any year. Meanwhile the bag of trout continuously increased, and each year showed a better result than the previous one, and the average weight of the fish killed in 1911 was a little more than 1 lb. 10 oz., the size limit being 1¼ lb.

Having established the principle that the pike must be kept down, the next point to consider is the methods by which they should be secured. There are four means of getting out pike successfully, (1) Spinning, (2) Wiring, (3) Trimmering, and (4) Netting, and all of them should be persevered in and no efforts relaxed to render the

Methods of killing down the pike.

keeper and his master proficient in all of them. In the spring very small pike are seen basking in weed-choked carriers, and the wire is, under these conditions, the best if not the only means of dealing with them.

A past-master in pike-spinning can levy a heavy toll on the fish and at the **Spinning.** same time get a fair amount of sport out of it. He can use a natural bait or an artificial, and of the latter the *wagtail* is perhaps the most successful. On days when it is not taken, and when the natural bait does not seem to tempt the jack a spoon or phantom minnow may sometimes be tried with advantage. The great secret of spinning for pike is to keep the bait moving slowly and as deep down as is compatible with the quantity of weed in the water.

Wiring is a very deadly method in the hands of the expert. One, two, or three **Wiring.** strands of brass wire twisted together should be used, the number of strands being dependent on the size of the pike. It is a good plan to carry wires of different thicknesses, as one of three strands is not successful with very small pike, and the wire of a single strand will often be broken by the weight of a large one. An open loop or eye is worked at the end of the wire, which is passed through this eye to make a running noose, and is tied securely to the finer end of a bamboo of from twelve to sixteen, or even eighteen feet in length. At the fine end of the bamboo a notch or split is made, and the wire is pressed into this notch to steady it. The noose is adjusted to a smaller or larger diameter according to the size of the particular pike seen, and must run quite freely through the eye so as to close on the pike at the right moment.

Everything being ready, the keeper walks along with the fine end of the bamboo **Method of using** in his hand and the stout end **the wire.** trailing along on the ground. A calm sunny day is preferable, and he must walk quite slowly with his eyes glued to the water until he espies a jack lying basking in the sun. It is of the utmost importance that he should walk slowly, and that his every movement should be deliberate. Presently he catches sight of a pike and, slowly adjusting the noose to the diameter required, he moves with noiseless short steps until he is within reach of the fish. Keeping as still as possible, he places himself as nearly as he can opposite and at right angles to the fish, having carefully noted the direction in which the pike's head is located.

Looking intently at the fish he should slowly and deliberately lower the wire into the water at some small distance above his prey, quietly extending the bamboo and lowering the noose of the wire into the water a short distance ahead of the pike. Should the jack shift its position he must leisurely withdraw the wire noose and start *de novo*. When the fish remains quite still he must gradually work the noose over the fish's head, and when dealing with large pike, say, 6 lb. or upwards, the wire should tighten on it well forward of its centre, i.e. close behind the pectoral fins, when the fish will be dragged headlong through the water and up the bank with ease. With small pike when the wire is about the middle of the body, which is in front of the dorsal fin, standing with his body and arms inclining well forwards, he must quickly but without jerk draw the wiring pole backwards. The noose running up will secure the pike, and its weight keeping all taut he must sling it steadily underhanded on to the bank.

Until he positively draws the noose the operator cannot keep too still or be too slow in his movements. He should keep his eyes fixed on his prey and make quite sure that the pike is actually in the noose before drawing, and it is well to remember that one is always apt to locate the pike nearer the surface than it really is. Sometimes the jack will dart off just as the keeper is going to draw the wire. He must then note where it goes, and often he can poke the thick end of the pole into this place and start the pike again. When it has settled another attempt can be made, and this may be repeated several times before the pike is secured. It may, after two or three attempts, be scared and swim away out of sight, and the operation will have to be postponed to a later hour, or possibly to a subsequent day.

There are days when every pike will lie still and be taken by the wire, and there are other days when the fish seem endowed with an extra sense and are almost unapproachable. On the good days persevere and on the bad ones abandon the attempt and wait for a more favourable occasion! Altogether it is fascinating work, and during the many hours of a fine day when the trout are not rising quite good sport can be obtained by a keen fisherman searching every ditch and carrier and helping in the good work of keeping down the trout's enemies. As a general rule, afternoons, dull and windy weather are unfavourable, and fine, calm forenoons favourable for wiring.

No doubt a number of pike in a trout-stream can be killed by spinning, and the wire is most efficacious wher-

Trimmering.

ever in the river or in carriers the jack are visible, but there are positions where neither is likely to be successful and where the trimmer is a most valuable adjunct. In a deep hole or an eddy or corner of the river, given any pike at all in the stream, one at least is almost sure to have taken up its quarters. The arrangement of a trimmer is a very simple matter. A withy or flexible bough, eight or ten feet long, is driven into the ground and bent over so as to project over the place where it is either probable that a pike is located or where it has positively been seen. A short length of strong water-cord is fastened to the upper end of this projecting stick, and is passed through a hole in the upper part part of the Y-shaped runner shown in Fig. 59. Ten or twelve yards of line, fastened at the upper end of the runner, are wound in and out of the arms, and the end of the slack is laid in a slit cut for this purpose at the lower end of one of the arms. Three or four feet of loose line are left hanging below the slit and a moderately large double gimp hook is fastened to the end of this loose line. A small lively dace or other live bait is threaded to the hook by a baiting needle, and the hook is passed diagonally upwards under the skin from a point near one of the ventral fins, coming out at the back on a line with the pectoral fins.

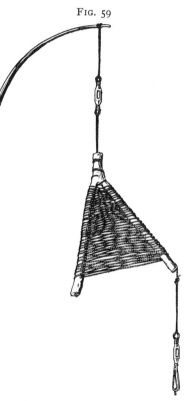

FIG. 59

The bait is dropped into the water and left to swim about without any lead or other contrivance to sink it.

If there is a pike in the hole, sooner or later it will seize the live bait, turn it over, and proceed to gorge it head first. The pull will release the line from the slit, let it unwind backwards and forwards from the arms of the Y, and in this way play the pike until it is exhausted. When the keeper comes round he will see that the line is unwound, and at once realize that there is a jack on the hook. He will steadily pull it in, land it, give it a smart tap on the summit of the spinal cord, and put on another bait to try to kill its mate in the hole.

A moderately large dace or roach of, say, four ounces, is the right-sized bait. Very small ones are not so good and occasionally kill large trout, and trimmering, say, after the early part of March, is a mistake, as at that time of the year trout are very likely to take the bait and get so injured that they have to be killed. A small pike is a good bait for a large one, but small grayling are not as a rule successful. A large pike in a hole is sure to succumb sooner or later to the trimmer, and in some cases it is a good policy to fasten a stone or bullet to the line and sink it with, say, a yard of slack line between the bullet and the bait. When the stone or bullet is on the bed of the river the bait will swim upwards and show well at a greater depth than the ordinary trimmer arrangement without a lead.

In a fishery much infested by rats or water-voles difficulty in keeping the trimmers set often occurs by reason **Rats and trimmer** of the propensity of these ver- **baits.** min of running up the rough withies on to the trimmer-forks, and there during the

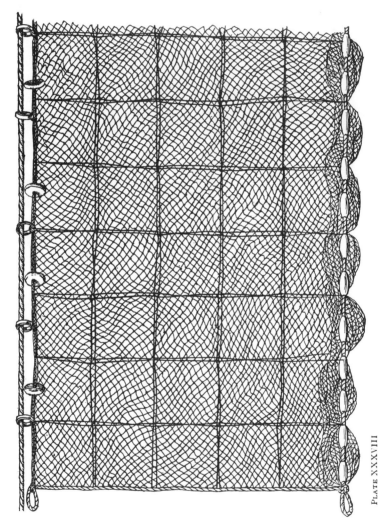

PLATE XXXVIII

TRAMMEL-NET

night gnawing the lines and cutting the whole trimmer adrift from the withy. My own keeper has on occasions been driven almost to despair by finding, morning after morning, his trimmers destroyed. The plan has been adopted of using bamboos instead of withies and fixing the trimmer-fork to the extremity with wire, allowing it to hang three or four inches below the top, with a swivel placed in the middle of the wire to prevent kinking. This method of arranging the trimmers has been found successful, and seems to completely baffle the would-be depredators.

In addition to all the methods referred to before, the thorough and efficient netting of every part of a really well-managed fishery on a trout-stream at least once in the early autumn, and possibly once or twice more before the spring, will prove most effectual in helping to kill down the pike and other coarse fish. All netting of the river must be finished before the end of February, as after that date the working of the nets over shallows will do a great amount of harm to the young trout alevins or fry.

Netting.

Three nets are required, of which preferably two should be trammel-nets and one a purse-net. A trammel-net, as shown in Plate XXXVIII, consists of a loose net of small meshes, called the sheeting or linnet, between two tighter nets of coarser twine and large square mesh called the walling. The

Nets required.

2 B

sheeting or linnet must be much deeper than the walling. The head-line carries a number of large bungs to float it, a second line is affixed to one end, and a series of horn rings are carried on the head-line; this second line is generally called the lock-line. The object of this arrangement of lines is, that when the net is being gathered in to the bank before being landed, the pulling in of the lock-line will close the net into a bag laterally, and prevent the escape of any fish in it. The lower side of the walling is a strong line armed with a number of leads to sink it to the bottom of the river.

The walling should be square, of very strong twine and coarse mesh, say, 15 in., and the sheeting or linnet of fine twine and 2 to $2\frac{1}{2}$ in. mesh. When a fish strikes the sheeting or linnet the effect is to drive it through the large square mesh of the walling, and the more it struggles the more does it get hung up and often killed in the meshes. For a river like the Test the nets should be about 20 yd. in length and 2 to 3 yd. in depth, and for smaller or shallower streams proportionately smaller. The net shown in Plate XXXVIII was made for me by Messrs. C. Farlow and Co., Ltd., to the following specification :—

Size.—To set 20 yd. long by 6 ft. deep.

Inner netting.—Best quality satin finished 6/3-hemp twine, tanned, 2-in. mesh (i.e. 1 in. from knot to knot), extra slack both in length and depth to allow for bagging.

Walls.—Square mesh, 12-in. bars on both sides.

Foot-rope leaded, equal to nine ¼-lb. leads per yard.

Head-rope corked and fitted with horn rings about 19 in. apart to allow the net to be drawn together in curtain-fashion.

Two of these trammel-nets are required, and the third or stop-net can be a **Purse-net.** trammel too, but I think a purse-net is preferable for this purpose. The purse-net is fitted with a head or cork line with bungs on it to float it, and a foot-line with plenty of leads to sink the lower end of the net. The net throughout is of a comparatively small mesh, say, two inches, and from a short distance at each side the netting is worked to form a long funnel-shaped bag or purse tapering to a point at the centre of the net. The end of the purse should be a square-shaped opening, say, eight inches in width, with a stout cord worked through the meshes a short distance above it. The fine end of the purse is then closed when the net is set, and when the net is hauled ashore by untying the cord the end of the purse is opened, and all fish or accumulation of weeds or rubbish in it can be easily taken out and the purse closed again before again setting the net in position.

When a date has been fixed and everything is ready for the netting, including, **Labour required.** of course, the cutting away of all weeds as closely as possible, a start should be made at a comparatively early hour in the morning. A competent man must supervise, and a considerable number of men are required to work the netting in a satisfactory manner. Three men for each of the trammel-nets, three or four boys in front of the trammel-nets while they are being dragged down to beat the water under the banks to drive out any pike lying up in such position, and a couple of extra men to help generally are absolutely necessary, or, say, eight men and four boys in all besides the keeper, who is supervising all. Plenty of spare ropes should be provided, and a wheelbarrow is very useful for carrying all kinds of gear from one draw to another. The ordinary pisciculturist's can is useful to keep any trout alive from the time they are taken from the net until returned to the stream. The keeper or his master should keep accurate records of the results of the netting.

Some days before netting the keeper must decide on the length of water he in-**Preparation for the** tends to work in the day, and **netting.** this should be a comparatively short stretch. The maximum length under the most favourable circumstances for an efficient day's work is perhaps three-quarters of a mile, but as a rule half a mile is quite sufficient. The lengths of each draw of the net, which should also be quite short, must be decided, and where possible, a place selected to land the nets where the water is shallow and where, if possible, the bank shelves. A perpendicular or overhung bank is very inconvenient. The rushes at the bank must be cut quite short and any brambles, large stones or boulders, boughs or other things likely to foul the net either in the river or on the bank must be carefully removed. The labourers or others assisting must be told that it is a serious business and not a picnic or excuse for beer-drinking—in fact, the less strong drink is given the better.

At the lower end of the upper length of the first draw to be netted the stop-net **Setting the stop-net.** is set with a line carried across to the landing-side. Care must be taken that the lead-line is well down and the net set correctly and without any twist or tangle. In the accompanying blocks, Figs. 60, 61, and 62, CC is the stop-net and c the end of the line on the landing-bank.

FIG. 60

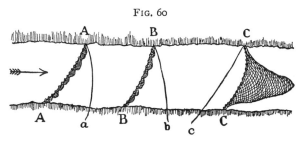

FIG. 61

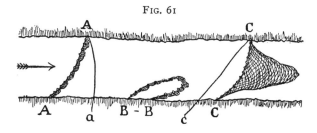

FIG. 62

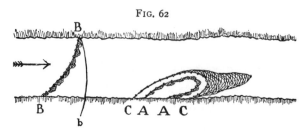

The upper trammel-net AA is then stretched across
the river at the upper end of
Setting the trammel- the first draw, and the line at
nets. the landing-bank attached to
it is marked a. The lower
trammel-net is then stretched across ten yards below
the upper one—it is marked BB, and the landing-line
from it, b. Care must be taken to set these nets properly and to see that the leads are down, the corks
along the surface, and everything in working order
before starting. It is a good plan to set the nets with
the end on the further side leading, or rather more
downstream than on the landing-side. The nets are
then in the positions shown in Fig. 60.

At a signal from the keeper, the men, one each at
AA and a, and one each at
Dragging the nets. BB and b, commence walking
downstream quite slowly. The
man on the further side at B should set the pace, and
all the rest should preserve their distances and move
at the same pace as he does. Meanwhile the boys
just in front of the nets at AA and BB will commence
beating the water with boughs or bamboos so as to

drive any pike from the banks. It is barely possible to drag too slowly, as the slower the nets go the more effectually will they catch the pike. When the net BB is within about twelve yards of the landing-place all dragging will cease, and, at a signal from the keeper, the man at the line b will draw the further side of the net round to the landing-bank. The position of the nets at this stage is shown in Fig. 61. The lock-line will be gathered in so as to make a bag of the entire net, and it will be lifted on to the bank. Any trout in it will be turned into a can which has been filled with fresh water, and the pike and other coarse fish knocked on the head. The net BB is then cleaned, and carried up to about ten yards above the net AA, and there stretched across the river.

Again, at the keeper's signal, the net AA is dragged down until it is about twelve yards above the landing-place. Simultaneously, the landing-lines of both nets AA, the trammel and CC, the purse- or stop-net are drawn in so that CC is carried round AA, as shown in Fig. 62. AA is landed first and then CC, the fish taken out, both nets cleaned, and the next length is then worked in precisely the same way.

If there is any doubt in the keeper's mind as to the netting having been effectual, **Dragging a length a second time.** or if by any chance a large pike has been seen and is not in the nets, it is a good plan to carry BB up to the starting-point and drag it down again, leaving AA and the stop-net CC in the positions shown in Fig. 61. Again, after all the nets have been landed, if he thinks it wise the keeper should have the nets set again as at the start, and the length dragged again with both nets. This is a most effectual plan of preventing the men dragging the nets too quickly and impressing on them the wise maxim of "slow and sure." The second time of dragging is often more effectual than the first, because the passage of the nets has stirred any mud and made the water so thick that the pike cannot see the net. On one occasion, netting in 1911, we saw a big fish, and it was only at the fifth time of dragging over the length that we secured a female pike of $6\frac{1}{2}$ lb. with the tail of a partially digested trout, quite $1\frac{1}{2}$ lb., projecting from its mouth.

The well-conditioned trout should, of course, be returned to the stream, but any

Advice as to the disposal of the fish. poor, black, deformed, blind or ill-conditioned ones should be at once knocked on the head. I would urge on every keeper or lessee of a fishery the policy of giving the trout knocked on the head, as well as the pike or other coarse fish, to the men working the nets. I am sure that they fully appreciate the attention, and the better they are treated the better they work—in fact, after the first season, any handy, willing men should be employed again and soon get quite interested in the work. In my experience, the keeper on a water I managed for some friends and myself took on a notorious poacher to cut and remove weeds and assist in netting. He did this because he thought that he might reform this man by treating him well and bringing him in contact with the respectable, hard-working men who constituted the rest of the netting gang, and in this case his judgment was correct, and the man was employed by us for several years. So far as the keeper knew he never poached our river after his first day with the nets.

CHAPTER V

STOCKING

A FEW years ago it might well have been necessary to open this chapter with an elaborate and carefully worked-out argument to prove that there was any need for stocking. Nowadays every expert, every fisherman, every keeper and even some of the free-holders are convinced that something of the kind must be attempted if the sport obtained is to bear any reasonable kind of ratio to the annual expense of any-thing like good dry-fly fishing. Some of our friends style it " restocking," but I beg leave to take exception to the term. Restocking means restoring the stock in the river to what it was at some anterior date and presupposes that in olden times the chalk-streams were fully stocked. Very little study of the question will convince the reader that the aggregate bag of the limited number of fishermen in former days was immeasurably less in quantity than what is obtained by the enormous number of anglers of the present time. It is true that, the fishermen being so far less numerous, the individual bags were greater, and thus we are told of the wonderful sport our ancestors had without stocking at all.

Once having admitted that stocking is necessary, it

is well to consider what are the available means of
doing this, and what are the

Methods of stocking.   respective advantages and disadvantages of these various
methods.   There are known to me six distinct methods,
and they are as follows : (1) With wild fish, (2) with
large stew-fed, artificially hatched fish which are sizable
or larger when turned in, (3) with two-year-olds, (4)
with yearlings, (5) with feeding-fry, and (6) with alevins
or eyed ova laid on artificial redds.

At the first blush it would almost appear that the
plan of using wild fish of

Stocking with wild   good average size is the most
fish.   desirable.   The fish are all
sizable and fit to kill from the
very outset, and being free from any possible taint
caused by artificial breeding or artificial rearing
should be far better able to take care of themselves
than any which have come from the pisciculturist's
ponds.   If there is any tangible foundation for the
theory that hand-feeding during adolescence is likely to
engender a disinclination on the part of the adult trout
to partake freely of surface food, these wild fish should
be likely to rise better than any which have been
grown in the trout-breeder's ponds.   So much for the
apparent advantages.

On the other side of the question there are two
unsurmountable obstacles to this method of stocking.
The first of these is that a few minutes' consideration
will convince the lessee of a fishery that if he is going

to purchase wild fish either from his own or from some other river for stocking purposes, there is one and only one possible means of their being procured, and that is by their being poached. In other words, he will buy from the poachers or their agents fish which have been illegally taken from other waters in the neighbourhood, or possibly even from his own, and he will in effect constitute himself a receiver of goods which, according to the extraordinary anomaly of the law, are not stolen but are clearly improperly obtained.

The second is an insuperable objection to the plan of attempting to stock with wild fish. In a fishery I managed there were two or three places where the number of trout always appeared to me too numerous, and there were other parts of the water lower down where the stock was evidently insufficient. We netted some of the overstocked reaches, put all the trout into cans and sent them down the stream in carts distances varying from three miles for some of them to as much as five miles for others. The experiment was on quite a large scale, and no less than 2283 wild trout were moved in this way and distributed among reaches lower down the same river. This work was carried out in the month of October, and the next spring we were surprised to find that the stock of fish in the lower reaches had not increased to any great extent, nor had we succeeded in reducing the number in the upper reaches. This is what invariably happens when wild fish are introduced or moved from one part of a fishery to another. They never seem to make themselves at

home in their new surroundings, are inveterate wan-
derers, and are thus of no advantage to the fishery.

The usual method of carrying out the plan of
stocking with large stew-fed
Stocking with large   fish is to buy yearlings from
stew-fed fish.   the pisciculturists, turn them
into stews constructed for the
purpose, and feed them very liberally until they are
two or three years old. The advantage claimed for
this method is that when the trout are turned in,
generally in the early spring, they are sizable and fit
to kill. The *pros* and *cons* of this plan, which has
been advised by some experts, will be treated in detail
in a subsequent part of this chapter in connection with
the question of what some of us term the *degeneration
of the chalk-stream trout.*

Stocking with two-year-olds purchased from the
trout-breeder and turned direct
Stocking with two-   into the river, is certainly the
year-olds.   least troublesome method of
stocking. If the best fed and
healthiest are selected, and if the pisciculturist who
raises them is up to his work and has not attempted to
force their growth by overfeeding, they are likely to
do well. Of course they are no better than their
parents, and it is of importance that the parent stock
should be of a good strain. It is probably a better
plan and less costly to purchase yearlings and grow
them up to two-year-olds in a stew on or near the
fishery.

Good healthy yearlings of, say, six inches in length are the best kind of stock to
Stocking with year- turn into most rivers, as they
lings. seem to get more easily ac-
climatized and used to their new surroundings than two-year-olds or larger fish. They are, as being of smaller size, less well able to take care of themselves than the two-year-olds, and are more likely to fall a prey to the ravages of the ubiquitous pike. Besides, too, one must remember that the yearlings will take fully two years to grow to a killable size in the river. If turned into stews and moderately fed they should be about ¾ lb. in weight by the following spring, when they could be turned in and in a few months would, under favourable conditions, grow to an average of 1 lb. in weight.

When turning out yearlings, two-year-olds, or larger fish it is very necessary to get
Turning out fish. the temperature of the water in the fish-carriers uniform
with that of the stream. To effect this pour about one third of the water out of the carriers and fill up with water from the river. Let them stand for some time, then empty half the contents of the carriers and fill up again. Continue this until the temperature of the water in the fish-carriers, as indicated by the thermometer, is identical with that of the stream. Then turn out the fish.

Mr. Corrie is further of opinion that " In many cases, too, one has to consider the differing qualities of the water dealt with. For instance, Itchen river water has hardly any iron in it, and if trout which had travelled in Itchen river water were first tipped out into a stream strongly or perhaps only slightly impregnated with iron the result would be alarming ; nor, of course, is iron the only difference which may exist."

I take it, too, that fish bred in very soft water would be prejudicially affected by being turned out of this into very hard water and *vice versa*.

Stocking with feeding-fry is often described as the most inexpensive method in general vogue. To my mind it is absolutely useless, and a man may as well throw his cash into the sea as waste it in this way. The ova have been hatched in troughs and the alevins, carefully watched until they have absorbed the umbilical sac, are induced to feed on finely grated liver or some of the many fish-foods prepared. When they have commenced to feed they are styled *feeding-fry*, and in this state are delivered. When turned into the river they are in the most helpless condition, quite unable to seek for their food and absent in experience of such every-day matters as the mere action of the currents in a stream. Then, too, they are at the stage when even in a state of nature the mortality is at the very highest, and with their total want of knowledge of the dangers to which they are exposed their chance is indeed a desperate one. I do not think that the late Mr. Andrews' opinion, often expressed to me, that

Stocking with feeding-fry.

not more than one in a thousand fry turned into a
stream is likely to celebrate the first anniversary of
its birth, was in any way exaggerated. Probably the
reason why artificial propagation and breeding of
salmon has proved so unsuccessful is that in the
majority of cases the young salmon have been turned
adrift in the rivers as feeding-fry.

The plan of making artificial redds and laying down
eyed ova within a week or even
Stocking with eyed ova less of their hatching out is so
or alevins. easy, so simple, and so inexpensive that it must commend
itself to all of us. The eggs hatch out in the water
of the stream in which the trout are destined to live ;
the helpless alevins, until they have absorbed the umbilical sac, are in comparative safety, and as they
reach the feeding stage will instinctively take up their
positions, locating themselves in shelter and generally
behind largish stones. They will dart out, seize the
tiny insect larvæ or nymphs, young shrimps, or other
minute creatures fit for their sustenance, dart back to
their hiding-places and thus elude a considerable proportion of their natural enemies. As they grow stronger
they will, of their own free will, swim out of the troughs
in which the artificial redds were made and distribute
themselves over suitable parts of the nearest shallows.

If there should be a difficulty in finding a suitable
place for the artificial redds, alevins may be purchased
just before they have absorbed the yolk sac and
planted out on the thinnest parts of the breeding

shallows. Nine years ago ten thousand eyed ova were planted in artificial redds, and when hatched out and feeding the fry made their way into water which has since been under careful observation. Early in 1906 five thousand alevins which had not quite reached the feeding stage were placed on the same shallows, and the result of the experiments has been quite remarkable. Nine years ago there were scarcely any small trout visible on this stretch of water, but a few years after the ova and alevins were introduced the shallows were thickly populated by some of the liveliest and hardiest little store fish with many sizable ones, and some of quite heavy weight. Many of these have come to maturity and reproduced in turn, and now practically all the fish on these shallows are in the pink of condition, feed freely on surface and other food, and are just as shy of the human presence as the wild fish on rivers where no stocking work has been undertaken.

It will be noticed that when stocking with the large stew-fed fish, growing up two-year-olds to sizable fish or keeping yearlings until they are two years old, it is neces-

The modern trout-stew.

sary either to have a stew or to go to the expense of the work being carried out by the pisciculturist. Proprietors and lessees of chalk-stream fisheries are practically all in accord as to the economy and benefits generally accruing from the judicious use of stews which are under their own control and management.

2 C

In the meadows adjoining most of the south-country chalk-streams there are numer-

Selection of a carrier for a stew. ous carriers, some natural and some artificial; the former selected by our ancestors to contribute to their scheme of water-meadow irrigation, and the latter dug out to perfect this scheme where the natural carriers were insufficient. The natural carriers are to be preferred, and in one of them the stew should be made. A little observation will soon show which are the most suitable, because they invariably contain a considerable number of small healthy trout. It is essential that the water supply should be constant (although perhaps slightly variable in quantity), and not subject to the caprice of millers or farmers.

If the fall is sufficient to enable the stew to be emptied of water when picking up the fish, it is a distinct advantage. Another point to be observed is that in every one of these natural carriers the water flows over hard solid gravel. To select a muddy ditch or one flowing over peat is unwise, and to go to the expense of putting down gravel over a clay or peat bottom is simply courting failure, because it is essentially a carrier unfit for the purpose. The making of the stew is a simple matter, and there is no possible advantage to be derived from constructing it with elaborate brick piers, solid brick sides, or other costly form of construction.

A description of the stew in which such satisfactory

results have been achieved in my case may probably
be of some service to the reader. A natural carrier
flowing over hard, clean gravel and with constant
water supply was selected. In it a length of 55
yards has been made into a stew by the placing
of proper screens at the upper and lower ends. It
is approximately 12 feet wide, and has a depth of
about 2 feet 6 inches, with the river at its ordinary
summer level. It is divided into four parts by intermediate screens properly and securely fixed.

The ideal arrangement of a stew divided into compartments is to put the yearlings in the uppermost,
the two-year-olds in the next, and the wild fish in
the third. These wild fish are some of the undersized trout of the river turned in here towards the
end of the fishing season instead of being replaced in
the river. These wild fish are fed during the autumn
and winter, and turned into the river in the following
spring. The fourth compartment is useful for ex-
perimental work. This arrangement is not carried
out in my stew, but if for any reason it had to be
reconstructed it would be rearranged on these lines.

I should advise anyone making a stew to purchase
his screens from one of the
Screens for the best pisciculturists in the king-
stew. dom, and to see that he gets
the very best material and
workmanship somewhat regardless of cost. To use
screens made by a local blacksmith, even the most
capable, is to court disaster. My screens, which were

made for me and purchased from the Itchen River Trout Breeding Establishment at Chilland, are 9 feet in length with upright bars securely fixed to the top and bottom of the frame of the screen and to an intermediate iron cross-piece. They are throughout of galvanized iron. For the yearlings the bars are spaced $\frac{1}{4}$ in. apart, and for the two-year-olds $\frac{3}{4}$ in. The necessity of keeping the bars free from weed or other obstruction must be impressed on the keeper, and he will require to clean them at least twice a day, and more frequently in the summer or when weed-cutting is in progress.

Most of the necessary work in making the stew is at the points where the screens **Construction of the** (top, bottom, or intermediate) **stew.** are fixed. Boarding the sides is an advantage, and not very costly ; it makes it easier to pick up the fish, and saves all anxiety as to the existence of rat holes, which permit the trout to stray from one division to another, or even to escape at the upper or lower ends. All woodwork used in the construction should be charred or tarred, and if the latter it should be left to soak in the water for several weeks before using so as to get rid of all the dangerous oils, etc., in the tar.

Begin by cutting back the bank on either side immediately below the place at which the various screens are to be fixed. These spaces cut out are generally called the *wings*, and in good solid ground they should extend for 2 feet into the bank and 2 feet

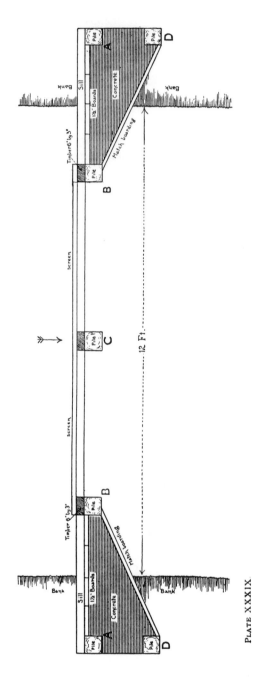

PLATE XXXIX

PLAN OF STEW, SHOWING SCREEN, PIERS, ETC.

down the stream from the sill against which the screen in each case is to be fixed. If the ground is loose or peaty the wings must be cut out further into the bank and further down the stream. The wings must be cut down to the hard gravel at the bottom of the stew and the ground must be made level from side to side along the line of the sill. The sill, which should be of good, solid, well-matured English oak, 4 in. by 3 in., is set on edge and firmly bedded in the gravel. Mr. Corrie suggests that for a sill, which is at all times under water, green elm or green beech (i.e. unseasoned timber) will outlast the best matured oak. It must be long enough to extend to the pile at the inner end of the wings on each side.

Close behind the sill at the place where the end of the screen will come, drive an elm pile 6 inches square on each side, marked A in Plate XXXIX, a similar pile in a line with it at the inner end of the wing marked B, and another similar pile at the lower end of the wing marked D on each side. Another pile marked C is driven immediately behind the sill in the centre of the stew, and all these piles are cut off at about 3 feet above the summer level of the water. Nail the sill firmly to the piles marked A, B, and in front of the sill lay 2 inches of concrete on the upper side on the bed of the stew, thus leaving the face of the sill against which the screen is fixed projecting 2 inches pointing upstream. Where there is much fall of level in rear of the screen the footing of the sill must be made secure by driving a row of beech piles on the upstream side of the sill. The beech piling is driven so that the top of it is level with the centre of the sill, and the screen rests on the top of the beech piling.

Drive $1\frac{1}{2}$-in. boards, pointed at the base like piles at each side, to fill up the space between the pile B at the end of the screen and the pile A at the inner end of the wing, and cut them off at a convenient level above the surface of the water. Match-board the space from the pile B at the end of the screen diagonally to the pile D at the lower end of the wing on each side, down to the gravel and up to the level of the $1\frac{1}{2}$-in. boards. A triangular compartment will thus be formed, on each side of the stew, by the $1\frac{1}{2}$-in. boards, the bank and the match-boarding. These triangular spaces should be filled with concrete (of one part cement to three of clean gravel) which, when set, will form piers as solid as any brickwork. A reference to the plan, Plate XXXIX, showing the arrangement and construction of the piers, sill, and screen, will assist the reader and enable any moderately handy and intelligent man to carry out the work.

The handrails across each screen are nailed to the piles. A length of timber 6 in. by 3 in. (long enough to reach from the head of the pile to the surface of the sill) must be nailed to each of the three piles to which the screen is to be attached. Planks laid across the stew at the screens are useful for feeding or other purposes. The screens themselves are fastened in place by screws or staples to the sill at the bottom, and to the three piles—one at the centre and two at the ends—and the work is complete.

To give shade to the fish, nail some half-saplings into frames to lie across the stew, fasten galvanized-wire netting to them with small staples, and cover them with old sacks, or sedge tied on like thatch. Any rough carpenter can do the work, and the cost is quite trifling.

The feeding question is a very serious one, and the one fault to avoid is that of **The feeding question.** giving the fish in a stew too liberal a diet. One hears of two-year-olds weighing $1\frac{1}{2}$ to 2 lb., and three-year-olds of 3 lb., and even greater weight, which are turned out at or about the commencement of the fishing season. As will be shown later on, these are overgrown, unhealthy stock, and in every way undesirable additions to the trout in the river.

There are many forms of food suited for the purpose, the best of which perhaps is bullocks' lights thoroughly boiled and passed through a small inexpensive mincing-machine. Unfortunately, it is often difficult, if not impossible, to get a regular supply of lights in country places, but boiled horseflesh can generally be obtained, and minced in the same way is a very good substitute. The food, whether lights or horseflesh, must be quite fresh—tainted meat is objectionable and not good for the fish in the stew. An occasional change of diet is desirable, and in my experience it is wise to mix with the minced horseflesh occasionally a small quantity of ground greaves or of the broken biscuit used for poultry food. In a stew containing 500 yearlings, 14 lb. per week is the maximum quantity which should be given, and in hot weather this quantity should be greatly reduced. A few of the largest of the fish, which would then be two-year-olds, could be turned out the following spring, and the remainder kept in the stew until they are three-year-olds.

In describing the stew I have referred to the division set apart for wild unsizable fish which in the ordinary way would be returned to the river. I have adopted the plan of keeping a certain proportion of the undersized trout caught in the latter part of the season for this purpose. I take the greatest care to select healthy, good-looking and good-conditioned trout of about $\frac{3}{4}$ lb., and when these are turned into the stew they will, after a few days, feed well and make the very best of wild fish for stocking in the following spring.

I am able, by the kind permission of the proprie-tors and editor of that invalu-**The degeneration of the** able paper, to give this and **chalk-stream trout.** other extracts from articles written by me for the " Field."

It must unfortunately be admitted by all who have given careful consideration to the subject that the trout of the south-country chalk-streams have gener-ally deteriorated. They do not grow to the dimensions of those we killed in bygone days, they do not rise as

freely, they do not play as well, they are not as handsome in shape, colour, or markings, and they are not
as palatable on the table. It is to be feared that unless
the most drastic remedies are applied without delay
this degeneration will continue and progress with ever-
increasing rapidity.

On some parts of the Test lessees have adopted the
ill-advised plan, before alluded to in this chapter, of
purchasing yearlings, keeping them in stews, giving
them an unduly liberal quantity of food, thus growing
them up to abnormally large and unhealthy two and
three-year-olds, and turning them into the river at, or
immediately before, the commencement of the spring
fishing. In and below the waters into which they are
introduced one almost invariably hears of great
numbers of large fish being killed in the spring, fish
which rise at any pattern of fly, give little or no
show of fight when hooked, turn dark or nearly
black soon after death, and are absolutely useless for
the table.

The reasons for this are not far to seek. Such fish
have been overfed in youth and are constitutionally
unhealthy. When first thrown on their own resources
they will take any fly offered to them, give little sport,
and a large proportion soon succumb to the wiles of
the dry-fly fisherman. Those that survive, never
having had to seek their own food, rapidly fall off in
condition and drop from the streamy water to deep
and comparatively sluggish reaches, when they rarely
feed on the surface of the stream. Many who have

gone to great expense to try this plan now see the error of their ways, and are giving instructions to their keepers to kill down these ugly brutes whenever, wherever, and however they can catch them. As far as I can ascertain, this method of stocking with overgrown, unhealthy, stew-fed fish has not often been tried on the Itchen.

Both on the Test and Itchen, however, the trout generally have distinctly deteriorated in late years, and to understand the position one must first of all grasp the scheme of the life history of a perfectly healthy and normal fish which has been hatched from one of a number of ova, deposited naturally on a spawning shallow by a healthy female and fertilized by the milt from an equally healthy and naturally bred male. In due course the eggs hatch, and the young trout at this stage is called an *alevin*. It is a most helpless little creature with a large ovoid sac attached to the central portion of its body. The mouth organs are not developed, so that it is unable to feed at this stage, and while the development of these mouth organs proceeds the alevin subsists on the contents of the yolk sac, which gradually shrinks and becomes absorbed.

Life history of a normal wild trout.

The fry, which is the name given to the young trout after the yolk sac has been absorbed, is in shape a small reproduction of the adult fish, and is able to take its food naturally. These young fry hide themselves in crevices among the stones, darting out to seize and devour any small crustaceans, mollusks, or water-bred fly larvæ, and at once returning to their hiding-places for safety. Those that escape the ravages of their numerous enemies (whether adult trout, pike, or other coarse fish, and even larvæ of water beetles) as they gradually increase in size seek places where the food on which they subsist is plentiful.

They continue growing in length and weight for a number of years, probably as many as six or seven, in rivers suited to them, until they have reached their prime and attained their maximum dimensions. They remain in their prime for a few years, and then gradually begin to lose condition and weight until old age creeps on and they get lanky and lean, their heads appear longer in proportion to their bodies, the teeth become more prominent, their colours dim, the spots lose their brilliancy, and at the last phase of old age they are dark or black in colour, and have completely lost the symmetry of form which is one of the most beautiful and attractive attributes of a perfect specimen of a chalk-stream trout.

Mr. E. Valentine Corrie, whose experience of the Itchen is greater than that of any other modern authority, and whose knowledge of the river dates back to an epoch anterior to that of any other living expert, has treated the subject briefly in an article in the

Mr. E. Valentine Corrie's opinion.

"Journal of the Fly-Fishers' Club," entitled "Re-stocking of Trout-Streams." He has also author-ized me to quote from a letter addressed by him to a correspondent dealing more in detail with his opinions on the subject in reference to the Itchen. In his letter he says: "This deterioration has been slow but sure for many years past, and during the last four or five seasons has rendered nearly valueless many miles of the river. The lower reaches of the Itchen first suffered, next the middle reaches, and now, although there are portions of the middle Itchen where good sport is obtained and the trout killed are handsome fish, these successes are hardly earned by most careful and skilled fishery management and con-stant restocking with the very pick of the trout-farmer's ready-grown trout; these trout, hand-reared until they are two or three years of age, are very short lived, and they make very bad parent fish. Thus with a slowly weakening strain among most of our artificially bred trout, and a rapid falling off in the health of our wild fish, the future of our Itchen fisheries looks gloomy indeed, and I venture to suggest that what has occurred on the lower Itchen and is now affecting the middle reaches of the same stream may at no distant date prove a source of danger to the upper part of the river also."

I want the reader to understand clearly Mr. Corrie's meaning, the more so as I am in every way in accord with him as to the causes of the evil and the sug-gested remedies. In order to illustrate the appear-

PLATE XL.

Typical Trout Male.

Leon Barritt, Engraving Co. Ltd.

ance of the normal as distinguished from the degenerate trout, I have selected and photographed four specimens killed on the Test in 1911. The reproductions of these photos are given in Plates XL, XLI, XLII and XLIII; Plate XL, a male of 1 lb. 12 oz., killed on June 24th, and Plate XLI, a female of 1 lb. 10 oz., killed on April 24th, are typical wild fish, and Plates XLII and XLIII are respectively degenerate specimens of male and female. I could easily have given shorter, thicker, and better-looking examples of the wild fish, but I consider these fair average examples of typical naturally bred Test trout. The male shown in Plate XLII, killed on April 11th, measured 20 inches in length, and weighed 2 lb. 7 oz. It is, in my opinion, a fair sample of one of these grossly overfed stew-fish, probably not above three years old, which had been turned out of the stew into the river in the early spring, and from that day to the day of its capture had dropped downstream and steadily deteriorated in weight and condition. Plate XLIII, a female of 1 lb. 8 oz., killed on May 1st, will, when compared with the typical naturally bred female Test trout given in Plate XLI, show what is meant here by a degenerate fish.

What is the cause of this degeneration? The necessity of stocking has for many years been brought home to all lessees of chalk-stream fisheries, because the natural reproduction cannot suffice to make up for the number killed, not only by the fisherman, but also by the other numerous enemies of the trout. The fish for stocking are usually purchased from one of the numerous pisciculturists, and turned in either as yearlings, two-year-olds, or even three-year-olds. It must be remembered that these fish have been hand-fed in stews for one, two, or three years, so that they have never had to find their own food under natural conditions, and the older they were when turned adrift the more they suffer from this inability to fend for themselves, and the more heavily they are handicapped against the wild fish in the river.

Then, too, as Mr. Corrie pertinently remarks in the "Journal of the Fly-Fishers' Club":—

"To-day the average wild mature trout in the open river is a bad fish to breed from; it has most probably been reared by artificial means, until one, two, or three years of age, and the older it was when turned out to fend for itself the worse parent fish it becomes. Nor at the trout-farmer's establishment is time friendly to our breed of trout. Instances there are when parent fish crossed with wild strains maintain the hardiness of their stock, but it becomes more difficult every year to obtain ova and milt from hardy wild stock, and, although artificially raised young trout make grand-looking fish so long as they are carefully tended and fed, the majority of them fail to thrive really well in the open river."

The pisciculturist does not as a rule assist us much in regard to this question of degeneration. Candidly, we cannot blame him. It has been the custom for the

PLATE XLI

Typical Trout Female

Swan Electric Engraving Co

various breeders to be placed in competition as to the prices of trout for stocking purposes. Too often the lessee or manager of a fishery wishes to obtain for a specified sum the maximum number of yearlings or older fish to turn into his river. Competition naturally lowers the price and necessitates more economical working in the hatcheries and ponds. As a result the selection of parent fish of good strain and of the right age, neither too young nor too old, has been neglected, and for too many years in succession the same breeding fish have been spawned and the ova fertilized from the same males. Yearlings and older fish, wanting in condition and stamina, have been delivered, and even some with deformities of jaws and gills have been sent out. Such fish never thrive, they are not good risers, they do not give good sport, they do not grow to the average size of the river, they are inferior for the table and the worst of ancestors for coming generations.

The ill-effects caused by the introduction of these degenerate trout do not end even with the reproduction of degenerate offspring. To quote once more from Mr. Corrie's letter: " The strongest and best of the parent fish are ever first on the spawning ground, and are followed there by the less mature and weakly spawners, which invariably make for the same nests and rout out most of the good ova already deposited, and in this connection the undesirable, hand-raised, interloping aliens are the worst offenders." *Ergo*, not only are we introducing a degenerate strain of trout,

but these fish, following their natural instinct of reproduction, positively destroy the eggs which have already
been laid in the redds by the naturally bred fish of the
river.

Just as the doctor who had diagnosed a specific
disease would be deemed a charlatan unless he
suggested a remedy, so it becomes the duty of those
who had drawn attention to the rapidly progressing
deterioration of chalk-stream trout to devise the means
of palliating or removing it. The first and most
obvious step must be a reversion to the old-fashioned
plan of taking the ova and milt from the very best
strains of naturally bred wild fish, and it is not
altogether easy to find them. It will not suffice for
the few owners and lessees of fisheries who have the
means of hatching out these ova to be the only ones
to adopt this course. The pisciculturist himself must
without delay proceed to breed a new race of trout
from the wild fish, keeping them to breed from and
doing away with the old worn-out and degenerate
spawning fish in his ponds. Even when he has succeeded in raising the necessary stock of breeding fish
he must, year after year, prevent their degeneration by
ever introducing fresh blood, either by fertilized ova or
milt, or both, from the best strains of naturally bred
fish available.

There is good reason to believe that, if necessary,
milt from the male fish can be expressed into a dry
bottle or tube, tightly corked, and transported any
distance not requiring more than, say, forty-eight hours

PLATE XLII

Degenerate Trout Male

in transit. It can then be used to fertilize ova taken from ripe spawning fish. I cannot say positively that this experiment has been made with trout, but I have before me some notes of experiments made on fertilization of salmon ova as far back as 1893. Ova from *Salmo salar* were successfully fertilized with milt which had been bottled for twenty-four hours, forty-eight hours, and ninety-six hours. Those which were treated with milt kept in the dry tubes for twenty-four and forty-eight hours were quite successfully fertilized, and the alevins hatched out in due course. The following is the note in reference to the ova fertilized with milt which had been bottled for ninety-six hours: " Milt from male salmon, 20 lb., taken at 1.15 p.m., on Monday, 19th December, 1893, in a dry bottle. Bottle kept in hatching tray so as to keep the temperature uniform. On the following Friday, 96 hours later, about 6000 eggs from a 16-lb. female were fertilized with this milt. These hatched out fairly well, and were healthy until they were turned into the Yorkshire Esk. The loss by *dead* ova was greater than in either of the previous experiments." This note was sent to me by Mr. J. W. Wheldon, who at that time resided at Burgate, Pickering, and was, I believe, keeper to the Costa Club, at Pickering, Yorkshire, and he was considered a very reliable and truthful observer.

I have thought it well to give this note *in extenso*, because if salmon milt can be kept dry in a properly corked bottle, and used forty-eight or ninety-six hours later to fertilize (and fertilize successfully) salmon eggs, there is every reason to believe that similar treatment with trout-milt would prove equally successful.

The exact method to be adopted by the managers of fisheries must depend in a great degree on the nature of their water. Given plenty of spawning shallows they should introduce eyed ova, turned down in suitable places a week or even less before they are due to hatch, and any trout-breeder can tell within a few days when a particular batch of eggs will hatch out. If preferred, the eggs can be hatched in the hatchery and the alevins turned down. It is most important that they should be laid down at the right moment, and Mr. Corrie, in the second part of his article on " Restocking of Trout Streams," in the " Journal of the Fly-Fishers' Club," is so explicit on this that I cannot do better than quote his words *verbatim*. " The age when alevins must be liberated into the water they are intended to stock is just before the little fish have quite absorbed the umbilical sac (an age about which the hatchery owner is unlikely to make any error). The alevins on being liberated will dart to the bed of the stream and take cover under the nearest stones they can find. They have, and will retain, all the instincts of self-preservation common to wild fry hatched in the open river, and have nearly as good a chance of growing to maturity as the hand-fed, pond-raised yearling of infinitely greater cost. Most fisheries have some places suitable for turning down trout fry ; the exact positions are easy to locate, and often

PLATE XLIII

Degenerate Trout Female

Swan Electric Engraving Co.

made very easy to spot by the disturbed beds of gravel where wild trout have already spawned, but if no redds are noticeable, any brightly gravelled shallow will serve where the water is not too swift and where the individual bits of stone and gravel forming the bed of the stream are not too tightly bound to allow the sheltering places for the alevins."

The expense of doing this is comparatively small, but it must be remembered that the mortality of fry in the natural state in the river is very great, so that the numbers required to be laid down must be proportionately large. As before remarked, on a fishery where this plan was adopted 10,000 eyed ova were laid down nine years ago and 5000 alevins three years later, and the result on a comparatively short length of good shallows was quite surprising.

If the fishery to be dealt with is very deficient in spawning shallows the best plan will be to grow the fry to the yearling stage in ordinary fry-ponds, and the great danger to be avoided is that of overfeeding. If the water has few shallows and long stretches of slow-running deep water the yearlings should, if possible, be kept a second year in a stew, and here again the amount of food to be given must be much less than is usually provided in the trout-breeders' ponds.

In a modern trout stew, selected and constructed on the principles laid down in an earlier part of this chapter, natural food will be plentiful and the quantity of hand-feeding reduced to a minimum. At the early stages for 500 yearlings, 7 lb. of minced cooked horseflesh per week will be sufficient, and during the hot weather even less than this amount. During the autumn the quantity can be gradually increased, and the maximum, as stated before, of 14 lb. per week should be reached, say, early in January, and the feeding should be continued on this scale until, say, the middle of March, when the two-year-olds should be turned into the stream.

The so-called Rainbow trout (*Salmo irideus*) was introduced to this country **Rainbow trout.** from the United States many years ago. It is probably the most beautiful fish of the genus. It is a grand fighter and grows rapidly to a great weight. It is also said to be the very best of all trout for the table. At first the English pisciculturists imagined that it might easily be acclimatized and would, in our rivers, prove a great boon to the angler. Unfortunately it has a decided propensity to work down the river, and in fact it is a moot point whether, at any rate in this country, it should not be classified among the migratory, or anadromous, species of the Salmonidæ.

When turned into lakes where this tendency to migrate can be defeated, it has proved to some extent a success. There is, however, a growing mass of evidence that in some lakes rainbow trout, after giving excellent sport to the angler for a time—say until they reach about 3 lb. in weight—cease to be in evidence, and in many cases disappear as absolutely as if they had gone to sea. Their disappearance, the impossi-

bility of discovering them by persuading them to take
fly or any other bait, and the failure to find their dead
bodies combine to make the question of rainbow trout
in lakes a puzzle and even a mystery. Upon these
points, however, we require more actual evidence than
has yet been forthcoming. At Blagdon and similar lakes
and reservoirs rainbow trout grow to a great average size
and are highly esteemed, but when turned into a river
they soon disappear, and as far as I can ascertain, have
not in this country been known to return from the sea
to the river in which they had passed their earlier days.

I tried an experiment with a comparatively small
number in the Test. Some five or six were taken on
pike-trimmers, and three rose to and were killed with
floating fly soon after they had been turned in. This
was, of course, in a stream where their desire to go to
the sea could not be restrained, and the next season
every one had disappeared.

I do not think they would be of any great benefit to
our chalk-streams because from their having, in my
limited experience, so often fallen victims to a live
bait on a trimmer, I take it that they have strongly
marked cannibalistic tendencies. My friend Corrie
concurs in what I have just said, and adds : "My idea
is that Rainbows deteriorate quickly under the normal
conditions they meet with in this country (I mean the
strain or breed deteriorates, and this, in my opinion,
is very often due to lack of suitable surroundings
for the breeding-fish), and unless a fish-farmer has
exceptional opportunities for raising Rainbows he

should often renew his stock by the purchase of ova from abroad."

The pisciculturist's yearlings and two-year-olds, when grown to large dimen- **Short gill-covers and** sions in stews, are at times **other deformities.** very disappointing. Frequently the mortality among these trout in the stew is somewhat alarming, and of the dead ones taken out quite a large proportion are found to have short gill-covers and other deformities. Short gill-covers are often deemed to be caused by overcrowding of the young trout at an early stage, and of course the fish-farmer who delivers such fish is *prima facie* guilty of a dire offence. He should, under no conditions, send out for stocking purposes trout which are in any way deformed, because these are never satisfactory, and a large proportion die in the stew. Mr. Corrie is of opinion that a large proportion of short gill-covers and other deformities are, according to his experience of practical hatchery work, due to partial suffocation of the embryo.

Fungus, which is a parasitic vegetable growth, is found at times in the stew, **Fungus on trout.** and occasionally even in the river. It is allied to the deadly salmon disease, and when once established is not easily cured. Immersion in strong brine is prescribed and is at times successful, but even under the most careful management trout once badly affected by fungus will generally succumb. The disease is believed to be contagious, but I have grave doubts whether thoroughly healthy fish are liable to catch it, and, on the other hand, unhealthy ones are almost certain to contract the disease when it is prevalent in the stew or in the river.

A small trammel-net is needed to pick up the trout from the stew, but when using it the greatest care is necessary. Trout generally get badly meshed in a trammel-net, and extracting them from the pockets formed by the sheeting or linnet being driven through the large-meshed walling is a delicate operation. It is, of course, better to construct stews so that the water-supply can be diverted and the stew emptied before picking up the fish, but this is in many cases impracticable owing to the fall or difference of level being insignificant.

Netting fish from the stew.

I am almost tempted to descant at length on this attractive subject. Transplanting a particular species of insect from one stream to another, or from one part of a stream to another part of the same stream, seems a fairly simple matter. The tyro would say : Take eggs or larvæ and convey them rapidly to the place where they are to be introduced, and if your judgment of the environment is sound, the problem would apparently be solved. In Part I, Chapter IV, " Choice of Pattern," when referring to the grannom, I have written on the subject : The experience of most enthusiasts who have at-

Transplanting fly.

tempted to acclimatize or transplant flies has been, like my own, so uniformly unsuccessful that I am reluctantly compelled to arrive at the conclusion that, although a most fascinating experiment, "le jeu ne vaut pas la chandelle."

In conclusion, I should like to add a few words of a personal nature. For more than thirty years I have devoted every spare moment to the study of the dry-fly fisherman's art, and have in this book striven to include everything which can in any way tend to elucidate the theory and practice of the fishing, the entomology, or the making and management of a dry-fly fishery. If I have omitted some essential point the reader must kindly credit me with having done so inadvertently, and not from *malice prepense*. I fully realize that, like every other form of sport, the cult of the dry-fly is likely in the future to be further developed and improved in matters of detail. Any such development or improvement which may perchance occur to me, or be suggested by any of my numerous friends, will, I hope, be incorporated in a series of supplements if my publishers, with their customary urbanity and desire to assist, will consent to publish such supplements.

INDEX